The Edges of Political Representation

The Edges of Political Representation

Mapping, Critiquing and
Pushing the Boundaries

Edited by Mihnea Tănăsescu and
Claire Dupont

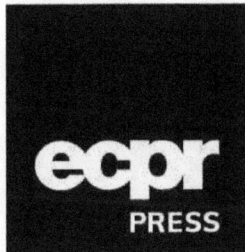

ecpr
PRESS

Published by the European Consortium for Political Research, Harbour House, 6–8 Hythe Quay, Colchester, CO2 8JF, United Kingdom

British Library Cataloguing in Publication Information
A catalogue record for this book is available from the British Library

ISBN: HB 978-1-78552-297-0

Library of Congress Cataloging-in-Publication Data Is Available

ISBN 978-1-78552-297-0 (cloth)
ISBN 978-1-5381-5681-0 (pbk)
ISBN 978-1-78552-298-7 (electronic)

ecpr.eu/shop

Contents

Acknowledgements

This book is the result of several years of fascinating discussions, debates and workshops among a dedicated group of researchers. All of the contributors to this book are excellent scholars with expertise in a variety of empirical and theoretical fields in democratic governance. Despite our heterogeneous interests and expertise, understanding the development of 'political representation' was a shared, key common issue. It quickly became the focus of our discussions: how is political representation understood, analyzed and assessed in each of our areas of expertise? How has this evolved over time? What can we learn about political representation in general by looking at it from the perspective of several different domains? We are delighted that we could pursue our line of investigation and work together to produce this book.

Without the support of the Vrije Universiteit Brussel's Strategic Research Fund, our explorations of political representation would not have been possible. Under the Strategic Research Programme 'EDGE' (Evaluating Democratic Governance in Europe), we were provided with the means, the time and the space to delve into this issue, and to learn from each other. The first iteration of the EDGE research programme ran from 2012 to 2017 and was expertly and delicately guided by Kris Deschouwer and Sebastian Oberthür, who provided the encouragement and engagement to ensure this book came to fruition.

Early drafts of the book were immensely improved thanks to the comments and feedback from three anonymous reviewers, and to the excellent support of Alexandra Segerberg at ECPR Press. We would like to thank all the ECPR Press editors and staff for their careful follow-up and close work on this project, which has helped yield a high-quality volume. We also were delighted with the enthusiastic response during our internal review process, and, as editors, we wish to thank our colleagues for their dedication to this project.

Academic work requires support not only from colleagues, but also from a wider network of friends and family. We thank the husbands, wives, partners, children, parents, brothers, sisters and friends of each of the contributors to this book for supporting our work. This book is dedicated to them, and especially to the new family members that joined us since we embarked on this common project: Aideen, Anna, Charlie Rose, Julinne, Lavinia, Maeve, Nneka, and Sophie.

Mihnea Tănăsescu, Brussels, Belgium
Claire Dupont, Ghent, Belgium
November 2018

Chapter One

Introduction

Mihnea Tănăsescu and Claire Dupont

In 2006, the Party for the Animals won its first seats in the Dutch parliament (Otjes, 2014). Voted for by humans, they had a platform built around the representation of non-humans. This was an electoral manifestation of a much wider phenomenon of non-human representation. In 2008, another stark example of this development came under the guise of constitutional rights for nature, in Ecuador (Tănăsescu, 2013, 2016). Finland, meanwhile, set up a Committee for the Future, thus effectively deciding to take the representation of the unborn in the Finnish parliament seriously (Groombridge, 2006). In Italy, a former comedian, who is the unofficial leader of a non-party, is one of the most powerful political figures in the country. Non-governmental organizations regularly lay claim to represent the general interest towards a better society (Rubenstein, 2013). And rock stars and Hollywood celebrities continue to speak for the supposed voiceless of the world, acting as their de facto representatives (Street, 2004). Political representation has clearly evolved considerably in practice, and theory has been working hard to catch up (Viera, 2017).

The type, shape and limits of political representation form a central element of any discussion of democratic political arrangements and their future. Both societal and scholarly debates delve into major questions around the legitimacy, fairness and effectiveness of new forms of political representation in democratic governance systems. These discussions are embedded in wider debates around the quality and boundaries of a democratic system as a whole (see Shapiro & Hacker-Cordón, 1999)—debates that have not yet been resolved, as the practice of democracy continues to evolve.

Despite the number of discussions and orientations on political representation (see Viera, 2017), there is still much to be explored and understood. The classical discussion of representation, from a theoretical point of view, is

1

Hanna Pitkin's *The Concept of Representation* (1967). This work set out to investigate the uses of the term *representation* in its political connotations. It remains one of the most influential works on the subject, and it has spawned a variety of interpretations that justify themselves in relation to the original work. These can be summed up by the nuanced assumption that representation is about making present something which is absent. Few discussions, however, have focused on how the concept of political representation has been pushed or stretched in theory and practice to accommodate ever more complex realities (Collier & Mahon, 1993). In this volume, we examine the edges of political representation from a variety of theoretical and empirical perspectives, shining a light on the complexity of modern representative democracy.

The practical array of cases that can be understood through the lens of representation has developed in tandem with theoretical scholarship that has expanded or stretched the concept greatly (Collier & Mahon, 1993; Sartori, 1970). Political representation therefore, as a concept, has had to shift to accommodate the evolving complexities of democratic governance, and to account for the realities of representation in practice, in an interconnected, interdependent world. Although representation and democracy are distinct concepts that can, and have, existed independently of one another (Manin, 1997; Urbinati, 2011, 2014), they have also intertwined in the last centuries in the form of representative democracy. The often-repeated judgement that this form of democratic rule is in crisis reflects the fact that the function of representation is being fundamentally challenged by several momentous social developments. Globalization, increasing inequality, the rise of nationalist sentiments in established liberal democracies, the perceived inability of nation states to manage crises, widespread economic and political turmoil, conflicts and global problems such as climate change all place strains on the quality of democratic governance and representative democracy (Bonanno, 2000; Diamond & Morlino, 2004; Schmitter & Karl, 1991). This, in turn, leads to heightened questions about legitimacy (in terms of both effectiveness and fairness): as representative democratic systems have proven inadequate to respond to these broader contexts, discontent grows and propels new responses, expanding the edges of the practice of political representation further. Hence a new cycle of theorizing begins, with scholars pushing the concept of political representation in response, both in order to keep up with the changing landscape and to challenge it to conform to particular norms.

Today, the concepts of representation and democracy are peeling apart, both conceptually and practically. This might mean an enduring divorce or, on the contrary, a more powerful union. What remains the case is that the representative element of representative democracy is increasingly contested. Where elected representatives embedded in national territorial units face challenges in responding to issues facing their citizens, new forms of representation have blossomed. The practice of actors outside the electoral system making claims of representation pushed scholars to rethink the theory of representation: it became necessary to develop tools to assess the democratic credentials of these new practices of representation (Montanaro, 2017; Saward, 2006).

This volume charts a course through this monumental questioning by itself asking one simple, trenchant question: what are the edges of political representation? There are at least two ways of interpreting the question, conceptually and practically, and both are relevant here. In the first instance, we are interested in clarifying what the conceptual boundaries of representation are, in order to be in a better position to imagine alternative democratic futures. Second, we are interested in the adaptations of representative institutions and practices to the changing social dynamics of contemporary democracies. We want to see how institutions and practices are responding and adapting to a world where the underlying social diversity is increasingly politically relevant.

We can understand an edge to be a delineation beyond which the phenomenon in question ends. It is that which gives the identity of what it encloses and, in doing so, separates it from the rest, sets it up against the different, which lies on the outside. Applied to the concept of representation, we do not assume that the edge is an actual border, a place that we could cross and all of a sudden find ourselves in non-representative terrain, but that the edges of representation are malleable and porous. This assumption is supported by the history of the concept and its multiple transformations, hybridizations and evolutions. As such, we do not view the 'edge' of political representation as a geographical or spatial delimitation of application, as the term was used in Ian Shapiro and Casiano Hacker-Cordón's 1999 edited volume on *Democracy's Edges*. Rather, we are interested in the ways in which the limits of the concept are pushed and challenged and expanded in multiple directions, as the reality of its practice evolves. This is necessarily an exercise in crossing boundaries as much as setting them.

By collecting contributions specifically designed to tease out the edges of the concept of representation, we hope to achieve a novel diagnosis of the problems of representation and to sketch out avenues for its future. The point is not to theorize the concept of edge to any great depth. Instead, we use this concept as a heuristic tool that helps us organize seemingly disparate aspects of political representation into a more coherent whole. Our claim is that the theory and practice of representation is being challenged in unprecedented ways. Investigating the edges of representation is a shortcut to finding out which pressure points seem to be most salient. For example, theories of representation tend to overlook the importance of parties (see Chapter 2). Theorizing political representation beyond its usual edges is itself an important task (as exemplified in Chapters 5, 6 and 7), but old edges, like the crucial role of political parties, endure.

Seen in this fashion, puzzling representative practices take on new meanings. New and small parties have never had an easier time getting into some governments, while governing parties reliably lose elections after governing. The usual interpretation of this as electorates being fed up with the representative process misses the point of the representative process itself attempting to morph in ways that will redefine electoral (and, more widely, political) allegiances. In other words, along the electoral/non-electoral and party/non-party edge there is an energetic reformulation of what representation means, both theoretically and practically.

Similarly, political representation at its most abstract is a process of selection, and this aspect, without which the process cannot be thought, has itself become a contested edge. The fact that representation is, in a sense, necessarily also about exclusion (see Chapters 3 and 5) challenges the democratic ideal of equal inclusion in decision-making processes. In the case of women, for example, Karen Celis shows that descriptive representation—the presence of female candidates and their election to office—is not enough to ensure the representation of women. In other words, there is an exclusion/ inclusion edge around which the concept of representation is articulated, and one that we try to explicitly (and in multiple ways) bring to light, such that it becomes central to future discussions of representative theory and practice.

Thus, the edges of representation should not be understood as its boundaries, but rather as its most salient articulations, the conceptual spaces where representation hybridizes and therefore develops. In Chapter 9, for example, the discussion shows how traditionally separate ways of organizing democracy (representative and participatory, but one can also think of deliberative democracy) are in fact spliced and rearticulated in new forms. In the case of supranational representation, participatory and representative mechanisms are mixed with the help of new technologies of communication in order to shorten the representative chains (also tackled in Chapter 4) that separate citizens from representatives.

It bears saying that all contributions to this volume come from a broadly political angle. Though we mix and set in dialogue with each other various ways of doing political science, we do not offer possibilities of hybridizing the senses of political representation with, for example, legal concepts. The fact that we do not do it here does not mean that it cannot be done, and we encourage more interdisciplinary studies of the concept of representation.

The volume tackles its task in eight chapters, each dealing with a particular edge of representation. Though far from exhaustive, each individual contribution approaches the question of the edges of representation from one important thematic angle. Together, they represent a partial but crucial overview of the main axes of change in the development of political representation. We look forward to future scholarship filling the gaps that are unavoidably left open in this volume.

Kris Deschouwer begins the investigation with the bedrock of representative democracy as we know it, namely the institution of elections, in Chapter 2. Representation theory has rightly developed past electoral representation alone, but it still remains the case that, both conceptually and practically, the organization of elections is a crucial axis of representative politics. Despite the importance of elections for the concept of representation, scholarship has been mostly segregated either along a conceptual representation axis, or along an empirical party politics one. In other words, few scholars have taken into account the complexities of representation and its organization via the party system together. Deschouwer points out that this oversight in the literature allows party scholars to hold the implicit assumption that representation functioned best in the so-called golden era of party politics, the age of the mass party (roughly, mid-20th century). This assumption obscures two important things: the meaning of representation over and beyond mass party politics, and the underlying reasons, many of them valid on democratic grounds, for the dramatic changes in party structures. The chapter explores these implications and shows that one important edge of representation is delineated by the changing function and structure of political parties.

The above-mentioned golden age of party politics was a decidedly male affair. This also means that, for the half of humanity that is not male, there has never been a golden age. Karen Celis shows, in Chapter 3, how the dynamics of exclusion and inclusion in the representative process have constituted, and still do constitute, an enduring edge of the concept and practice of representation. By charting the history of the feminist struggle for inclusion in representative politics, Celis is able to historically ground a trenchant critique of contemporary exclusionary practices. By advancing the concept of reflexivity in representation, she proposes ways of continuing the struggle for inclusion and therefore pushing the boundaries of representation further.

Whether electoral or otherwise, representation is usually understood against the background of more or less stable fora. These have traditionally been nation states, though discussions of representation have also focused on sub-levels. However, representative practices have outrun theory when developing at supranational levels, often reliant on shifting agreements and changing constellations. This is the case for the representation of the European Union in international negotiations, and Sebastian Oberthür gives a detailed account of what it means to represent a supranational entity in the international community in Chapter 4. When the EU takes part in international processes, does it represent itself, its member states, the citizens of its member states, or all of these? As Oberthür shows, this practice of supranational representation challenges our understanding of representation in at least two ways: it introduces different modes of representation (supranational and intergovernmental), and it stretches the distance between representative and represented to such an extent that questions of legitimacy and accountability become urgent.

One of the most salient developments that have challenged the union between representation and democracy has been the increased political significance of social heterogeneity. Societies have always been widely diverse, encompassing both inter- and within-group heterogeneity. In modern representative democracies, this basic social fact has come to have deep political implications. One particularly trenchant question when examining the edges of representation is who the rightfully represented is under conditions of recognized and acknowledged extreme diversity. Chapters 5 to 7 give different answers to this fundamental question for representation today. In Chapter 5, Mihnea Tănăsescu postulates the person as the basic unit of representation and, starting from there, examines whether and in what sense persons themselves can be represented. Eline Severs argues for the enduring salience of groups in political representation in Chapter 6. By contrasting feminist, constructivist and liberal approaches to theorizing representation, she offers a powerful set of arguments for why groups are the rightful recipients of representation, despite their intrinsic diversity. Contemporary societal challenges also mean that politics can no longer be concerned exclusively with the short-term interests of those currently alive. Intergenerational issues such as climate change and enduring environmental degradation have pushed scholars to consider the practice of representation across time and beyond current generations. The question of how, and whether, future generations should be represented is tackled by Claire Dupont in Chapter 7. She shows that the practical implementation of such representation is particularly complex, but that mechanisms of representation can and may indeed contribute, but only in part, to the inclusion of future generations in present decisions. Here, the link between representation and democracy is once again shown to be in precarious transformation. Though we have become accustomed to thinking of democracy as primarily representative, it is by no means the case that representative politics exhausts the possibilities of democratic practice.

The final two chapters chart this particularly salient edge of representation, at the intersection with democratic practice, in two different ways. In Chapter 8, Ilke Adam, Soumia Akachar, Karen Celis, Serena D'Agostino and Eline Severs together examine the concept of symbolic representation and propose that it might be a much more important aspect of representation than previously thought. Its importance derives from its transformative power and, by examining the case of Black Pete in the Netherlands, the authors show how the self-image of society changes through symbolic contestation. This holds immense potential for the radical transformation of representative practices.

Ferran Davesa and Jamal Shahin continue pushing the concept of representation beyond its ordinary meaning in Chapter 9 by examining how, in the supranational context of the European Commission and the European Parliament, representation is hybridized with participation, precisely in order to achieve a level of democratic legitimacy that standard representative practices have lost. Through various forms of e-participation that the authors analyze, supranational institutions are attempting to include direct citizen voices in decision-making, though some measure of representation remains unavoidable. These new hybrid practices are not, in themselves, successful. Rather, they are poignant examples of the pressure under which representative politics currently exists.

Taken together, the contributions to this volume chart the major pressure points of the concept of representation and show ways forward for both theory and practice. As such, we present the contributions in this volume as engaged in an ongoing dialogue with scholarly work and empirical reality. We wrap up the volume by briefly drawing out these insights and suggesting possibilities for future research. The volume highlights how representation is being stretched along several conceptual edges, but the clear interrelations between democracy and representation require further elaboration. Research to understand the link between the challenges facing both representation and democracy, understood as highly dynamic and evolving concepts, is now of clear importance.

REFERENCES

Bonanno, A. (2000). The crisis of representation: The limits of liberal democracy in the global era. *Journal of Rural Studies*, *16*(3), 305–23.

Collier, D., & Mahon, J. E. (1993). Conceptual "stretching" revisited: Adapting categories in comparative analysis. *American Political Science Review*, *87*(4), 845–55.

Diamond, L., & Morlino, L. (2004). The quality of democracy: An overview. *Journal of Democracy*, *15*(4), 20–31.

Groombridge, B. (2006). Parliament and the future: Learning from Finland. *Political Quarterly*, *77*(2), 273–80.

Manin, B. (1997). *Principles of representative government*. Cambridge: Cambridge University Press.

Montanaro, L. (2017). Representing affected interests. In M. B. Vieira (Ed.), *Reclaiming representation: Contemporary advances in the theory of political representation*. Abingdon, Oxon: Routledge.

Otjes, S. (2014). Animal party politics in Parliament. In M. Wissenburg and D. Schlosberg (Eds.), *Political Animals and Animal Politics* (pp. 107–22). New York: Palgrave Macmillan.

Pitkin, H. F. (1967). *The concept of representation*. Berkeley and Los Angeles: University of California Press.

Rubenstein, J. C. (2013). The misuse of power, not bad representation: Why it is beside the point that no one elected Oxfam. *Journal of Political Philosophy*, *22*(2), 204–30.

Sartori, G. (1970). Concept misformation in comparative politics. *American Political Science Review*, *64*(4), 1033–53.

Saward, M. (2006). The representative claim. *Contemporary Political Theory*, *5*, 297–318.

Schmitter, P. C., & Karl, T. L. (1991). What democracy is . . . and is not. *Journal of Democracy*, *2*(3), 75–88.

Shapiro, I., & Hacker-Cordón, C. (Eds.). (1999). *Democracy's edges*. Cambridge: Cambridge University Press.

Street, J. (2004). Celebrity politicians: Popular culture and political representation. *The British Journal of Politics and International Relations*, *6*(4), 435–452. https://doi.org/10.1111/j.1467-856X.2004.00149.x

Tănăsescu, M. (2013). The rights of nature in Ecuador: The making of an idea. *International Journal of Environmental Studies*, *70*(6), 846–61.

Tănăsescu, M. (2016). *Environment, political representation, and the challenge of rights*. London: Palgrave Macmillan.

Urbinati, N. (2011). Representative democracy and its critics. In S. Alonso, J. Keane, & W. Merkel (Eds.), *The future of representative democracy* (23–49). Cambridge: Cambridge University Press.

Urbinati, N. (2014). *Democracy disfigured: Opinion, truth, and the people*. Cambridge, MA: Harvard University Press.

Viera, M. B. (Ed.). (2017). *Reclaiming representation: Contemporary advances in the theory of political representation*. Abingdon, Oxon: Routledge.

Chapter Two

Electoral Representation

Kris Deschouwer

Democracy appears to be in crisis. Anyone who browses today through the recent social science literature on democratic governance can only conclude that democracy is in rather bad shape. There are many debates and discussions on democratic deficits, on challenges to democracy or even on the possible death of democracy (e.g. Crouch, 2004; Della Porta, 2013; Huizinga, 2016; Keane, 2009; Mastropaolo, 2012; Urbinati, 2014). It therefore needs to be rethought, recalibrated, renewed or rejuvenated. This widespread concern is certainly not about the very principle of democracy. The implicit assumption in most writings is that democracy is a valuable project and that it needs to be cherished and defended. That is exactly why the tone has turned more negative: the way in which modern democracy now functions raises concerns about its quality.

There are certainly also more nuanced voices that refer, for instance, to the constant inherent tensions of democracy (Rosanvallon, 2006) or to the development of new forms of democratic control (Keane, 2011), but when *electoral representation* as an important form and practice of modern democracy is being discussed, the diagnosis is most often formulated in terms that express deep concern (Van Reybrouck, 2016). If the only political movement that can look back at decades of constant growth is the group of those who do not turn out to vote, there must be something wrong. If political parties that have governed a country are almost certain to be severely punished at the polls—irrespective of the policies that they conducted—this probably reveals a deep distrust towards just any policy conducted and defended by party government. If voters are easily attracted by candidates who mobilize sceptical attitudes about those who were elected last time, this is a strong indicator of disaffection. All this suggests a lack of legitimacy and a poor responsiveness of the actors who have been selected through the electoral process and who have in this way been given the right to govern in the name of those who were invited to participate in the election.

The focus on elections in the critical voices on democracy is no surprise: they are a key feature of democracy. Modern democracy is—at least in the way it is organized by public authorities—mainly *representative* democracy, and the representation is formally organized by electing the representatives of the people. That does not mean that democracy, representation and elections naturally belong together. Democracy can also be organized without representation, and not all forms of representation are democratic (Alonso, Keane, & Merkel, 2011). Yet both principles and practices have become historically intertwined. Elections have become the standard procedure for selecting those who govern, and exactly because they are elected they can claim to legitimately represent the people. Electoral representation is at the heart of modern democracy, and an assessment of why and how modern democracy is believed to be in crisis must therefore focus on how elections and representation relate to each other.

This chapter will discuss the relation between elections and representation by looking at three historical periods. Following Manin (1997), we start by describing the origins of electoral representation. The choice for electing the governing elites was a conscious one that has built several features into the functioning of democracy. Typical for the early days of electoral representation are limited voting rights and a focus on the quality of the persons who are elected to represent. The second period marks the shift towards mass democracy and party democracy. Candidates for election are grouped into parties that present competing proposals about the way in which society should be organized. The typical party of this phase of electoral representation is the mass party, deeply rooted in a societal subgroup defined by the political cleavages that developed in the process of modernization. The third period—starting in the 1970s—is marked by the erosion of the old cleavages, by increasing volatility and the rise of new parties mobilizing on other than the traditional class and religious cleavages. It is also the period during which parties and elections are increasingly being seen as not properly fulfilling their democratic functions.

The concerns about the functioning of electoral representation today are indeed—be it often only implicitly—voiced by comparing the most recent period with the period of mass democracy and the mass party. Indicators used for describing the evolutions in party organization and voting behaviour stress the fact that the recent figures are—sometimes spectacularly—different from the ones in the heyday of party democracy. We will in this chapter summarize the findings of that literature and reflect on the way in which it refers to the quality of representation. We want to stress two important points. The first is that the literature on political parties and electoral representation has developed quite independently from the literature on political representation in general. It does make assumptions about representation—both its forms and its quality—but very seldom by using the language that is familiar to the scholars of political representation. The second point that will be made in this overview of the parties and elections literature is the fact that when the consequences of the changes in the functioning of democratic representation are discussed, it explicitly or implicitly uses the period of party democracy not only as a point of reference but also as the normative yardstick with which good democratic representation can be evaluated. Democracy and representation are too easily identified and evaluated in the terms of this time-bound institutional practice, which leads to a negative evaluation of new developments and turns a blind eye on the (many) imperfections of political representation in the age of mass parties.

THE NATURE OF ELECTIONS
AND EARLY PARLIAMENTARISM

There are different ways in which people can select other people to represent them. In ancient Athens and throughout the Middle Ages a selection at random was often used to select persons who had to represent their city or certain groups of it. This selection by lot was however gradually abandoned and replaced by election. Electoral representation was not introduced by accident but was a deliberate choice made in full consciousness of its possible consequences (Manin, 1997).

The most important effect of random selection is that every citizen has an equal chance of being selected as a governor. Elections cannot bring about this equality. To the contrary, if winning elections is a condition for being selected as a governor, then those who are selected are different from those who have not been selected, and they become different from those who have made the selection. Elected representatives are always better than the others at least in getting elected, whatever it takes to reach that goal. Election creates a difference between the representatives and the represented and therefore always and by nature produces an assembly that does not perfectly represent, in a descriptive way (Pitkin, 1967), the members of society. Random selection, however, is able to produce this good reflection of the variety of people and groups in society. With a perfectly randomized selection all different subgroups and categories are present and represented according to their relative size. If the founding fathers of different revolutions (American and French, in particular) opted for election and not for random selection, it is because they did not prioritize this equality of chances to be selected nor the descriptive representativeness of the people selected to govern. The choice for election was based on the fact that elections are a procedure by which the selection of the representatives is an act of will, a choice for one option and not for the others. Elections—combined with a limited term and the possibility to be re-elected—introduce a dialogue between the citizens and the governors. Those who want to run for election have to convince voters that they are better suited for the job, and if they seek re-election they need to convince voters that they have done their job in a more than satisfactory way. Elections organize the authorization to govern and the responsiveness and accountability of those elected. "Elections simultaneously separate and link citizens and government" (Urbinati, 2011, p. 24). Random selection cannot do this.

There are three important characteristics of political representation as it developed in these early stages of parliamentary democracy. The first is territorial logic. Members of parliament are elected in relatively small constituencies for which they become the representative. They represent the territory and its voters in a parliament that, however, governs the full territory of the state. This gradually transforms the early parliaments from arenas and forums where local and particular interests were defended and discussed to a forum for discussing and governing the nation. The idea that members of parliament are supposed to represent the nation and not local or particular interests has made its way into the constitutions of democratizing states and remains, to this day, a normative yardstick for defining the scope of representation in parliaments.

The famous speech of Edmund Burke to the electors of Bristol (1774) formulates the principle quite well: "Parliament is not a congress of ambassadors from different and hostile interests, which interests each must maintain, as an agent and advocate, against other agents and advocate; but Parliament is a deliberative assembly of one nation, with one interest, that of the whole—where not local purposes, not local prejudices, ought to guide, but the general good, resulting from the general reason of the whole". This actually does not only present a clear view on the territorial scope of representation that is considered to be the good one, but also on the style. Burke formulates here what has later been labelled the trustee style (Eulau, Wahlke, Buchana, & Ferguson, 1959) of representation. Elected representatives should be elected not because of the interest that they will represent as good advocates or 'delegates', but they are entrusted with the right to govern because they have the capacity and ability to do so. They have the time (because they have the money), they have the expertise needed, and they have the wisdom to deliberate with others and to find with the other elected trustees the best solution for the problems of government.

Next to this trustee style and nationwide scope of representation, the actor who represents the voter in the early days of elected democracy is clearly an individual. It is an individual person who receives the right (and the honour) to represent, and whose capacities and performances are linked to his or her person. Exactly these capacities mark the difference between the voters and the elected representatives. Elected representation creates an elected aristocracy, a group of people who are better than the others at winning office. And in the early days of elected representation, the qualities that were needed to win an election were exactly those of the wise trustee who is—like the good governors in Plato's view—able to see and to defend the common good. That common good, though, is of course only the common good of the small stratum of privileged citizens having the right to vote in these early days of elected representation. The demos of that time is small and fairly homogenous.

ELECTORAL REPRESENTATION IN MASS DEMOCRACY

Carving up gradual historical evolutions into neatly separated periods never does justice to nuances. The picture of the early democracy sketched above is obviously way too blunt. It is however meant to identify its core features and to highlight important changes over time. The core features are in the first place the introduction and diffusion of the electoral procedures which allow for a dialogue of authorization and accountability. The second is the creation of an elected aristocracy, as opposed to equal chances for all citizens (voters) to become part of the selected governors. These two features belong to the very nature of elections and are thus solidly built into the electoral procedure. They cannot be avoided.

The third characteristic is the importance of the individual representative who is supposed to act as a trustee. And the fourth is a fairly homogenous—in terms of social background—electorate. The two latter characteristics are those that will change with the introduction of mass suffrage. While the nature of the electoral procedure does not change, its context does, and the consequences of that have been very important.

The gradual expansion of the right to vote is not a minor development. It has at the same time enlarged the scale at which electoral representation had to be organized and changed the nature of the electorate. The lowering of the thresholds for participation has allowed for the mobilization of the electorate along major cleavages based on class, religion and peripheral identities (Lipset & Rokkan, 1967). The most visible by-product and henceforth central and crucial actor of this mass democracy is the political party. According to the often-cited Elmer Eric Schattschneider (1942, p. 1), "political parties created democracy and modern democracy is unthinkable save in terms of parties". That might be slightly exaggerated (and today increasingly questioned), but it does illustrate at the same time the centrality of parties in the structuring of the competition for elected office and for governing power, and a normative appreciation of the functions fulfilled by parties. Political parties are the collective actors that represent the people, and questions on how representation functions therefore need to look at how parties perform.

With respect to electoral representation, the parties' function is mainly the structuring of the dialogue between the citizens and those who represent them. Political parties provide communication shortcuts to the voters. They do so by aggregating a variety of smaller issues and demands into a broad ideological package. The party ideologies and programmes cover several aspects of the citizens' life and link those together into a coherent story about who they are, what their interests in society are and what kind of policies are to be preferred to defend their interests.

Good representation in such a context is based on congruence (Louwerse, 2012; Thomassen & Van Ham, 2014). There is an obvious and historical match between the interests of the voters and the policy proposals of the party for which they vote. The relationship between voters and parties is therefore not in the first place one of trust—like in the trustee style of the individual representative—but one in which the substance matters. Political parties represent their voters mainly in a delegate style; that is, they receive a mandate to represent and possibly to govern according to clearly announced specific interests. Parties do also act as trustees, certainly in systems where the formation of majorities to govern requires the collaboration of different parties who have received different and to a certain extent always conflicting mandates. The trust given to parties and to those who act for and in the party is however a bounded one, where the party ideology defines the boundaries of what can be accepted. If parties sometimes face hard choices (Müller & Strøm, 1999), it is because they know that they lose votes if they too easily sacrifice their policy promises for the winning of office.

The central role of parties in the dialogue of representation moves the focus away from individual representatives. Although elected representative assemblies are still populated by persons, these members of parliament follow the cues they receive from the parties to which they belong. Even in electoral systems where members are elected in single-member districts, the competition for seats is between parties, and the selection of the candidates is done by the political parties. And parties select on the basis of ideological closeness; they educate and socialize their candidates. This selection of candidates is a first and very strong guarantee for the coherence of the parties in parliament. It is indeed quite striking to see that when members of parliament vote, they usually do so as if they were one single body. Dissident voting behaviour is in most parliaments a rare exception. Parties have means—for instance, candidates have to be re-selected if they want to be re-elected—to discipline a parliamentary group. Yet discipline is seldom needed, because the unity is produced by sheer agreement on the issues or—if there is lack of agreement—by the acceptance of the very norm that representatives need to act in unison with the others who have been elected on the same party ticket

(Depauw & Martin, 2009; Kam, 2009; Sieberer, 2006; Van Vonno, 2016; Van Vonno et al., 2014).

It is this very predictable partisan behaviour of members of parliament that allows for the good functioning of the responsive party model (American Political Science Association, 1950; Thomassen, 2004). This model— a normative prescription for a good functioning mass democracy—assumes that political parties offer alternative options to the voters and subsequently govern in line with these promises. If parties are incoherent, the dialogue is impossible and the cycle of authorization and accountability cannot be properly closed.

The responsive party model also supposes that the competition between parties within one public authority—most typically the national state—is fairly homogenous all over the territory. This means that the same parties should be present in all or most electoral districts and that voters vote according to the signals sent out by the national level of the parties. This process of the nationalization of electoral politics (Caramani, 2004) has indeed taken place. It has reinforced the meaning of the national parliaments as forums and arenas for politics and policies aimed at all citizens of the country, and it has reinforced the role of political parties as the organizing and intermediate actors between the citizens and the public authorities that govern their society.

The typical model of the political party in this context is the mass party (Duverger, 1951). It is characterized by a strong formal organization and written statutes, high membership numbers (possibly through collective membership of affiliate organizations), a widespread network of local sections, a clear party doctrine, and a strong and centralized leadership. The contrast made by Duverger between this mass party and the cadre party is also one between the early days of electoral representation and the era of mass politics. The cadre party was very much a loose association of members of parliament and the small number of voters that needed to be mobilized. The mass party that organizes and mobilizes the members of a subgroup of society is the main and central actor of a democracy in which the demos (gradually and sometimes reluctantly) includes all the members of society.

THE MALAISE OF ELECTORAL REPRESENTATION

This—again, sketchy—picture of electoral representation in mass democracy is needed to properly understand the ongoing discussions about it being in crisis. Recent developments are evaluated against the background of what is sometimes referred to as the 'golden age' of party government (Farrell, 2014) and of well-functioning electoral representation. That golden age is fading away because the clear and easy link between parties and the electorate appears to have become difficult to maintain. After the alignment of voters and parties along the major societal cleavages, we have been entering a time of dealignment (Crewe & Denver, 1985; Franklin, 1992; Franklin, Mackie, & Valen, 1992). One of the first books that started the analysis of electoral dealignment and the increasing volatility of voters was titled *Voters Begin to Choose* (Rose & McAllister, 1986). It suggests that voters until then did not so much choose their party because they agreed with the policy proposals (because of issue congruence), but because they identified with their party, because they belonged to their party, believed in their party and had been socialized to vote for their party. The relative predictability and stability of electoral representation and its outcome was in other words not only (and maybe not mainly) based on issue congruence and delegation but also on some form of symbolic representation (Pitkin, 1967). The parties could refer to a set of meanings, interests, persons, affiliated organizations and senses of belonging that were recognized as the symbols representing one's position in society (see also Chapter 8 on symbolic representation). Whatever the basis of the solid link between voters and parties, one can today establish that parties and voters are facing difficulties in finding each other or in keeping a long-lasting relationship alive. The dialogue has become increasingly difficult.

THE VOLATILE VOTER

There are several indicators that can be used and that are abundantly used in the party literature to illustrate the changing relationship between parties and voters. A first set of indicators look at voting behaviour. And within that category there are two evolutions. First there is voter turnout (Franklin, 2004). The number of registered voters who do cast a vote at elections has been gradually decreasing over the past few decades. The figures do fluctuate, but the lowest turnout figures for all countries are to be found among the most recent elections. Turnout remains highest at the national level and is lower at the subnational level. Especially European elections have a dramatically low turnout (43% in 2014). The meaning of that evolution can be debated, but most scholars agree that it illustrates a lack of interest and a lack of trust in the electoral channel of representation. If people do not want to produce the very limited effort of turning out to vote once every few years, it means that they believe it is not worthwhile. Low turnout illustrates a lack of trust in what elections can do. A growing number of citizens show no interest in the way in which they are electorally represented in parliament. Low turnout also has very clear effects on who is being represented. Those who turn out less are people with lower education, lower interest in politics, and lower political knowledge. They therefore also belong to the socially less privileged groups. If elections are meant to be a mechanism for producing policies that respond to the demands of voters, then they risk being oriented increasingly towards the more privileged groups in society. Decreasing voter turnout means that—at a systemic level and for specific groups—representation does not function well.

A second statistic that captures changes in voting behaviour is electoral volatility (Dassonneville, Blais, & Dejaeghere, 2015; Pedersen, 1979). Electoral volatility refers to the movement of voters between parties between elections. Volatility increases when between two consecutive elections more people move from one party to another. Volatility has been increasing gradually, and the highest figures are again found for the most recent elections. It is generally measured at the aggregate level—by looking at election results—but is confirmed by research at the individual level. It does show without any doubt that parties and voters are no longer able to build long-lasting relationships with each other. Voters choose time and time again, and apparently many of them decide that the previous choice was not a good one. Part of that larger category of increasing volatility is the increasing 'cost of ruling' (Narud & Valen, 2009; Paldam, 1986). It means that parties that have governed are almost certain to pay a price at the next election. Incumbent governments that are able to keep or increase their previous electoral score have become rare exceptions. And yet another way of tapping into the same phenomenon is looking at parties themselves and at the evolutions of their electoral score. They have become increasingly unstable, jumping up and down with sometimes quite spectacular changes. Old parties are not sure that they will be able to mobilize their voters at the next election. New parties easily enter the scene and sometimes grow very rapidly, only to disappear again one or two electoral cycles later (Bolleyer, 2013).

A related evolution in electoral behaviour is the phenomenon labelled as personalization or presidentialization (Karvonen, 2010; McAllister, 2007; Poguntke & Webb, 2005). It suggests that the relation between parties and voters is increasingly based on the personal characteristics of the candidates. Personalization refers to candidates using their personal characteristics and qualities to differentiate themselves from other candidates, including those of their own party. They do so because they fear that association with the party label might be more harmful than helpful to them. Presidentialization refers to personalization for the top candidates only. It points at an evolution in electoral campaigns towards a confrontation between individual candidates who claim the right to lead the country. In presidential systems, this type of competition is obvious, but it has also made its way into parliamentary and multiparty ones.

Decreasing turnout, increasing volatility and increasing personalization of campaigns can all be seen as indicators of the same broader phenomenon of the loosening of partisan ties between voters and elected representatives. The parties appear to be less able than before to offer meaningful information shortcuts. Several related explanations have been put forward to understand how and why this is happening. They refer to important societal and institutional evolutions. Among these are the erosion of the cleavages along which the political parties developed (Evans, 1999). Class and religious divisions have lost their strong and encompassing nature and therefore fail to offer a clear and lasting point of reference for giving sense to many or most daily activities and for defining the crucial identities and interests that need to be represented and defended. These traditional cleavages developed within the boundaries of the nation state, while today's opening up of these boundaries—in economic, demographic and cultural terms—redefines interests in society and generates a gap between the winners and the losers of this globalization (Kriesi et al., 2006). While the latter suggests that older cleavages can be transformed or surpassed by new cleavages, volatile voting behaviour can also be explained by a mere increase in the importance of short-term factors like—see above—the personal characteristics of candidates or the ever changing and shifting short-term issues that are rapidly propelled to the top of the agenda by the variety of new media of communication, only to be replaced by others at an equally high speed. Election results then offer a picture of society that risks being outdated before it is properly taken.

Together with these societal changes that blur the lines between parties and the public, there have been important institutional developments that have affected the meaning of elections. The institutions, rules and procedures of electoral representative democracy have been developed at the level of the national state. The boundaries of the national state have defined citizenship and given shape to the specific development of the societal cleavages along which the political parties have developed. This process of nationalization of politics has also created a concentration of power at the level of the national state, which therefore became the obvious locus for the democratic struggle for power (Bartolini, 2005).

Yet the national state where the democratic battle is fought has lost (some) of its centrality and henceforth its power. Decentralization to substate organizations has spread the power and made lines of representation and accountability less clear (Tuschoff, 1999). More important though is the gradual transfer of competencies to the European Union, which has removed crucial macroeconomic policy instruments from the state level. National politicians are—to quote Peter Mair (2013)—'ruling the void'. They compete for office, while the power is moving elsewhere. That 'elsewhere' is not only the European Union—which is in fact created and controlled by the national states—but also the international economic actors and the financial markets deciding on the credibility of national states. This reduction of the power to conduct policies at the national level is reinforced by the fact that important policy choices have been made in the past—like a social security scheme, a

schooling system, public infrastructure, energy, mobility or environment—
that can today only be changed in a piecemeal way. Many big choices have
been made, and those elected to govern have to a large extent the task to keep
things going. Governments are the administrators of previously made
choices. And when the policy choices are limited, the chances increase that
there is a disconnection between electoral promises and real policy. This
explains why we witness a certain 'depoliticization' of government (Mair,
2013), that is, a legitimation of policies in terms of good governance rather
than in terms referring to electoral pledges and promises. This is what is also
captured by the idea that 'input legitimacy' makes place for 'output legitimacy' (Scharpf, 1999). Parties and governments defend and legitimize policies
in terms of 'what is needed' rather than in terms of 'what has been asked'.
Parties and party government keep order rather than give voice; they stress
the importance of persons who can do the job rather than the party ideology
(Bardi, Bartolini, & Trechsel, 2014).

PARTIES BETWEEN SOCIETY AND THE STATE

A second set of indicators—next to electoral behaviour—looks at the political parties and how they organize. These indicators substantiate the fact that
the archetypical mass party has faded away and has been replaced by 'cartel'
parties (Katz & Mair, 1995) or 'modern cadre parties' (Koole, 1996). The
most spectacular evolution in the way in which parties organize is the development of membership numbers. They have simply been plummeting (Katz
et al., 1992). One of the core characteristics of the mass party—its mass
membership—has therefore rapidly disappeared. The crumbling of membership numbers is another strong illustration of the loosening links between
parties and society. Rather than being membership organizations the political
parties tend to focus their attention—and their organizational resources—on
their role in the state (Katz & Mair, 1995). This migration from society to the
state, or from representing to governing organizations (see also below), is the
core characteristic of the 'cartel party'. It not only focuses very much on its
role as (potential) governing party but also needs to be present in parliament
and possibly in government because that is a crucial source of funding for the
party. The 'cartel' in the party label actually refers to the collusion among the
parties that have in common their need of the state for providing them with
resources (like state subsidies and paid personnel).

This shift in the role and nature of political parties is very important for
understanding the debate about the crisis of representative democracy. The
type of party that has developed has become to a large extent a public utility
(Van Biezen, 2004), an organization regulated and financed by the state that
provides and defends state policies. It is an agent of the state rather than an

agent of the public. And that says something important about representation. The literature on the development of political parties (especially Mair, 2009, 2013) voices concerns about democratic representation because the actors that are supposed to represent the people—the parties—do not represent them but mainly govern them. Yet for parties to have the legitimate right to govern, they must have received the authorization to govern.

This evolution of the former mass parties to cartel parties and their gradual migration from society to the state has left a gap that has been filled by new parties. These come in many different forms and either aim at purifying an ideological position that has been abandoned by the mass parties or at mobilizing new values and ideas that the mass parties—given their lack of solid links with society—fail to pick up (Lucardie, 2000). Especially parties that favour a populist discourse—whether on the right or on the left—are believed to be major challengers of the mainstream parties and of the very logic of political representation, or actually the lack thereof, that the traditional parties have allowed to come about (Mudde, 2007). The challenger parties or niche parties (Meguid, 2007) do claim to represent—do claim to talk in the name of—the people and blame the mainstream and governing parties for misrepresenting them and for conducting policies that have not been asked for by the citizens. The most obvious examples of these 'unwanted' policies are the opening of boundaries to immigration or the transfer of crucial tools of the state's economic power to the European Union.

Enroth (2015) remarks that two concepts are presented here as each other's opposite: representation on the one hand and governing on the other. If parties concentrate on one thing, they cannot do the other. They either represent, or they govern, well. By following that line of reasoning, though—which is widespread in the recent literature on party types and electoral behaviour—one actually limits representation, and especially good and legitimate representation, to the way in which it was done by mass parties. In an implicit way this approach states that representation must be based on predefined interests and identities and that its legitimacy must be deduced from the degree of substantive congruence of these interests and identities between parties and voters. This normative assumption about the way in which representation can be democratic has obviously been forged in the age of mass democracy.

The literature on party politics and the literature on political representation do not often talk to each other (but see Enroth, 2015; Thomassen & Van Ham, 2014), and this shows. The party literature uses a rather static definition of *representation* and has not been in dialogue with developments in the representation literature which suggest that representation is a dynamic process, where representatives not only follow predefined interests of their constituents but also actively make and create them through the process of representation itself (Saward, 2010). The party literature with its yardstick for measuring good representation based on the mass party suggests that representation can only be good and legitimate when it is substantive, that is, when there is congruence between objectively measured interests and promises and policies produced by the parties. Good representation by the parties must then also mainly have a delegate style. Parties using the language of output legitimacy—by referring to the general will rather than to specific partisan demands—are in this perspective not representing at all.

CONCLUSIONS

In this chapter, we have described and reflected on the debates about the alleged crisis of democracy. In particular, we have explored how in these debates the functioning of electoral representation is being questioned. When that is the case, there is always an obvious actor to blame: political parties. It is political parties that are supposed to produce the electoral representational link between citizens and politics, and this link is no longer satisfactory. Political parties fail to produce good representation. That is the consequence of the increasingly loose and short-term ties between voters and parties, which is itself a consequence of societal changes, particularly changes that have led to the erosion of the traditional cleavages on which parties and party systems have been anchored. Society has become more diverse and heterogeneous, and that diversity itself has become an issue with high political relevance. If parties are seen as performing poorly at their representative role, that is also the consequence of the difficulties that they are facing when they govern. They have to do so in an increasingly complex and multilevel context, in which they need to be responsive to several principals, of which the electorate is only one. Parties that govern are constrained by international rules and organizations and by sunk costs of past decisions. Parties focus on governing and therefore cannot properly represent. That is the (very) short summary of the debates in the literature on parties, party systems and electoral behaviour.

It leads to two concluding thoughts. The first is about the relation between elections and representation. The general assessment that the evolutions of the past few decades have led to a deterioration of the quality of representation by elections and by political parties uses the past as a normative yardstick. It states that electoral representation was functioning well—or certainly better than today—in the period of the mass party. Electoral representation was good representation until the beginning of dealignment in the 1970s. That good representation was based on policy congruence, on the similarity between the options and demands of the voters and the positions of the parties. This congruence was the consequence of the cleavage base of parties, of the clear alignment of voters along societal division lines. In the language of representation theory, this was basically representation by delegation. It was representation that focused on an ex ante legitimation or on input legitimacy.

The gradual migration of parties from society to the state, that is, the loosening of the clear and solid ties between parties and voters and the increasing concentration of parties on their role as governors, has undermined this legitimacy. The depoliticization of the legitimacy claims, the reference to responsibility rather than to responsiveness, the stressing of longer-term needs over short-term electoral demands, the accountability to other principals than citizens, often outside the national state, are all indicators of a shift that is in the party literature explained and interpreted as a move away from representation and a replacement of the representational role of parties by their governing role. This actually means that an input-based, cleavage-based and delegate style of representation is not only good electoral representation, but that it is the very definition of electoral representation itself.

It is important to point out this assumption made in the party literature (see especially Enroth, 2015). Representation by parties that use more of a trustee style, rely on output legitimacy or stress the importance of the quality of the political personnel needed to steer the ship through difficult, complex and unpredictable times, is—so the general assumption goes—not representation but governing. Representation theory however would recognize this as a style of representation, quite similar to the style that was dominant in the early and pre-partisan days of electoral representation. It might be more useful and fruitful therefore if the reflections on the evolutions in electoral representation would liaise more explicitly and more often to the representation literature. That could lead to fruitful discussions on the question of whether a trustee style of representation and a more personalized representation can function well for a demos that has not the high degree of homogeneity of the time before the expansion of voting rights. How is, for instance, the increased (and still increasing) heterogeneity and fragmentation of society related to the successful discourses of those who claim to talk in the name of, and thus to truly represent, the people? There is without any doubt much room for interesting exchanges that could include both party and representation scholars (but see Enroth, 2015; Thomassen & Van Ham, 2014).

A second thought also refers to the way in which the era of the mass party is being used as a point of reference and as a normative yardstick for the evaluation of electoral representation. Not only has this reduced the meaning of representation to one of its possible forms, but it has also led to a belief that the past was better than the present. Yet by using the past as a positive point of reference one might also too easily glorify one particular form of democratic governance in general. "The corollary of fixating on a particular model of party is a tendency to pay undue homage to a style of democracy that may well be past its sell-by date. . . . When looking back to a Golden Age there is a risk of doing so through rose-tinted glasses" (Farrell, 2014, p. 443). There are at least two major aspects of this 'good' electoral representation that deserve attention. First there is the apparent importance of stability and predictability. The 'decline' discourse refers to volatile voters who are thus not committed to one single party, to the rise and success of new parties that mobilize on new issues or that try to purify the discourse on old issues. 'Good' electoral representation was in the first place indeed cleavage based, and therefore also relatively stable and predictable. Cleavage-based electoral politics have however a fairly low degree of competition. And one should be aware that by elevating that cleavage-based representation to a gold standard, one assumes that democracy works better when competition is limited, when voters identify rather than choose (Dalton, Flanagan, & Beck, 2011; Rose & McAllister, 1986; Thomassen & Van Ham, 2014). This actually also qualifies the normative assumption that political representation by mass parties was truly a representation by delegation and thus a conscious choice for a package of policy proposals that was well known by the voters. The political stability of the mass party era was also the result of the institutionalization of both parties and party systems, whereby the act of voting was not so much a substance-based authorization to represent and to govern, but also to a large extent a confirmation of a relation of trust between voters and parties.

Secondly, one should also be aware that electoral representation in the age of the mass party was to a large extent a top-down, elite-driven (see Michels, 1911), and male middle-class affair with procedures—like electoral systems and internal party processes—that kept reproducing the same bias. The norm that is used to evaluate the quality of electoral representation should therefore also be scrutinized from that angle, from the invisible edge that has lent political representation its supposed past success (see also Chapter 3 in this volume).

REFERENCES

Alonso, S., Keane, J., & Merkel, W. (Eds.). (2011). *The future of representative democracy.* Cambridge: Cambridge University Press.

American Political Science Association Committee on Political Parties. (1950). Towards a more responsible two-party system: A report of the Committee on Political Parties. *American Political Science Review, 44*(3), part 2 supplement.

Bardi, L., Bartolini, L., & Trechsel, A. (2014). Responsive and responsible? The role of parties in twenty-first century politics. *West European Politics, 37*(2), 235–52.

Bartolini, S. (2005). *Restructuring Europe: Centre formation, system building and political structuring between the nation state and the EU.* Oxford: Oxford University Press.

Bolleyer, N. (2013). *New parties in old party systems: Persistence and decline in seventeen democracies.* Oxford: Oxford University Press.

Caramani, D. (2004). *The nationalization of politics: The formation of national electorates and party systems in Western Europe.* Cambridge: Cambridge University Press.

Crewe, I., & Denver, D. T. (1985). *Electoral change in Western democracies*. New York: St. Martin's.

Crouch, C. (2004). *Post-democracy*. Cambridge: Polity.

Dalton, R. J., Flanagan, S., & Beck, P. A. (Eds.). (1984). *Electoral change in advanced industrial democracies: Realignment or dealignment?* Princeton, NJ: Princeton University Press.

Dassonneville, R., Blais, A., & Dejaeghere, Y. (2015). Staying with the party, switching or exiting? A comparative analysis of determinants of party switching and abstaining. *Journal of Elections, Public Opinion & Parties, 25*(3), 387–405.

Della Porta, D. (2013). *Can democracy be saved?* Cambridge: Polity.

Depauw, S., & Martin, S. (2009). Legislative party discipline and cohesion in comparative perspective. In D. Giannetti & K. Benoit (Eds.), *Intra-party politics and coalition governments* (pp. 103–20). London: Routledge.

Duverger, M. (1951). *Les Partis politiques*. Paris: Armand Colin.

Enroth, H. (2015). Cartelization versus representation? On a misconception in contemporary party theory. *Party Politics, 23*(2). doi:10.1177/1354068815576293.

Eulau, H., Wahlke, J., Buchana, W., & Ferguson, L. (1959, September). The role of the representative: Some empirical observations about the theory of Edmund Burke. *American Political Science Review*, pp. 742–56.

Evans, G. (Ed.). (1999). *The end of class politics? Class voting in comparative context*. Oxford: Oxford University Press.

Farrell, D. (2014). 'Stripped down' or reconfigured democracy. *West European Politics, 37*(2): 439–55.

Franklin, M. (1992). The decline of cleavage politics. In M. Franklin, T. Mackie, & H. Valen (Eds.), *Electoral change: Responses to evolving social and attitudinal structures in Western countries*. Cambridge: Cambridge University Press.

Franklin, M. (2004). *Voter turnout and the dynamics of electoral competition in established democracies since 1945*. New York: Cambridge University Press.

Franklin, M., Mackie, T., & Valen, H. (1992). *Electoral change: Responses to evolving social and attitudinal structures in Western countries*. Cambridge: Cambridge University Press.

Huizinga, T. (2016), *The new totalitarian temptation: Global governance and the crisis of democracy in Europe*. New York: Encounter Books.

Kam, C. J. (2009). *Party discipline and parliamentary politics*. Cambridge: Cambridge University Press.

Karvonen, L. (2010). *The personalisation of politics: A study of parliamentary democracies*. Colchester: ECPR Press.

Katz, R. S., & Mair, P. (1995). Changing models of party organization: The emergence of the cartel party. *Party Politics, 1*(1), 5–28.

Katz, R. S., Mair, P., Bardi, L., Bille, L., Deschouwer, K., Farrell, D., . . . Widfeldt, A. (1992). The membership of political parties in European democracies, 1960–1990. *European Journal of Political Research, 22*(3), 329–45.

Keane, J. (2009). *The life and death of democracy*. London: Simon & Schuster.

Keane, J. (2011). Monitory democracy? In S. Alonso, J. Keane, & W. Merkel, *The future of representative democracy* (pp. 212–35). Cambridge: Cambridge University Press.

Koole, R. (1996). Cadre, catch-all or cartel? A comment on the notion of cartel party. *Party Politics, 2*(4): 507–23.

Kriesi, H., Grande, E., Lachat, R., Dolezal, M., Bornschier, S., & Frey, T. (2006). Globalization and the transformation of the national political space: Six European countries compared. *European Journal of Political Research, 45*(6): 921–56.

Lipset, S. M., & Rokkan, S. (1967). Cleavage structures, party systems and voter alignments: An introduction. In S. M. Lipset & S. Rokkan (Eds.), *Party systems and voter alignments* (pp. 1–64). Glencoe, IL: Free Press.

Louwerse, T. (2012), Mechanisms of issue congruence: The democratic party mandate. *West European Politics, 35*(6): 1249–71.

Lucardie, P. (2000). Prophets, purifiers and prolocutors: Towards a theory on the emergence of new parties. *Party Politics, 6*(2), 175–85.

Mair, P. (2009). *Representative versus responsible government*. MPIfG Working Paper 09/8, Cologne.

Mair, P. (2013). *Ruling the void: The hollowing of Western democracy*. London: Verso.

Manin, B. (1997). *Principles of representative government*. Cambridge: Cambridge University Press.

Mastropaolo, A. (2012). *Is democracy a lost cause? Paradoxes of an imperfect invention*. Colchester: ECPR Press.

McAllister, I. (2007). The personalization of politics. In R. J. Dalton & H. D. Klingemann (Eds.), *Oxford handbook of political behavior* (pp. 571–88). Oxford: Oxford University Press.

Meguid, B. (2007). *Party competition between unequals: Strategies and electoral fortunes in Western Europe*. Cambridge: Cambridge University Press.

Michels, R. (2011). *Zur Soziologie des Parteiwesens in der modernen Demokratie; Untersuchungen über die oligarchischen Tendenzen des Gruppenlebens*. Leipzig: W. Klinkhardt.

Mudde, C. (2007). *Populist radical right parties in Europe*. Cambridge: Cambridge University Press.

Müller, W., and Strøm, K. (1999). *Policy, office, or votes? How political parties in Western Europe make hard decisions*. Cambridge: Cambridge University Press.

Narud, H. M., & Valen, H. (2009). Coalition membership and electoral performance. In K. Strøm, W. C. Müller, & T. Bergmann (Eds.), *Cabinets and coalition bargaining* (369–402). Oxford: Oxford University Press.

Paldam, M. (1986). The distribution of election results and the two explanations of the cost of ruling. *European Journal of Political Economy, 2*(1): 5–24.

Pedersen, M. (1979). The dynamics of European party systems: Changing patterns of electoral volatility. *European Journal of Political Research, 7*(1): 1–25.

Pitkin, H. (1967). *The concept of political representation*. Berkeley: University of California Press.

Poguntke, T., & Webb, P. (Eds.). (2005). *The presidentialization of politics: A comparative study of modern democracies*. Oxford: Oxford University Press.

Rosanvallon, P. (2006). *La contre-démocratie. La politique à l'âge de la défiance*. Paris: Seuil.

Rose, R., & McAllister, I. (1986). *Voters begin to choose*. Beverly Hills: Sage.

Saward, M. (2010). *The representative claim*. Oxford: Oxford University Press.

Scharpf, F. (1999). *Governing in Europe: Effective and democratic?* Oxford: Oxford University Press.

Schattschneider, E. E. (1942). *Party government*. New York: Holt, Rinehart & Winston.

Sieberer, U. (2006). Party unity in parliamentary democracies: A comparative analysis. *Journal of Legislative Studies, 12*(2): 150–78.

Thomassen, J. (2004), Empirical research into political representation: Failing democracy or failing models? In K. M. Jennings & T. Mann (Eds.), *Elections at home and abroad: Essays in honour of Warren Miller* (pp. 237–64). Ann Arbor: University of Michigan Press.

Thomassen, J., & Van Ham, C. (2014). Failing political representation or a change in kind? Models of representation and empirical trends in Europe. *West European Politics, 37*(2): 400–419.

Tuschhoff, C. (1999). The compounding effect: The effect of federalism on the concept of representation. In J. B. Brzinski, T. D. Lancaster, & C. Tuschhoff (Eds.), *Compounded Representation in Western European Federations* (pp. 16–33). London: Frank Cass.

Urbinati, N. (2011). Representative democracy and its critics. In S. Alonso, J. Keane, & W. Merkel (Eds.), *The future of representative democracy* (23–49). Cambridge: Cambridge University Press.

Urbinati, N. (2014). *Democracy disfigured: Opinion, truth, and the people*. Cambridge, MA: Harvard University Press.

Van Biezen, I. (2004). Political parties as public utilities. *Party Politics, 10*(6): 701–22.

Van Reybrouck, D. (2016). *Against elections: The case for democracy*. London: Bodley Head.

Van Vonno, C. (2016). *Achieving party unity: A sequential approach to why MPs act in concert* (Doctoral dissertation, Leiden University).

Van Vonno, C., Itzkovitch-Malka, R., Depauw, S., Hazan, R., & Andeweg, R. (2014). Agreement, loyalty, and discipline: A sequential approach to party unity. In K. Deschouwer, & S. Depauw (Eds.), *Representing the People: a Survey among Members of Statewide and Substate Parliaments.* (pp. 110-136). Oxford: Oxford University Press.

Chapter Three

Exclusion and Representation

Women's Struggle for Inclusion

Karen Celis

> Women's exclusion is ubiquitous, operated through layer upon layer of male
> dominated political institutions (not least political parties) that are insulated by
> layer upon layer of formal and informal rules of exclusion.
> —Childs & Lovenduski, 2013, p. 507

Exclusion is the common ground of many of today's crises of electoral representation (see Chapter 2). Low voter turnout, voter dealignment, lack of responsiveness and congruence are all considered to be problematic because too many citizens, their concerns or interests, are increasingly excluded from representation processes, resulting in an overall poor linkage between citizens and representatives.

Exclusion from representation is highly problematic from a democratic perspective for at least two reasons. First, it is problematic because of the cumulative material effects of exclusion. Exclusion from political power makes the excluded vulnerable to further oppression. Indeed, political power can be used—strategically or out of ignorance—for denying rights and equal standing, and for overlooking the specific needs and wishes of the powerless and the excluded. Inclusion, by contrast, provides the opportunity to fight and avoid exclusion and to obtain equality in all spheres of life, both public and personal, through laws and policies. Second, exclusion disempowers symbolically: it sends the message that the excluded are 'second-class citizens'; equal inclusion in political representation, on the contrary, is a recognition of full citizenship (Phillips, 1995; Young, 2000). As a consequence, exclusion results in a lack of trust and an overall decrease in the legitimacy of democratic institutions (Dovi, 2007; Williams, 1998).

The historical and contemporary exclusion of women from electoral representation is well documented. Only few women feature amongst the elected aristocracy and selected governors. This has not drastically changed with mass democracy and the growing importance of political parties in electoral democracy. Whatever form these parties have taken over time, women's stark numerical underrepresentation remained. Furthermore, and again notwithstanding the many shifts and turns occurring in electoral representation, its actors and institutions, the inclusion of women's needs and interests remained (and remain) lacking.

Feminists have been fighting women's exclusion from representative institutions for well over a century. The feminist struggle for women's inclusion in politics has developed over different phases, each featuring a distinct theoretical account about the nature of women's exclusion and a distinct set of tools and measures to overcome gender inequality. In contrast to the evaluation of electoral representation insightfully discussed in Chapter 2 by Deschouwer, in which the past is used as a normative yardstick, feminists have always been future oriented and mobilized to overcome the next layer of exclusion. They do not look backwards to the 'good times' of the mass party when policy congruence naturally followed from the clear alignment of voters with cleavage-based parties. Given that gender equality never existed in any polis, feminists do not consider any past situation to be the ideal after which many things went wrong. Quite the contrary. According to feminists, the wrong is situated in the past and the present, and full political inclusion and gender-equal political representation is yet to be achieved.

Hence, the feminist experience and expertise with dealing with exclusion in a future-oriented fashion might well be of interest to those who seek to overcome problematic forms of exclusion in contemporary representative democracies. To that end, this chapter first tells the story of the ongoing Western feminist struggle for inclusion in the processes and institutions involved in political representation and the multiple refinements of the feminist ideal of full inclusion through time. It is an endeavour in which feminist scholars, political actors and practitioners joined forces. Building from this overview, the conclusion asks the question of what we can learn from the feminist struggle for inclusion in order to overcome contemporary problems of exclusion.

GENDER-EQUAL POLITICAL
REPRESENTATION IN THE 20TH CENTURY

Women's Enfranchisement and Equal Numbers of Female Representatives

When women knocked at the doors of political institutions, these had already, *grosso modo*, taken the shape that we know today. Political representation was operationalized through elections, and political parties had already become the pivotal actors in mass democracies that they remain today. The right to vote and to run as candidates was the evident first stride of the first feminist wave of the end of the 19th century (Paxton, 2000). It resulted in women's enfranchisement worldwide in the course of the 20th century. Enfranchisement was considered to be a means to provide full political citizenship to women. Liberal feminists assumed that it would suffice to obtain equality in politics: once women were granted full voting rights—the right to vote and to stand as candidates—time would do the rest of the work (Kantola, 2006).

Radical feminists were however more pessimistic (Kantola, 2006). They warned that political institutions are inherently patriarchal, and simply including women would not change them. It would be the other way around: women would get co-opted and marginalized by the institutions, and the power status quo would be maintained. Women would not only be unable to bring change and exert power in and through the institutions, but they would also be used to legitimize oppressive mechanisms. Later, new institutionalist studies (Pierson, 2000), and feminist institutionalism more specifically (Kenny, 2007), proved radical feminist theorists to be closer to reality than their liberal sisters. Positions of privilege and marginalization, together with gender power relations, are institutionalized and hence hard to change. Institutions provide power resources such as rules, regulations, norms and standing operating procedures to advantaged groups—privileged men—that enable them to resist feminist change.

Women's enfranchisement was indeed found to not be as transformative as feminists had hoped: it did not automatically result in equal numbers of male and female electoral candidates and elected representatives. A vast number of cultural, socio-economic and political factors and conditions accounted for the prevalence of women's underrepresentation: non-egalitarian cultures, religiosity, low levels of women in the pipeline professions and how electoral systems function in practice (Childs & Lovenduski, 2013, pp. 495–96).

Party organization, rules and ideology were found to play a crucial role in maintaining low descriptive representation of women in elected assemblies (Norris & Lovenduski, 1995). Out of pure sexism or gender blindness, party selectorates deemed men to better fit the criteria of 'the good candidate' (Murray, 2015). Parties were found to prefer candidates who had already proven themselves in terms of legislative capacities and electoral potential, and who could enhance parties' internal and external effectiveness accordingly (for a discussion, see Celis & Erzeel, 2017). This 'incumbency advantage' has been known to quickly turn into an incumbency disadvantage for new groups in politics, such as women (Schwindt-Bayer, 2005).

'Vote for women' campaigns by the women's movement (both party-internal and party-external) were not able to overcome women's underrepresentation. They were found to be inefficient, but increasingly also conceptually wrong. Such campaigns hold individual women responsible for solving a structural problem that they are the victims of. Feminist political theorists developed a new understanding of gender equality that had two major implications for establishing women's equality. First, it reversed the guilt logic. The underrepresentation of women was theorized as a structural problem, hence requiring a structural solution (Squires, 2013). Political institutions, not women themselves, came to be seen as the ones responsible for abolishing formal or informal rules that generate gender inequality and for implementing processes and tools to obtain it. Second, equality was approached as a political or cultural matter, implying recognition of different identities, for instance gender identities (Phillips, 1999). This 'equality as recognition' was a shift away from 'equality as redistribution', the dominant understanding of equality through much of the 20th century. The latter strand understood inequality primarily as a class phenomenon, something to do with the distribution of income and wealth and the effects of private property. And whereas economic equality was very much about erasing (class) differences, the newer understanding of political equality acknowledged difference. Understanding equality as recognition constituted an important turn in gender and politics activism and scholarship. The argument that women were different had foremost been used as a tool to discriminate against women. In the newer understanding of gender equality, in contrast, it was used to question and challenge the 'male norm' embedded in political institutions.

Understanding women's underrepresentation as structural and the positive recognition of difference made possible tools to increase women's representation that go beyond formal equality and equal opportunities. More precisely, it provided legitimacy for strategies aiming at equal outcomes. This conceptual shift underpinned the introduction of gender quotas (and also the creation of women's policy agencies and the introduction of gender mainstreaming, which we discuss further on) (Squires, 2007). Gender quotas became a global phenomenon, and worldwide over 100 countries have implemented them (Krook, 2010). Gender quotas often did increase the levels of women's representation, however not always to a great extent, nor in a linear way or in all contexts. Like women's enfranchisement, gender quotas were found not to be a sufficient condition to reach full gender equality in representation. Nevertheless, all efforts together did lead to an increase in the numerical representation of women, although there still exist important regional differences.

Women's Substantive Representation

Once women were present in elected assemblies, new burning questions arose: did it matter, and did women representatives represent women? These concerns directed feminists to the next layer of representation: substantive representation. Next to formal (voting rights) and descriptive equality (equal numbers of men and women candidates and elected representatives), equal consideration for women's issues was deemed to be the cornerstone of gender equality in representation.

Feminist political theorists in the 1980s and 1990s engaged with this concern by discussing what the 'women's issues' that needed to be represented were and the way and extent to which women's descriptive representation (women representatives) led to women's substantive representation (i.e. of women's issues). Concerning the first issue—the 'what' of women's substantive representation—it proved to be very difficult to neatly demarcate women's issues. In the 1980s debates took place over whether women's substantive representation was about representing specific women's *interests* linked to their socio-economic positions defined by the 'private distribution of labour' (i.e. the tasks of giving birth to and caring for children) or also included more broadly distinct *wants* and *needs* originating in female values and psyche (Diamond & Hartsock, 1981; Sapiro, 1981). The scholars of group representation of the 1990s, in contrast, embraced the view that the content of substantive representation could not be defined in a universal way. It results from the diversified life experiences of different groups of women (Phillips, 1995, 1998) and their social perspective as a group deriving from its structural position in society (Young, 1997, 2000).

Concerning the second question—the relationship between descriptive and substantive representation—an important shift occurred during the 1980s and 1990s. The 'critical mass theory' coined by Drude Dahlerup in 1988 and its interpretations (and misinterpretations) later on predicted a rather firm link between being female and acting for women (for a discussion, see Childs & Krook, 2006). When women make up a critical mass of about 30%, they can and will make a difference and substantively represent women. Anne Phillips's 'politics of presence' theory of the 1990s (Phillips, 1995, 1998), on the contrary, contended that the link between women representatives and the political representation of women is only 'half-fastened': the *possibility* that women are represented increases when women are present, but there is no guarantee (see also Jónasdóttir, 1988; Mansbridge, 1999; Williams, 1998).

Women's shared gendered life experience provides 'resources' in terms of consciousness and expertise for the substantive representation of women, and it also influences their priorities and engagement for representing women. Most importantly, the presence of women also enables a 'politics of transformation': interests and needs take shape during political decision-making. Only in the most optimal circumstances, in particular when a group is systematically present in the process of working out alternatives, is it capable of formulating new subjects and challenging dominant conventions. Similarly, Young (1994, 2000) contends that making the social perspective of women present can only be achieved by persons who share the experience that goes with a structural position in society, as the people in this position are sensible to certain subjects, questions or events.

There exists but little proof for the critical mass effect on women's substantive representation (for a discussion, see Celis, 2009). Nevertheless, it became a powerful argument for claiming more female representatives, for example, through the implementation of gender quotas (Childs & Krook, 2006). In contrast, the 'politics of presence' theory was supported by a vast body of empirical research (see Celis, 2009, for a discussion). It confirmed that women representatives did substantively represent women's issues and interests, but not everywhere and under all circumstances. Women representatives were indeed found to have a greater potential to represent women because, more than men, they recognized the existence of women's interests and felt a responsibility to devote attention to and prioritize them. Women representatives also featured higher levels of congruence with the views of women MPs on the one hand and female citizens and the women's movement on the other. However, such attitudinal differences were not always applicable to all women MPs or for every attitudinal dimension. Some studies confirm that female representatives' roll-call voting behaviour is, compared to men, more favourable for women, that they speak more often in favour of women and work more on legislation in favour of women. Other studies discard the existence of such a connection. These studies point at a multitude of political, parliamentary, social and individual conditions and situations hampering the wish to represent women in practice or interfering with its contents. Party affiliation often seems to be the most influential factor. In that sense, it was yet another lesson learned about the stickiness of political institutions and how hard it is to change them.

Given these varying levels of success in increasing women's substantive representation through an increase in their numerical representation, other venues were explored: women's sections in political parties, women's policy agencies within the state and gender mainstreaming policy. First, women established women's internal party organizations (party women's sections or auxiliaries) (Kittilson, 2013). These often had already existed for a long time, and they mainly had a coffee service and other types of supportive and entertaining function. When women became enfranchised, they served to elicit women voters' support. From the 1980s onwards, they were increasingly used by party women for promoting women for office and to articulate women's demands. This integration strategy was found to be quite productive. In some Nordic countries where women chose this kind of party politics avenue early on, women's representation reached high levels. In other parties these women's sections, however, resulted in the ghettoization and marginalization of party women.

Second, women's policy agencies (WPAs) are undoubtedly amongst the key actors in substantive representation to have developed in recent decades. WPAs are special units charged with promoting women's rights, including offices, commissions, agencies, ministries, committees, secretaries, and advisers for the status of women (McBride Stetson & Mazur, 1995). In 1975 the UN World Conference on Women in Mexico City recommended that all governments establish WPAs, and this request has been repeated at every UN World Conference on Women since, and also promoted by international women's groups. Nearly 30 years later, 164 countries around the world had established WPAs (Squires, 2007). Notwithstanding their scepticism about the bureaucratization that it would engender, the women's movement did mobilize the establishment of WPAs. But WPAs were also established for reasons other than a true commitment to establishing equality, for example, the strategic interests of political elites and international pressure, which set limits to their performativity.

WPAs are highly effective in the substantive representation of women and perhaps even a more successful strategy than increasing women in elected politics (Htun & Weldon, 2012; Weldon, 2002). The WPAs were found to be important allies within the state for women's movement activists. In the early days of the WPAs the linkage between elected representatives, members of the executive, academic experts, women's movement actors and public officers working in the WPAs (the so-called femocrats) was based on a shared feminist perspective, a shared descriptive identity (i.e. being a woman) and a shared history (Woodward, 2004). These networks were dubbed 'velvet triangles' due to the highly informal policy processes that this collective of female and feminist actors engaged in. According to Woodward (2004), gender studies experts, public officers and women's movement activists worked together in a dynamic triangular relationship to foster equal opportunities for women and men and to establish and implement equality policies. Furthermore, it was found that being a woman and having feminist attitudes were common characteristics of WPA members, gender experts and politicians active at the regional, national and international policy levels. Collectively, these constellations of people fostered the substantive representation of women (Holli, 2008).

Until the mid-1990s, WPAs were mostly engaged in lawmaking, producing sectorial equality policies and positive action targeting women. In the mid-1990s an important shift occurred when WPAs became the key actor in a new type of gender equality policy that was quickly and widely adopted. This new policy, known as gender mainstreaming, was launched during the 1995 UN World Conference on Women in Beijing and soon became the dominant equality policy strategy due to its promotion by the Council of Europe and the European Commission (Verloo, 2005). Gender mainstreaming is a multifaceted, holistic, long-term strategy that aims at establishing gender equality between women and men by including a gender perspective in all policy domains (Walby, 2005). It therefore applies a set of tools and processes designed to integrate a gender perspective into all policies at the planning stage by considering the likely effects of policies on the respective situation of women and men, and then revising the policies if necessary such that they promote gender equality rather than establish, produce or reproduce gender inequality (Squires, 2007).

THE CHALLENGES OF THE 21ST CENTURY: DIVERSITY AND INEQUALITY AMONGST WOMEN [1]

By the end of the 20th century it was commonly accepted amongst scholars, activists, politicians and policy actors alike that gender equal representation required equal participation of women in elections, equal presence in representative institutions, equal consideration for women's issues and interests and the furthering of gender equality in all policy domains. Supported by an understanding of equality as a recognition of gender difference and requiring more than formal rights, a global consensus also developed concerning the tools for establishing gender equal representation, such as gender quotas, women's party sections, WPAs, and gender mainstreaming. Notwithstanding all these successes and achievements, new challenges arose due to an increased acknowledgement that women are not a homogeneous bloc, and that also within the group of women, processes of privileging and marginalization occur.

The 20th-century politics of gender equality was predominantly underpinned by men-women binary logics. Notwithstanding the acknowledgement that there is no such thing as 'the' woman or man, and that 'women' and 'men' are highly heterogeneous categories, theories and praxis to improve women's political representation applied a men-women binary nonetheless. The implications of the diversity within these categories for what gender equal political representation actually is and for its implementation only recently became a concern of the theories, empirical investigations and implementation of gender equal representation. What is problematized is the fact that older views on gender equal representation, using the men-women binary, can support claims that equality is reached even when large groups of women, perhaps even the majority of women, are not represented, or are structurally underrepresented (see also Celis & Mügge, 2017). That is because the ideological diversity and power differences amongst women were not considered to be a major issue for gender equal political representation; they were not considered political. Instead, the gender and politics scholarship considered 'women' as a unitary category and applied a universal and singular understanding of women's issues. Ironically, by not seeing the ideological and power dimension of diversity, and by consequence deeming it safe to work with singular and universal categories and concepts, it fell into the same trap that they fought for decades: by ignoring difference they made gendered power inequalities and conflicts of interests invisible, and by doing so they contributed to generating and maintaining inequality.

We now turn to discussing two ongoing scholarly debates about diversity and gender equal representation. The first one focuses on ideological diversity amongst women and was put on the agenda by the rise of conservative women in politics and gendered claims by conservatives. The second one focuses on structural power inequalities between women. The latter debate comes from the theoretical innovations brought by intersectionality theory. After briefly presenting these scholarly debates, we turn to discussing their implication for the implementation of gender equality in practice.

Ideological Diversity Amongst Women: Conservatives and Women's Representation

At the turn of the century a new phenomenon occurred with regard to women's representation: conservative parties selected and elected greater numbers of women representatives and articulated explicitly gendered discourses on women and gender relations (Celis & Childs, 2014). Changes in gender roles in society, conservative women's party sections and competition from left-wing parties championing a women-friendly label incentivized right-wing parties to reconsider (some) traditional gender roles and to feminize (Childs & Webb, 2012; Schreiber, 2014).

Party feminization and gendered representation seem to be able to coexist, albeit often uneasily, with rightist ideologies, even populist radical right ones. Including women representatives and women's issues implied a stretching and bending of conservative ideology and practices because traditional ideas about what is appropriate for women and in particular about women's participation in the political sphere challenge the very presence of conservative women in politics. Conservative women negotiated these public/private tensions in various ways, for instance by claiming one's motherhood as the basis for one's participation in politics and for the articulation of a conservative inspired set of women's interests. A good number of populist radical right actors are also making strong claims about gender equality (Akkerman, 2015). They often present an intriguing mix of advocacy of more traditional gender roles, especially regarding the private sphere, and apparently feminist notions of gender equality as central to a national identity in need of protection from an Islam that is anti-feminist/anti-gender equality (De Lange & Mügge, 2015).

The greater presence of conservative women political actors and conservative claims to act for women disconcerted many feminist activists and scholars. Albeit often implicit, what was conceived as women's interests and gender equality was embedded in a progressive, leftist feminist ideology: it was in the first instance about granting rights to women as individuals (not as mothers or wives) and establishing equality between men and women (not complementarity and equal worth). This feminist ideology historically had its roots in the fight for women's gender equality in which, especially in the later decades of the 20th century, progressive and left-wing actors and organizations were most visible and successful within the women's movement. Their understanding of what gender equality entails in political representation had also heavily influenced scholarly debates, and especially empirical investigations. The presence of conservative women representatives and conservative claims for women and gender equality was at odds with the existing consensus amongst scholars and activists about what it entailed to represent women.

The result of this ideological bias in the scholarship was that the specific struggles of conservative women politicians and their contribution to women's representation was less studied (but see, for instance, Childs & Webb, 2012; Schreiber, 2008; Wiliarty, 2010). Furthermore, the focus on leftist women's issues and themes (such as the legalization of abortion) had foremost drawn attention to anti-feminist interventions by conservatives, and to the 'exceptional' conservative (women) representative that acted as an ally with the feminist sisters. This way of measuring against feminist standards had potentially underscored the conservative politics of presence, that is, conservative women's efforts and specific strategies to further conservative women's representation.

The 'progressive/leftist' bias of the feminist scholarship—or the problematic conflation of women's and feminist substantive representation—that the conservative women's representational contribution exposed prompted a revision of the conceptual framework on women's substantive representation (Celis & Childs, 2012). The straightforward logic underpinning the conceptual revision was that conservative women also had a democratic right to be represented on their own terms. A conceptual distinction was made between feminist and gendered claims for women. The latter category includes those claims that address women's concerns and perspectives but do so in ways distinct from traditionally understood feminism. Instead, these can be under-pinned by a commitment to women's traditional roles and see women's public role as an extension of their private role as, for instance, mothers or caregivers. Like feminist claims, they might give voice to women's organiza-tions, in this case conservative women's organizations. They might well be framed in terms of valuing women's difference and improving women's status and lives, rather than seeking to transform gender roles and norms in a progressive, feminist sense.

The major advantage of this conceptual framework is that it is fit to include plural, and potentially oppositional, interpretations of what is in the interests of women. The conceptual inclusion of varying claims for women that are responsive to different and perhaps opposing groups in society con-stitutes an important shift in the struggle for gender equality in political representation. Establishing gender equality often was, and still is, a struggle between women as the marginalized and underrepresented group and men as the overrepresented and dominant group in politics. Recognizing that power struggles are not only occurring between men and women, but also amongst women, raises a new requirement for gender equality in politics. Next to addressing women's underrepresentation vis-à-vis men, establishing gender equality also implies that the views of some women and feminists do not erase the issues and interest of other women. Fair representation requires the representation of women as a diverse group (also see Chapter 6).

Intersectionality: Within-Group Advantage and Disadvantage

At the turn of the century the traditional interpretation of the principle of gender equality was also challenged by globalization and multiculturalism (Squires, 2013). These evolutions draw attention to the fact that the category of women was (and admittedly always has been) a very heterogeneous group, and, most importantly, that within-group differences went hand in hand with within-group privileged and disadvantaged positions. For instance, black women face different forms of oppression than black men or white women given that they experience racism and sexism simultaneously. This intersect-ing of multiple discriminatory strands is captured by the intersectionality concept. It contends that categories are 'always permeated by other catego-ries, fluid and changing, always in the process of creating and being created by dynamics of power' (Cho, Crenshaw, & McCall, 2013, p. 795). In other words, one's identity and structural position in society is never constituted on the basis of, for example, one's gender alone. Positions are always influenced by the combination of identities such as gender, race, class, sexuality, age, ethnicity and ability (Crenshaw, 1991; Hill Collins, 1998). Such intersections generate positions of marginalization as well as privilege, depending on the specific time, context and space in which they operate.

The feminist scholarship on gender and representation predominantly using the singular categories 'men' and 'women' was critiqued for making the
underrepresentation of subgroups of women invisible. When, for instance,
measuring gender equality, it was quite often by comparing white, majoritarian, highly educated, heterosexual women and men. Based on this counting,
claims about gender equality would be made (Celis & Mügge, 2017). The
level of gender equality for other, marginalized groups of women and men,
and how gender mechanisms worked out for them, was ignored. By doing so
the feminist scholarship was accused of contributing to the privileging of
dominant groups of women and maintaining the oppression of others.

White, middle-class, heterosexual women were not only the implicit
norm; this privileged group of women also reaped the benefits of the tools
that were implemented to increase women's representation. Parties' wom-
en's sections were criticized for being too 'white', and gender quotas for
above all furthering the representation of privileged (e.g. ethnic majority/
white) women (Celis & Erzeel, 2017; Celis, Erzeel, & Mügge, 2015). WPAs
were found to privilege the concerns of white, highly educated, working
women (Hakim, 2000; Squires, 2008), and equality policies that fit dominant
policy frames indirectly favoured already privileged groups of women (Bedford, 2006; Franceschet, 2002).

In sum, the presence of a partial group of women in elected political
institutions, and the representation of a particular reading of women's interests and of gender equality, is increasingly rejected as an indicator of gender
equal representation. Successful representation can no longer be limited to
legislators furthering a 'universal' agenda of interests that all group members
share—for instance, a leftist feminist one in the case of women. Therefore, it
became increasingly important to explore the possibility of competition and
conflict—not just collaboration, mutual reinforcement, and reciprocity—
between actors that may have alternative, if not directly opposing, conceptions of what the substantive representation of the (sub)group means in terms
of its content, direction and purpose.

Good Substantive Representation of Women and Gender Equal Representation

As a result of the debates about the ideological and power differences
amongst women, scholars have started revising the notion of gender equal
political representation. The main focus of this ongoing investigation is on
substantive representation, but it also has implications for descriptive representation. Its goal is to elaborate an understanding of good substantive representation that does not assume that all women share the same interests but
that, instead, is able to cope with an ideologically diverse and potentially
conflicting set of women's interests. This approach to women's representa-

tion requires two kinds of guarantees: it should be all-inclusive and rightfully inclusive (Celis & Childs, 2018).

First, good substantive representation of women should be all-inclusive. This requirement is about ensuring that disadvantaged groups of women and women who do not self-identify as progressive feminists are equally represented. Incorporating these ideas implies that the quality of women's substantive representation is defined by the extent to which it is responsive to and inclusive of a wide variety of women and their interests, and that they receive equal respect and consideration (Celis & Childs, 2018; Disch, 2011; Severs, 2012; Weldon, 2002).

The all-inclusive requirement sheds new light on the traditional tools for implementing gender equality. The gender equality devices should be used and sequenced to enhance the political system's reflexivity when it concerns women (Disch, 2011). The reflexivity of the system determines the extent to which individuals' reflective control—their capacity to guide, inform and restrain their representatives—is warranted. Reflexive systems require (1) the recognition of contestation and dissent as positive features (not as 'betrayal' or 'not being loyal to the women's cause'), because they bring individuals to a clearer understanding of what is at stake and hence can draw them into the representation process; (2) regular and structured ways for taking objections into account; and (3) the interlocking of representative actors and institutions (media, parties, state institutions, Internet forums, and so on) so that intervention by one triggers the reaction of others, collating individuals' reactions into subsequently broader assemblies, and therefore broadening the scope of the conflict.

Translating these general ideas to the specific gender equality tools in political representation implies intensifying and complicating the efforts for descriptiveness, "to press, not just for proportionate representation along *one* social axis—gender, class, race, caste—but for a proportionality that recognizes the cross-cutting intersections of the full range" (Phillips, 2012, 516). Gender quotas are hence foremost desirable when they are adopted by all parties, that is, both the parties on the left and on the right on the ideological continuum. Given that chances for women's substantive representation increase parallel to an increase in women's descriptive representation, responsiveness to a wide variety of women might also increase when all parties implement gender quotas. Idem for women's party sections and the feminization of parties: in light of all-inclusive women's representation, these are as desirable in right-wing parties as in left-wing ones. All-inclusiveness should also be a priority of WPAs and gender mainstreaming. When specific issues are on the political agenda, they must make sure that the voices and perspectives of all women involved are included, for instance by including representatives of a wide variety of women's organizations or by including a diverse set of experts. Instead of perceiving WPAs as allies of feminist women's organizations, they could provide a forum for discussion and deliberation about women's interests and issues as part of a participative and deliberative gender mainstreaming strategy.

Second, women's representation should be rightfully inclusive. This requirement is about making sure that what is included is still women's representation. An inclusive understanding of women's representation does not imply that whatever, for instance, a populist radical right representative says and does in the name of women is automatically accepted as contributing to women's representation. Rightful inclusion requires mechanisms for exclusion, albeit not the progressive feminist standards of the past. Instead, rightful inclusion/exclusion can be based on the extent to which representative claims relate to claims made by women's organizations in society and the mutual relationships between representatives and those they claim to represent (Dovi, 2002); correspondence between a particular claim and subsequent action, or at least the intention to deliver on the claims made (Dodson, 2006); or how a particular claim 'fits' with others claims made at the same time by the same actor (or closely related actors) (Celis & Childs, 2018). Only actors that meet these requirements deserve a seat at the table where women's issues and interests are discussed.

This new take on good substantive representation of women contributes to gender equality in political representation in a double way. First, as mentioned above, by acknowledging ideological diversity and power differences amongst women due to the intersection of gender with other inequality mechanisms, gender equality is secured for all women. Put simply, it increases gender equal representation by granting it to more women. Secondly, and most importantly, it furthers gender equal political representation because it claims a fully-fledged political status for women's issues and interests. It shifts women's representation from the margin to the heart of politics where ideological conflict and power struggles take place.

Gender equality in substantive representation is no longer similar to a straightforward interest representation. For a long time, it was necessary for feminists to join forces and focus on a single issue and perspective due to the numerical underrepresentation of women and the low legitimacy of women's issues. Claiming the right to disagree and the revision of the political institutions because of ideological diversity and power struggles amongst women, equal to all other members of the polity, brings the quest for gender equal political representation to a fourth phase, following the ones focusing on enfranchisement and descriptive and substantive representation. The political representation of women as a diverse group is a new challenge for the establishment of gender equality. It constitutes a new frontier, or edge of representation, given that it requires a more sophisticated understanding of what constitutes fair representation. Moreover, our representative institutions need to be redesigned in order to allow for the representation of women as a diverse group.

CONCLUSION

What can we learn from the feminist struggle for solving today's crisis of representative democracy? As mentioned, this question is grounded in the observation that the stride for gender equality and many contemporary debates about the crisis of representation have exclusion as a common ground. Obviously not all problems with democratic representation boil down to the issue of exclusion, but arguably many do. As discussed in Chapter 2, exclusion is a common denominator of contemporary debates about a missing link between citizens and politics, trust, legitimacy and responsiveness. This concluding section explores what can be learned from the feminist struggle for inclusive democratic institutions with its long history marked by various phases where different thoughts and solutions have been tried out, evaluated, and improved. We would like to draw attention to three general insights that could travel from the feminist undertaking for making representation more inclusive to the overarching contemporary debates about the crisis of representative democracy. They concern the nature of exclusion, the scope of the endeavour required to make representation more inclusive, and the kind of representation and representative institutions it asks for.

First, as the history of gender equal representation shows, increasing inclusiveness only occurred once exclusiveness was understood to be a structural phenomenon. As long as it was considered to be an individual problem requiring a solution at the individual level, not much progress was made. Individual voting rights for women and campaigns urging women to vote for women did not result in drastically more inclusive institutions. More important progress was made once exclusion was seen as a structural feature of political institutions, praxis and culture. Most importantly in that respect is that it paved the way for shifting the responsibility for erasing exclusion away from individual women and towards political institutions. It enabled structural measures reforming the institutions that cause exclusion.

A second general insight that can be drawn from the feminist political history concerns the stickiness of institutions. Exclusionary mechanisms are hard to break. Increasing inclusiveness requires more than establishing formal equality; it requires—some would argue drastic—measures that change the political and institutional culture. As discussed above, the right to vote for women and to stand as a candidate did not automatically erase gender biases in the electoral system and political culture. Equal descriptive representation of men and women was therefore sought through the implementation of gender quotas and the establishment of women's sections within political parties. Equal representation of women's issues and interests and the gendering of the general interest required strategies like the establishment of women's party sections, women's policy agencies and gender mainstreaming. The formal, descriptive and substantive inclusion of citizens that are systematically excluded requires coordinated action at various levels and sites; in the case of women these included revising electoral laws, party reorganization, establishment of public administration bodies and rules about the policymaking process.

Thirdly, the ongoing scholarly debates on gender equal representation in times of ideological diversity and intersectionality point to the fact that inclusive representation requires more than increasing the diversity of the inhabitants of the representative institutions. What is equally needed is more deliberation as part of representation. As discussed above, the quality of representation increases when inclusive deliberations regarding political issues are set up, including a wide variety of concerned voices. This requires reflexive representative institutions that support contestation, dissent and objections.

We by no means claim that these three insights are final recipes for solving all of today's issues with democratic representation. They should be read as avenues that deserve further thought and explorations in the quest for making representation more inclusive. In light of the crises that representative democracy faces, it is an important task that is worth our intellectual and political investment. Nevertheless, it will remain a job unfinished. The desired level of inclusiveness that is needed and wanted is not objectively given and static. As the feminist history discussed in this chapter shows, how inclusive representation must be in order to be democratic, and how it should be brought about, is part and parcel of political debates and societal and scholarly evolutions. Societal and political debates about inclusiveness are likely here to stay.

Moreover, we should acknowledge that there are limits to how inclusive representative democracy can be. Citizens can never be fully included in representation and made present in all of their diversity. First, there are obviously practical limits to, for instance, how inclusive a representative institution can be. Political institutions can only include a certain number of elected representatives, which sets a limit to how many identities can be embodied by our representatives. Second, and more importantly, representation is not really representation without exclusion. Representation requires the absence of the represented in order to generate agency for deliberation on the part of the representatives to deliberate and reach a decision (Urbinati, 2008). Even if the interests, views and perspectives of all affected citizens are included, some might well not be in the final decision concluding the deliberative process. The absence of the represented, however, also generates the agency on behalf of the citizens to judge its representatives, laws and representative institutions. Political representation thus designates a form of political process as a continuum that is structured in terms of circularity between representative institutions and society over time. It is in that way an engine for the entire democratic process (Urbinati, 2006, pp. 28–31). As Chapters 7 and 5 by Dupont and Tănăsescu in this volume demonstrate, this representational paradox (i.e. that representation is making the absent present in some way) should be embraced in order to acknowledge the specific democratic function of representation. These are enduring edges of representation; it requires the absence of the represented, and exclusion is inherent to it.

NOTE

1. This section greatly draws from my current work with Sarah Childs and publications such as Celis and Childs 2012, 2014, 2018.

REFERENCES

Akkerman, T. (2015). Gender and the radical right in Western Europe: A comparative analysis of policy agendas. *Patterns of Prejudice, 49*(1–2), 37–60.

Bedford, K. (2006). The imperative of male inclusion: How institutional context influences World Bank gender policy. *International Feminist Journal of Politics, 9*(3), 289–311.

Celis, K. (2009). Substantive representation of women (and improving it): What is and should it be about? *Comparative European Politics, 6*(4), 95–113.

Celis, K., & Childs, S. (2012). The substantive representation of women: What to do with conservative's claims? *Political Studies, 60*(1), 213–25.

Celis, K., & Childs, S. (Eds.). (2014). *Gender, conservatism and political representation.* Colchester: ECPR Press.

Celis, K., & Childs, S. (2018). Conservatism, conservatives and the recasting of women's political representation. *Politics and Gender.*

Celis, K., & Erzeel, S. (2017). The complementarity advantage: Parties, representativeness and newcomers' access to power. *Parliamentary Affairs, 70*(1), 43–61. doi:10.1093/pa/gsv043

Celis, K., Erzeel, S., & Mügge, L. (2015). Intersectional puzzles: Understanding inclusion and equality in political recruitment. *Politics & Gender, 11*(4), 765–70.

Celis, K., & Mügge, L. (2017). Intersectional group representation: A new inductive approach. *Politics.* doi:10.1177/0263395716684527

Childs, S., & Krook, M. (2006). Should feminists give up on critical mass? A contingent yes. *Politics & Gender, 2*(4), 522–30.

Childs, S., & Lovenduski, J. (2013). Political representation. In K. Celis, J. Kantola, G. Waylen, & L. Weldon (Eds.), *The Oxford handbook of gender and politics* (489–513). New York: Oxford University Press.

Childs, S., & Webb, P. (2012). *Sex, gender and the Conservative Party: From iron ladies to kitten heels.* Basingstoke: Palgrave.

Cho, S., Crenshaw, K., & McCall, L. (2013). Toward a field of intersectionality studies: Theory, applications, and praxis. *Signs, 38*(4), 785–810.

Crenshaw, K. (1991). Mapping the margins: Intersectionality, identity politics, and violence against women of color. *Stanford Law Review, 43*, 1241–99.

De Lange, S., & Mügge, L. (2015). Gender and right-wing populism in the Low Countries: Ideological variations across parties and time. *Patterns of Prejudice, 49*(1–2), 61–80.

Diamond, I., & Hartsock, N. (1981). Beyond interests in politics: A comment on Virginia Sapiro's 'When are interests interesting? The problem of political representation of women'. *American Political Science Review, 75*(3), 717–21.

Disch, L. (2011). Toward a mobilization conception of democratic representation. *American Political Science Review, 105*(1), 100–114.

Dodson, D. (2006). *The impact of women in Congress.* Oxford: Oxford University Press.

Dovi, S. (2002). Preferable descriptive representatives: Will just any woman, black, or Latino do? *American Political Science Review, 96*(4), 729–43.

Dovi, S. (2007). *The good representative.* Oxford: Blackwell.

Franceschet, S. (2002). State feminism and social movements: The impact of Chile's Servicio Nacional de la Mujer on women's activism. *Latin American Research Review, 38*(1), 9–40.

Hakim, C. (2000). *Work-lifestyle choices in the 21st century: Preference theory.* Oxford: Oxford University Press.

Hill Collins, P. (1998). It's all in the family: Intersections of gender, race, and nation. *Hypatia, 13*(3), 62–68.

Holli, A. (2008). Feminist triangles: A conceptual analysis. *Representation, 44*(2), 169–85.

Htun, M., & Weldon, L. (2012). The civic origins of progressive policy change: Combating violence against women in global perspective, 1975–2005. *American Political Science Review, 106*(3), 548–69.

Jónasdóttir, A. G. (1988). On the concept of interests, women's interests, and the limitation of interest theory. In K. B. Jones & A. G. Jónasdóttir (Eds.), *The political interests of gender.* London: Sage.

Kantola, J. (2006). *Feminists theorize the state.* Basingstoke: Palgrave Macmillan.

Kenny, M. (2007). Gender, institutions and power: A critical review. *Politics, 27*(2), 91–100.

Kittilson, M. C. (2013). Party politics. In K. Celis, J. Kantola, G. Waylen, & L. Weldon (Eds.), *The Oxford handbook of gender and politics* (pp. 536–53). New York: Oxford University Press.

Krook, M. L. (2010). *Quotas for women in politics: Gender and candidate selection reform worldwide.* Oxford: Oxford University Press.

Mansbridge, J. (1999). Should blacks represent blacks and women represent women? A contingent "yes". *Journal of Politics, 61*(3), 628–57.

McBride Stetson, D., & Mazur, A. (1995). *Comparative state feminism.* Thousand Oaks, CA: Sage.

Murray, R. (2015). What makes a good politician? Reassessing the criteria used for political recruitment. *Politics & Gender, 11*(4), 770–76.

Norris, P., & Lovenduski, J. (1995). *Political recruitment: Gender, race and class in the British Parliament.* Cambridge: Cambridge University Press.

Paxton, P. (2000). Women's suffrage in the measurement of democracy: Problems of operationalization. *Studies in Comparative International Development, 35*(3), 92–111.

Phillips, A. (1995). *The politics of presence.* Oxford: Clarendon Press.

Phillips, A. (1998). Democracy and representation: Or, why should it matter who our representatives are? In A. Phillips (Ed.), *Feminism and politics* (pp. 224–40). New York: Oxford University Press.

Phillips, A. (1999). *Which equalities matter?* Cambridge: Polity Press.

Pierson, P. (2000). Increasing returns, path dependence, and the study of politics. *American Political Science Review, 94*(2), 251–67.

Sapiro, Virginia. (1981). When are interests interesting? The problem of political representation of women. *American Political Science Review, 75*(3), 701–16.

Schreiber, R. (2008). *Righting feminism.* Oxford, New York: Oxford University Press.

Schreiber, R. (2014). Motherhood, representation and politics: Conservative women's groups negotiate ideology and strategy. In K. Celis & S. Childs (Eds.), *Gender, conservatism and political representation* (pp. 121–40). Colchester: ECPR Press.

Schwindt-Bayer, L. (2005). The incumbency disadvantage and women's election to legislative office. *Electoral Studies, 24*, 227–44.

Severs, E. (2012). Substantive representation through a claims-making lens: A strategy for the identification and analysis of substantive claims. *Representation, 48*(2), 169–81.

Squires, J. (2007). *The new politics of gender equality.* London: Palgrave.

Squires, J. (2008). The constitutive representation of gender: Extra-parliamentary re-presentations of gender relations. *Representation, 44*(2), 187–204.

Squires, J. (2013). Equality and universalism. In G. Waylen, K. Celis, J. Kantola, & L. Weldon (Eds.), *The Oxford handbook on gender and politics* (pp. 731–55). Oxford: Oxford University Press.

Urbinati, N. (2006). *Representative democracy: Principles and genealogy.* Chicago: University of Chicago Press.

Verloo, M. (2005). Displacement and empowerment: Reflections on the concept and practice of the Council of Europe approach to gender mainstreaming and gender equality. *Social Politics, 12*(3), 344–65.

Walby, S. (2005). Gender mainstreaming: Productive tensions in theory and practice. *Social Politics, 12*(3), 321–43.

Weldon, L. (2002). *Protest, policy and the problem of violence against women.* Pittsburgh: University of Pittsburgh Press.

Wiliarty, S. (2010). *The CDU and the politics of gender in Germany: Bringing women to the party.* New York: Cambridge University Press.

Williams, M. (1998). *Voice, trust, and memory: The failings of liberal representation.* Princeton, NJ: Princeton University Press.

Woodward, A. (2004). Building velvet triangles: Gender and informal governance. In T. Christiansen & S. Piattoni (Eds.), *Informal governance and the European Union* (pp. 76–93). London: Edward Elgar.

Young, I. M. (1994). Gender as seriality: Thinking about women as a social collective. *Signs: Journal of Women in Culture and Society, 19*(3), 713–38.

Young, I. M. (1997). Deferring group representation. In I. Shapiro & W. Kymlicka (Eds.), *Ethnicity and group rights. Nomos 39. Yearbook of the American Society for Political and Legal Philosophy* (349–76). New York: New York University Press.

Young, I. M. (2000). *Inclusion and democracy.* Oxford: Oxford University Press.

Chapter Four

Representation and Accountability of the European Union in Global Governance Institutions

Sebastian Oberthür

Over the past decades, the European Union (EU) has increasingly emerged as an important actor on the international scene (Bretherton & Vogler, 2006; Drieskens, 2017; Jupille & Caporaso, 1998). A major part of the EU's international 'actorness' has materialized in international negotiations, frequently conducted within international institutions. Relevant international institutions include both formal international organizations, such as the United Nations (UN) or the World Health Organization, and international treaty systems, frequently referred to as 'international regimes'. Examples of relevant treaties include the Non-Proliferation Treaty, the UN Convention on the Law of the Sea and the UN Framework Convention on Climate Change. They typically establish permanent negotiating systems in which countries develop applicable rules and norms over time. The EU (and its member states) has become a major actor in many such institutions (Jørgensen, 2009; Jørgensen & Laatikainen, 2013; Laatikainen & Smith, 2006; Oberthür, Jørgensen, & Shahin, 2012).

It should be useful to clarify up front that, for the purposes of this chapter, the EU or 'Europe' as an international actor can take different shapes. First, the 'European Union' is, strictly legally, a supranational organization established by its member states with its own legal personality separate from the member states, that can act and be represented as such (usually by the European Commission) internationally. Second, the EU, politically speaking, also acts and is represented internationally, if the EU member states act in concert, even outside the supranational EU apparatus.[1] Third, the EU and its currently 28 member states—and thus a total of 29 entities—in practice frequently act together and in coordinated ways on the international plane. In each of these cases—whether formally acting on behalf of the EU itself, the EU member states, or the EU and its member states—'Europe' or the EU (in simplified speak) are represented as a political unit. As further discussed in section 3, the choice of concrete representative arrangements is frequently contentious, as it relates to the distribution of competences between the EU itself and the member states. The following analysis will relate to all these sub-cases and shapes. To enhance clarity, I will hence attempt to refer to 'the EU itself', 'the EU member states', and 'the EU and its member states' as and where appropriate—while referring to 'the EU' (without 'itself') also as encompassing all three different constellations.

The analysis in particular zooms in on and applies to the broad range of regulatory policies that the EU and its member states pursue. These include a variety of policies directly or more indirectly related to the EU internal market (including environmental policy, common commercial policy, health policy, monetary policy, asylum policy, etc.). The analysis excludes the EU's Common Foreign and Security Policy (CFSP) and Common Security and Defence Policy (CSDP) that have both remained far less regulatory and far less 'Europeanized', with greater authority and discretion retained for national policymaking (and hence a different *problematique* as regards external representation of 'Europe'). As a result, the EU's international actorness has remained far more constrained in this area (Smith, 2014).

This chapter investigates a particular aspect of the EU's role in international institutions and multilateral negotiations in general, namely the EU's political representation and democratic accountability and legitimacy. It thus addresses an aspect that is rarely in the limelight of analyses of the EU's role in international institutions/negotiations. The literature has in particular zoomed in on the EU's success, effectiveness and performance in relevant international negotiations, the EU's international 'actorness', its leadership and processes of delegation to and control of the EU negotiator (Delreux, 2011; Drieskens, 2017; Jørgensen & Laatikainen, 2013; Koops & Macaj, 2015; Meunier, 2005; Oberthür et al., 2012; Van Schaik, 2013). The question of who acts and speaks on behalf of the EU (and its member states) in international negotiations has always formed part of this broader discussion. However, it has rarely been explored through the lens of political representation and democratic accountability. To what extent do arrangements for external representation and policymaking of the EU enable and ensure democratic accountability and legitimacy?

I argue in particular that the accountability of EU external policy is based on rather long chains of representation. As a result, there is a particularly large distance between those representing and deciding on behalf of the EU externally and those eventually to be represented, the people. This constitutes challenges for democratic accountability and legitimacy that become particularly pronounced and problematic where the policy at stake is or becomes subject to contestation. Possible approaches to addressing these challenges include a strengthening of intergovernmental and supranational channels of representation and participation as well as enhanced direct involvement in EU and international decision-making by EU citizens. Their potential to successfully counter the existing shortcomings remains, however, limited (see Chapter 8 in this volume for a fuller discussion).

The argument is developed in three steps. First, the next section demonstrates that both global governance and the role of the EU in relevant international negotiations and institutions have grown tremendously over the past decades. Hence, EU external policymaking has politically become increasingly significant, enhancing the potential for political contestation. The subsequent section then analyzes and presents in more detail the arrangements for the representation and policymaking of the EU and/or its member states in international negotiations in accordance with the relevant provisions of the Lisbon Treaty (2007), which is composed of the Treaty on European Union (TEU) and, in our context particularly relevant, the Treaty on the Functioning of the European Union (TFEU). In force since December 2009, this current legal basis builds on similar provisions in preceding European treaties including the Maastricht Treaty (1992), the Amsterdam Treaty (1997) and the Nice Treaty (2001). The analysis of these two sections provides the foundation for exploring the logics and chains of representation from the individual to 'the EU' in external relations in the fourth section of this chapter, highlighting and discussing the problems that arise for political accountability and legitimacy. The fifth section then turns to exploring a number of routes which may help enhance political accountability and legitimacy in EU external representation in global governance institutions.

THE RISE OF GLOBAL GOVERNANCE AND THE EU AS AN INTERNATIONAL ACTOR

In much of the literature on global governance, the strong growth of international organizations and institutions over the past decades is commonplace. It is well established that the number of international organizations and 'international regimes' has increased tremendously. For example, the number of multilateral environmental agreements has grown from a few dozen in 1950 to a few hundred in 1980 to nearly 1,300 in 2016 (Mitchell, 2018). More generally, the number of international treaties has been found to have increased fourfold since 1960 alone (Zürn, Ecker-Ehrhardt, & Radtke, 2007; see also UN Treaty Collection at https://treaties.un.org/). Two noteworthy features of the 'legalization' of international relations has been a rise of procedures and mechanisms for rule implementation and enforcement (Keohane, Moravcsik, & Slaughter, 2000) and the emergence of institutional complexes in which international institutions interact to co-govern particular policy areas (Biermann, Pattberg, Van Asselt, & Zelli, 2009; Gehring & Faude, 2013; Oberthür & Stokke, 2011). This trend indicates a growth not only of international rules, but also of international fora for policymaking, since many, if not most, relevant international treaties establish decision-making procedures and processes through which their parties develop policy over time. Hence, an increasingly dense web of international institutions enables and develops responses to globalization, thereby limiting the room for manoeuvre for national (and subnational) regulators.

As part of this process, global governance has also seen a qualitative change in that international regulation has increasingly deeply and profoundly intruded on domestic policies and regulations 'behind the borders' (Zürn, 2004). For example, whereas regulation of international trade (since 1994 in the framework of the World Trade Organization) originally aimed primarily at reducing trade tariffs at the border, it has over time increasingly addressed non-tariff barriers, services and product standards in domestic law (and hence 'behind the border'). Similarly, international environmental policy and law has seen a gradual shift from addressing transboundary flows of pollution and other such issues to shaping domestic policies, measures and frameworks. Much the same could be said about other policy areas and has, for example, led to the emergence of and calls for global administrative law (Esty, 2006; Kingsbury, Krisch, & Stewart, 2005). Hence, global governance has not only expanded and grown denser, but it has also deepened so that it increasingly shapes and constrains policymaking at lower levels of governance.

In parallel with the growth of global governance, EU policymaking has dramatically expanded and deepened over the past decades. This intensifying European integration is not least reflected in the various rounds of changes to the European treaties since the 1980s: the Single European Act of 1987, the Maastricht Treaty of 1992, the Amsterdam Treaty of 1997, the Nice Treaty of 2001 and the Lisbon Treaty of 2007. Starting from the internal market, the EU has as a result acquired competences and developed policies and legislation in many other policy fields, including environmental policy, energy policy, monetary policy, fisheries policy, transport policy, cohesion policy, social policy, health policy, agricultural policy, and the area of freedom, security and justice (including asylum and immigration policy and judicial cooperation) (see TFEU, especially Articles 3 and 4; see also Nugent, 2010).

As a 'supranational' governance system beyond the nation state, the EU has itself become a major actor in international/global governance (Bretherton & Vogler, 2006; Jørgensen & Laatikainen, 2013). The rise of the EU as an international actor and negotiator has a major root and rationale in the aforementioned growth of EU competences for internal policymaking. For example, a common internal market implies common external customs tariffs and does not leave room for unilateral action by individual member states on external tariffs. For the internal market to function, cars, for example, cannot face different import tariffs in, say, Spain than in Portugal or Poland; and if they faced different national import tariffs, importers would look for the member state with the lowest rate. This provides a major rationale for the EU itself (represented by the European Commission), rather than individual member states, to conduct international trade negotiations, be it in the World Trade Organization or in bilateral contexts such as the EU-Canada Comprehensive Economic and Trade Agreement (CETA) concluded in 2017. In general, internal EU competences and common internal EU regulations require EU involvement in related international negotiations, because any agreement would need to be (also) implemented at the EU level (even if at times action at the member state level may also be required). This logic has long been established as a rule by the jurisdiction of the European Court of Justice (ECJ) and has, with the entry into force of the Lisbon Treaty in 2009, been codified in the TFEU: Accordingly, paragraph 1 of Article 216 TFEU permits and requires the EU itself to be involved in international negotiations where their outcome 'is likely to affect common rules or alter their scope'.

Consequently, the EU itself, usually represented by the European Commission, has become involved in many relevant international negotiations in addition to the member states. This has not been a development without impediments. First and foremost, the EU as a supranational organization is not automatically recognized as an inter-*national* actor by other countries, as international treaties traditionally are concluded between states. Hence, many international organizations do not provide for membership of actors other than states. However, where the EU itself holds significant governance competences, it has gradually been recognized by other states either formally (as a 'regional economic integration organization' or otherwise) or informally (e.g. by de facto discussing matters with the European Commission even where the EU is not a formal member). Thus, the EU itself has become an important actor in many, if not most, areas of global governance, routinely participating in multilateral negotiations on trade, fisheries, agriculture, climate change and others of the aforementioned policy areas in which it possesses internal competences and has significant governance resources at its disposal (Gehring, Oberthür, & Mühleck, 2013; Jørgensen & Laatikainen, 2013).

Also beyond the areas in which the EU itself, usually represented by the European Commission, acts internationally, there is hardly an area of regulatory policy in global governance in which EU representation does not play an (increasing) role. As can be derived from Article 4 and various provisions under Title V of the TEU containing the general provisions on the EU's external action, EU member states are under an obligation to coordinate their

external policies in international institutions also where they retain significant competence (as opposed to the EU itself) (Eeckhout, 2011). Europe or
'the EU' is thus also represented and acting beyond the areas with exclusive
EU competence for internal policymaking, formally as a coalition of the EU
member states increasingly speaking with one voice or, at least, one message
(with some variation; Da Conceição-Heldt & Meunier, 2014). Under conditions of 'mixity' (with both the EU itself and the member states holding
competences), Europe also increasingly speaks with one voice as 'the EU
and its member states'. Hence, EU member states have been found to become increasingly coherent in their voting behaviour in fora such as the UN
General Assembly, especially on non-security items (Blavoukos, Bourantanis, Galariotis, & Gianniou, 2016; Bouchard & Drieskens, 2013), and coordinate their policymaking and negotiating strategy in most global governance
fora (Jørgensen, 2009; Jørgensen & Laatikainen, 2013). Leaving aside fora
related to the EU's CFSP, including the UN Security Council (as mentioned
before), remaining pockets of incomplete coordination especially relate to
established old international institutions that do not foresee EU participation
and facilitate gaming by EU member states wishing to preserve established
influence (e.g. the International Monetary Fund; see Wouters & Van Kerckhoven, 2013).

In conclusion, the rise of global governance and of the EU as an international actor in it is constitutive of the problem in focus here, namely the
democratic accountability and legitimacy of the arrangements for the EU's
external representation and policymaking. Global governance has acquired
increasing political significance, and the EU has become a major actor in
related policymaking processes (alongside individual member states). The
growth of international legislation and policymaking has put increasing constraints on policymaking at lower levels of governance. And the increasing
role of the EU in external representation and policymaking limits the inde-
pendence of individual EU member states. This increasing importance of
international and European policymaking beyond the nation state provides a
strong rationale of its increasing contestation and results in a rising demand
for their (democratic) legitimacy/legitimation (Zürn, 2004). As a result, the
question of the accountability of those who represent the EU and its member
states in international negotiations/institutions and decide on their external
policies arises and gains particular relevance.

ARRANGEMENTS FOR THE EXTERNAL
REPRESENTATION AND POLICYMAKING OF THE EU

The external representation of the EU and its member states in international
negotiations can follow two different routes, primarily depending on the

distribution of competences between the EU itself and its member states. As further discussed in this section, the EU and its member states are thus usually represented internationally either by the European Commission or by the Council presidency (or, occasionally, by individual member states). In either case, policy is commonly coordinated with and/or among member states in a special committee of member state representatives. Member states in the Council of Ministers are also involved in defining the negotiating objectives and in deciding on the eventual acceptance of an agreement. In comparison to the European Commission and the EU Council, the role of the European Parliament, albeit growing, has remained more limited.

Where competences of the EU itself exist, the European Commission is commonly in the lead on external representation and policymaking.[2] This 'supranational' mode follows the procedures for the negotiation of international treaties laid down in Article 218 TFEU (previously Article 300 EC Treaty). Accordingly, the European Commission first submits a recommendation to open negotiations and for negotiating directives to the Council of Ministers of EU member states. On this basis, the member states in the Council are to decide on the launching of negotiations and the more specific negotiating mandate, that is, the objectives to be pursued and achieved by the European Commission as the chief negotiator. Furthermore, the European Commission generally must conduct the negotiations in coordination with a special committee of member state representatives. In practice, such coordination involves discussions in an appropriate existing working party of the EU Council of Ministers, assembling ministerial officials from all member states, as well as '*sur place*' at international negotiating sessions. Once the international negotiations have led to an agreement, the EU member states in the Council (as well as the European Parliament—see below) have to accept this international agreement for the EU itself to be able to sign and ratify it. While the European Commission is in the lead, the arrangements thus involve coordination with, and ensure a strong role for, the EU member states. Importantly, council decisions in each step of the procedure are to be taken by qualified majority, unless internal policymaking requires unanimity (Eeckhout, 2011).

While Article 218 TFEU principally only applies to the negotiation of formal international treaties, the relevant coordination and representation procedures, once established, are usually also followed for lower-level negotiations that commonly occur *in the framework of* the relevant treaties and organizations. For example, regular, frequently annual 'conferences of the parties' (COPs) to multilateral environmental agreements commonly take significant decisions concerning the interpretation and implementation of the agreements concerned (e.g. Brunnée, 2002; Gehring, 2007). Parties to the Paris Agreement on climate change, for instance, adopted important implementing provisions for the agreement in 2018. Similarly, international fisheries management organizations such as the International Commission for the Conservation of Atlantic Tunas regularly take important decisions on catch quotas. The European Commission and the EU member states pragmatically apply the same 'supranational' arrangements for the external representation and policymaking, adapted as appropriate to their changed context: the Commission is in the lead and coordinates with the member states, while negotiating directives are not formally adopted and no formal decision on the acceptance of the outcome of the negotiations is taken (since it is not required).

Where competences rest with the member states, the presidency of the Council of Ministers, that rotates among the EU member states every six months, usually takes the lead in external representation. In this 'intergovernmental' mode of representation, coordination mechanisms within a special committee of EU member states within the Council of Ministers otherwise commonly very much resemble the ones under Article 218 TFEU just described. However, negotiating objectives and directives are agreed in the form of Council Conclusions (as compared to a formal council decision on a negotiating mandate) and, hence, are decided by consensus (as opposed to qualified majority in the case of Article 218 TFEU—see above).

While the locus of competences thus principally determines who represents the EU and its member states in international negotiations/institutions, reality is in at least two respects not as clear cut. First, the EU itself (represented by the European Commission) is not a member of all relevant international institutions, which at times do not provide for membership of parties other than states. In these cases, the EU itself may not formally be represented. Second, competences are usually not nicely delimited along the borders of international treaties. Instead, many international agreements encompass areas of EU and of member state competence and thus constitute 'mixed agreements'. Where possible, representation may then be divided per international agenda item (with e.g. the Council presidency speaking on finance issues that fall under member state competence). However, this may not always be possible since individual agenda items may touch upon competences of both the EU itself and the member states.

The EU's response to these complications of the real world has to a large extent been pragmatism. For example, where the EU itself is not recognized as a member within an international governance institution, the EU has formally been represented by the Council presidency or another member state— even in areas of exclusive EU competence (with the European Commission being actively involved in the making of the substance of the external policy). Similarly, in settings where only a subset of member states is party to an institution (e.g. a regional convention such as the Alpine Convention) or represented in its governing body (e.g. the International Monetary Fund), one of the relevant EU member states (or all relevant EU member states jointly supported by coordination) may represent the EU. Pragmatic arrangements have also been developed in the international climate negotiations to informally appoint a mixed team of lead negotiators. The Council presidency to this end usually appoints, in coordination with the other member states and the European Commission, so-called lead negotiators (supported by expert issue leaders) from among the government officials of various member states and the European Commission (Delreux & Van den Brande, 2013). These informal arrangements have helped ensure that member states, who eventually have to implement international and European regulations, remain actively involved in external policymaking and representation (Delreux & Keukeleire, 2017).

Although not formally involved in external representation or policymaking as such, the role of the European Parliament has grown over the years. Based on a different representational logic, the Parliament previously only had consultative rights. The Lisbon Treaty in Article 218 TFEU then established that the Parliament's consent be required for the ratification of most international treaties. It also determined that the European Parliament 'shall be immediately and fully informed at all stages of the procedure' (paragraph 10). The European Parliament thus has information rights and veto power that it can employ to advance its role in external policymaking and to press for its views to be taken into account in international treaty negotiations. The Parliament has used this veto power to this end, for example by rejecting the Anti-Counterfeiting Trade Agreement (ACTA) in 2012, not least on the grounds that its views had not been taken into account in the negotiations. It has also played an active role in discussions on contested agreements such as CETA and the EU-US Transatlantic Trade and Investment Partnership (TTIP). Although expanding, the European Parliament's role in external policymaking has nevertheless remained clearly more limited than that of the European Commission and the member states in the EU Council.[3]

It may not be surprising that the arrangements for the EU's international representation have been subject to significant political and societal contestation. Different arrangements may provide different levels of autonomy to the 'agents' from their 'principals' and may lead to varying outcomes of international negotiations. That different arrangements produce significantly different outcomes provides a major rationale for related debates and conflicts. Consequently, related conflicts between the European Commission and member states have led to several judgements of the European Court of Justice (Eeckhout, 2011). Furthermore, international trade negotiations with Canada (CETA) and the Unites States (TTIP) have seen a rising contestation of representation arrangements and the role of the European Commission.

CHAINS OF REPRESENTATION
AND PROBLEMS OF ACCOUNTABILITY

In a globalized world in which regulatory authority has increasingly shifted to the international level (see previous discussion), the traditional prerogative of the executive power (i.e. national governments) over foreign policy and external relations becomes problematic itself. This prerogative of the executive may have had a stronger rationale in a world in which the relations between states concerned a more limited set of topics, primarily related to issues 'at the border' (such as tariffs in trade). Governments could generally be empowered to manage these issues, with national parliaments stepping in and controlling governments on matters of particular importance. With the expansion and deepening of global governance through proliferating international institutions, the rationale for the traditionally large degree of discretion of governments in external relations has been weakened, and national parliaments have stepped up efforts to be involved (Bajtay, 2015).

However, parliamentary efforts at controlling national governments in global governance face serious limitations, especially as regards multilateral institutions and fora. Compared to domestic legislation/debates, accountability of governments for their actions in global governance is more limited. In 'purely' domestic policymaking (in representative democracies), the representatives elected by the people (i.e. parliaments) eventually take the decision. Where far-reaching decisions (that condition national regulation and policy) are taken at the international level, however, they can only partially be ascribed to particular participating governments, so that accountability towards national parliaments is more diffuse. National governments can broaden their room for manoeuvre in this 'two-level game'. While Robert Putnam first introduced the 'two-level game' metaphor primarily to illustrate how governments are bound by and can exploit national-level restrictions in international negotiations (Putnam, 1988), the game may also work the other way around: national governments can 'sell' international decisions by pointing out that they were only one among several or many involved in the decision-making. This is a well-known phenomenon in EU decision-making where individual governments have frequently played the game of blaming 'Brussels' for decisions that are unpopular at home.

While these limitations apply to all political systems represented in global governance, they are particularly pronounced in the case of the EU as an international actor. The accountability and representation chain gets even longer in the case of EU external relations, which may rather constitute a 'three-level game'. The additional level of EU decision-making further increases the distance between decision-making and elected representatives in national parliaments. The latter are first of all represented by their national governments in EU discussions within the special committees in the context of the EU Council of Ministers that serves to determine and develop the EU's position and strategy in international negotiations (see above). These discussions provide a first opportunity to diffuse accountability along the lines highlighted above: member state governments can point out that compromises needed to be struck and can blame 'Brussels' for any unwanted elements. In addition, however, the international negotiations in which the EU and its member states are represented by the European Commission and/or the rotating presidency of the Council of Ministers (see above) serve to further diffuse accountability and representation. Here, the same game can be played again: it can be claimed that the EU was just one among several players and since compromises were required, the result of the negotiations was the best deal available.

The problem is that those represented have very limited capacity to check whether the claims at both the EU and the international levels are appropriate and whether and to what extent other concessions and outcomes might have been possible. To start with, decision-making within the EU Council of Ministers is comparatively opaque and hardly facilitates participation and input by stakeholders and others. Discussions are for the most part held, and decisions taken, in private. There are also hardly any opportunities for other forms of participation and input of civil society. Thus, the Council of Ministers is generally considered the EU institution that is least open vis-à-vis societal interests (Uçarer, 2018, p. 460). Beyond that, the transparency of EU action in global governance is limited in two respects. First, even the member states—who are consulted by the EU negotiator—suffer from information asymmetries. The leeway of the lead negotiator is one of the major reasons for the not uncommon conflicts between the European Commission (as the representative of the EU itself in international negotiations) and the member states over who should represent the EU (and its member states) in international negotiations (Hoffmeister, 2017). National parliamentarians may be in an even more difficult situation since they often rely to a large extent on their governments for information, and access by others to the core of international negotiations has remained severely limited (despite a trend towards increased participation and openness to societal interests). Overall, it is difficult to see the EU's representatives in global governance as representing and being accountable to the European electorate, as this may only be the case in a very indirect and mediated way in a long chain leading from the lead negotiator over member states' governments to their respective parliaments.

The relative decline of the EU and its member states in international politics over the past decades may further aggravate the problem. This decline has resulted from the rise of the emerging powers, including China, India, Brazil and others. As a result, the EU has lost weight relative to others in many areas of global governance, including international trade, climate change and others—as measured by indicators such as its share in world

GDP, world population or greenhouse gas emissions (Bretherton & Vogler, 2006; Oberthür, 2016). Whereas the EU was used to being a crucial actor whose participation was essential in many fields, it has increasingly become part of a more multipolar setting (with China and the United States as the two main heavyweights) in which it is one among many/several. This enhances the claim of the EU negotiator that certain EU interests could not be carried through, while making it even more difficult for those represented to check such claims.

Legitimacy problems arising out of these long chains of representation and accountability are aggravated, or at least not sufficiently mitigated, by some other key features of the EU's decision-making system relating to the three main European institutions (the Council of Ministers, the European Commission, and the European Parliament). As already mentioned, it is rather difficult for citizens and national parliaments to hold governments accountable for their behaviour in the EU Council. The European Commission as the second European institution involved in external representation and policymaking also remains deficient in the two functions it has in this regard. First, it makes proposals for core international policies (formally to the EU Council of Ministers and the European Parliament), including for any negotiating mandate to be issued under Article 218 TFEU (see above). Second, the European Commission acts as the EU's main negotiator in various international negotiations. As regards the former, the Commission frequently conducts stakeholder consultations at the European level, thereby trying to incorporate societal input. In its role as an international negotiator, the European Commission has been criticized for providing for rather limited amounts of transparency, for example in the context of trade negotiations on CETA and TTIP. Arguably, it faces a dilemma in this respect since negotiating effectively requires holding the cards to your chest to some extent. At the same time, the criticism is a clear sign of shortcomings of the existing representative arrangements, especially where the issues under negotiation are deeply contested in society (so that contestation spills over from substance to the political system and its arrangements as such; also see Chapter 9).

The European Parliament, finally, has so far had a rather limited role in external policymaking. Directly elected by EU citizens, the European Parliament could in principle strengthen the direct accountability of external policymaking (even if electorates seem to pay more attention to national parliaments than to the European Parliament; see also Chapter 2). Although somewhat strengthened in the Lisbon Treaty, the European Parliament's authority remains sharply limited (see above). The Parliament, in principle, has veto power and is regularly informed by the European Commission/EU negotiator about the status of negotiations, but it has little power to shape the EU's external policies—even though it may use its veto power to some extent to gain influence. However, it does not control the EU negotiator to the same extent as national parliaments control their governments. In other words, the direct representative link from the electorate to the European Parliament does not easily extend to EU external policymaking and negotiations.

Overall, EU external representation and policymaking are therefore characterized by very long chains of what amounts to rather indirect representation and, as a consequence, rather limited direct accountability. Chains of representation run from the individual citizen through members of national parliaments and governments coordinating in the EU Council of Ministers to the EU representative in international negotiations (be it the European Commission or a member state). Alternative chains of representation and accountability, through access to the EU Council of Ministers or the European Commission and participation of the European Parliament, exist in a rather nascent state, at best. This leaves EU participation in global governance with a problem of legitimacy that is compounded as compared with national political systems due to the additional level of policymaking involved.

TOEHOLDS FOR POSSIBLE IMPROVEMENTS

How could representation and accountability of EU external decision-making in global governance be improved? In exploring the field, we may think along the two representative modes that characterize EU external policymaking. It is probably fair to assume that both the intergovernmentalist and the supranational logic of representation will continue to coexist and interact in the EU's external representation. They reflect the hybrid character and state of the European integration project between a union of member states and a supranational entity more generally. In addition to thinking along these two logics, enhancing the transparency of global governance institutions and advancing EU policies and frameworks may also serve to improve the situation.

With respect to the intergovernmental mode of representation, a couple of toeholds for future improvements can be identified. To start with, informal arrangements have generally served to align the EU institutions (notably the Commission frequently leading negotiations) with the member states and keep the latter involved in such external relations (beyond the letters of the Lisbon Treaty). Enhancing member state ownership and buy-in, this has also had the effect of enhancing the legitimacy of EU external relations in the eyes of the EU member states (Delreux & Keukeleire, 2017). Second, the intergovernmental arm of the EU in global governance may become more accountable through increased participation and deliberation. There should be room for increased direct involvement and input by those concerned (i.e. stakeholders and the public) in the deliberations of the EU Council. As mentioned above, the EU Council so far hardly allows for any such input. Who qualifies as a stakeholder obviously would need to be clarified, since access raises the question of the legitimation of those who can enjoy that privilege. Issues in this respect also provide a strong rationale for granting stakeholders a 'voice' and 'ear' in deliberations but no formal voting rights in decision-making.

As to the supranational mode of representation and accountability, also two options for improvement can be highlighted. First, the European Parliament could get further competences with respect to external policymaking, as this would strengthen the somewhat shorter chain of 'electoral representation'. Even without being in charge of the international negotiations itself, the Parliament could be given the opportunity to formally provide input and participate in decision-making on external policies. Second, the accountability of the European Commission as an international negotiator could be further strengthened through regularizing and formalizing opportunities for input and participation of stakeholders and the public (in parallel with the suggestions regarding the EU Council above).

Two more toeholds deserve mentioning. First, further enhancing opportunities for participation of stakeholders in, and access of the public to, decision-making in global governance would not only support the legitimacy of global governance (building on existing progress in this respect), but would also facilitate holding EU representatives acting within these processes to account as information about these decision-making processes and the role of the EU's representatives in them would become more widely available. Second, systematically advancing internal policies and frameworks holds a significant potential. Such internal policies also provide a firm foundation for the EU's external policies, including a unifying effect among EU member states and stakeholders sharing an interest in the internationalization of European standards. Such support for the substance of external policies can effectively facilitate trust in the EU negotiator, ensure acceptance and support for the EU's role in global governance institutions and limit the demand for transparency and accountability. In other words, strong 'output legitimacy' may to some extent be able to balance demands for enhanced 'input legitimacy'.

While the potential of each discussed element remains limited, their combination may go some way towards advancing the situation. Each of the toeholds just addresses one part of a broader complex. The options for enhancing direct involvement and input into European decision-making and for a strengthening of the European Parliament would each address the problem of long representational chains to some extent. However, none of them can make up for the—perceived and factual—length of the causal chain. In combination, their impact may be enhanced, but they would hardly ensure satisfactory accountability. The other elements (advancing internal policy frameworks, direct involvement/input in global governance institutions) could further improve the situation, while issues and limitations remain (e.g. concerning the selection of stakeholders who may be able to provide input and participate). Advancing on these suggestions in combination may nevertheless enable significant progress in a stepwise process that may lay the foundation for further learning by doing in the future.

CONCLUSIONS

Two very different but not necessarily mutually exclusive logics seem to coexist and be at work in the external representation and policymaking of the EU. On the one side, a 'traditional' intergovernmentalist representative logic is enshrined and still predominant in EU international policymaking. Accordingly, EU member state governments—traditionally the leading powers in foreign policy—determine external policies. These governments are themselves accountable to their national parliaments and publics. On the other side, a 'supranational' logic of representation connects European policymaking in a shorter chain with the public/individuals, presupposing the existence of a European public and polity. This logic is visible in some consultation mechanisms of the European Commission and the—limited—role of the European Parliament.[4]

Beyond the wider problems that electoral representation is facing more generally (see Chapter 2), this EU set-up encompasses particular and more severe challenges to representation and accountability in global decision-making when compared to nation states. The intergovernmentalist chain of representation, through adding the level of the EU Council of Ministers, is particularly long (running from the individual citizen through members of national parliaments and governments coordinating in the EU Council of Ministers to the EU representative in international negotiations) and thereby significantly diffuses accountability. This long chain exposes the legitimacy of EU policymaking on and representation in policy fields such as international trade policy, human rights protection and global climate governance. The supranational mechanisms are more nascent than mature in the current structures. As a result, they cannot at present be considered to make up for the lack of direct accountability.

Globalization, the rise of global governance and deepened European integration further exacerbate the situation. The current arrangements for EU involvement in global governance may not have raised major concerns where external policy primarily concerned a limited number of border issues and the EU's role was more confined. However, contemporary global governance affects domestic policy choice in more fundamental ways which increase the demand for accountability. At the same time, under conditions of deepened European integration, the EU and its member states are bound to act jointly in many if not most global governance fora, which not only adds a level of policymaking but also moves the centre of decision-making further away from the individual at the bottom of the representational chain.[5]

A number of toeholds and options exist to try to improve the legitimacy and accountability of the EU in global governance institutions, especially if applied in combination. There are no easy answers and no silver bullets for addressing the challenges. The role of the European Parliament in external policymaking could be strengthened. Involvement of stakeholders in and public access to related decision-making by the European Commission and the EU Council as well as in global governance institutions could be enhanced. And advancing internal policy frameworks can serve to reduce contestation of substantive external policies. None of these steps in itself is likely to represent a quantum step forward for accountability. However, together they could significantly advance representative arrangements and accountability and pave the way to a stepwise process in which representation and accountability are further improved over time.

I take the liberty to end on a note of caution. In reforming current arrangements for the EU's engagement in global governance, policymakers are likely to face a trade-off between enhancing representation and accountability, on the one hand, and effectiveness in international negotiations, on the other. If not carefully designed, enhanced stakeholder and public involvement could compromise effectiveness since success in international negotiations requires the negotiator to have some level of discretion and be able to act strategically. Such a negative impact could also harm the legitimacy of the EU's role in global governance in its output dimension. Care should therefore be taken to design improvements that leave the ability of the EU to act as an effective international negotiator intact.

NOTES

1. This may, for example, be the case within international institutions to which the EU itself cannot be and is not a party, but several or all member states are. Examples include the Alpine Convention or the Convention on Migratory Species (CMS); see also the discussion on chains of representation and problems of accountability in this chapter.

2. As regards the CFSP, which is not considered here, the high representative of the Union for Foreign Affairs and Security Policy is in the lead instead of the European Commission. In the context of some political organs such as the UN General Assembly or the G7, the president of the European Commission and the president of the European Council also represent the EU externally; see also Article 17, paragraph 1, and Article 15, paragraph 6, of the TEU, respectively.

3. The European External Action Service (EEAS) established in the wake of the Lisbon Treaty is not discussed further here since its role in the regulatory policy fields in focus here is more limited, mainly focused on coordinating and supporting member states and the European Commission.

4. The distinction of the intergovernmentalist and supranational logics is reminiscent of the main protagonists of the debate on the democratic deficit of the EU (see Moravcsik 2002; Follesdal & Hix 2006).

5. See Tănăsescu, this volume, for a discussion of whether, and how, individuals themselves can be represented at all.

REFERENCES

Bajtay, P. (2015, July). Shaping and controlling foreign policy: Parliamentary diplomacy and oversight, and the role of the European Parliament. Retrieved from http://www.europarl.europa.eu/RegData/etudes/STUD/2015/549045/EXPO_STU(2015) 549045_EN.pdf

Biermann, F., Pattberg, P., Van Asselt, H., & Zelli, F. (2009). The fragmentation of global governance architectures: A framework for analysis. *Global Environmental Politics, 9*(4), 14–40.

Blavoukos, S., Bourantanis, D., Galariotis, I., & Gianniou, M. (2016). The European Union's visibility and coherence at the United Nations General Assembly. *Global Affairs, 2* (1), 1–11.

Bouchard, C., & Drieskens, E. (2013). The European Union in UN politics. In K. E. Jørgensen & K. V. Laatikainen (Eds.), *Routledge handbook on the European Union and international institutions: Performance, policy, power* (115–27). Abingdon: Routledge.

Bretherton, C., and Vogler, J. (2006). *The European Union as a global actor* (2nd ed.). London: Routledge.

Brunnée, J. (2002). COPing with consent: Law-making under multilateral environmental agreements. *Leiden Journal of International Law, 15*, 1–52.

Da Conceição-Heldt, E., & Meunier, S. (2014). Speaking with a single voice: Internal cohesiveness and external effectiveness of the EU in global governance. *Journal of European Public Policy, 21*(7), 961–79.

Delreux, T. (2011). *The EU as international environmental negotiator*. Aldershot: Ashgate.

Delreux, T., & Keukeleire, S. (2017). Division of labour and specialization in EU foreign policy-making. *Journal of European Public Policy, 24*(10), 1471–90.

Delreux, T., & Van den Brande, K. (2013). Taking the lead: Informal division of labour in the EU's external environmental policy-making. *Journal of European Public Policy, 20*(1), 113–31.

Drieskens, E. (2017). Golden or gilded jubilee? A research agenda for actorness. *Journal of European Public Policy, 24*(10), 1534–46.

Eeckhout, P. (2011). *EU external relations law* (2nd ed.). Oxford: Oxford University Press.

Esty, D. C. (2006). Good governance at the supranational scale: Globalizing administrative law. *Yale Law Journal, 115*(7), 1490–562.

Follesdal, A., & Hix, S. (2006). Why there is a democratic deficit in the EU: A response to Majone and Moravcsik. *Journal of Common Market Studies, 44*(3), 533–62.

Gehring, T. (2007). Treaty-making and treaty evolution. In D. Bodansky, J. Brunnée, & E. Hey (Eds.), *The Oxford Handbook of International Environmental Law* (pp. 467–97). New York: Oxford University Press.

Gehring, T., & Faude, B. (2013). The dynamics of regime complexes: Microfoundations and systemic effects. *Global Governance: A Review of Multilateralism and International Organizations, 19*(1), 119–30.

Gehring, T., Oberthür, S., & Mühleck, M. (2013). EU actorness in international institutions: Why the EU is recognized as an actor in some international institutions, but not in others. *Journal of Common Market Studies, 51*(5), 849–65.

Hoffmeister, F. (2017). Of presidents, high representatives and European commissioners—The external representation of the European Union seven years after Lisbon. *Europe and the World, 1*(1), 1–46. doi:10.14324/111.444.ewlj.2017.02

Jørgensen, K. E. (Ed). (2009). *The European Union and international organizations*. London: Routledge.

Jørgensen, K. E., & Laatikainen, K. V. (Eds.). (2013). *Routledge handbook on the European Union and international institutions: Performance, policy, power*. Abingdon: Routledge.

Jupille, J., & Caporaso, J. A. (1998). States, agency and rules: The European Union in global environmental politics. In C. Rhodes (Ed.), *The European Union in the World Community* (213–29). Boulder, CO: Lynne Rienner.

Keohane, R. O., Moravcsik, A., & Slaughter, A.-M. (2000). Legalized dispute resolution: Interstate and transnational. *International Organization, 54*(3), 457–88.

Kingsbury, B., Krisch, N., & Stewart, R. B. (2005). The emergence of global administrative law. *Law and Contemporary Problems, 68*(3/4), 15–61.

Koops, J., & Macaj, G. (Eds.). (2015). *The European Union as a diplomatic actor*. Houndmills: Palgrave Macmillan.

Laatikainen, K. V., & Smith, K. (Eds.). (2006). *The European Union at the United Nations: Intersecting multilateralisms*. Basingstoke: Palgrave Macmillan.

Meunier, S. (2005). *Trading voices: The European Union in international commercial negotiations*. Princeton, NJ: Princeton University Press.

Mitchell, R. B. (2018). International Environmental Agreements (IEA) Database Project. Retrieved January 10, 2018, from https://iea.uoregon.edu.

Moravcsik, A. (2002). In defence of the 'democratic deficit': Reassessing the legitimacy of the European Union. *Journal of Common Market Studies, 40*(4), 603–34.

Nugent, N. (2010). *The government and politics of the European Union* (7th ed.). Houndmills: Palgrave Macmillan.

Oberthür, S. (2016). Where to go from Paris? The European Union in climate geopolitics. *Global Affairs, 2*(2), 1–12.

Oberthür, S., Jørgensen, K. E., & Shahin, J. (Eds.). (2012). *The performance of the EU in international institutions*. Abingdon: Routledge.

Oberthür, S., & Stokke, O. S. (Eds.). (2011). *Managing institutional complexity: Regime interplay and global environmental change*. Cambridge, MA: MIT Press.

Putnam, R. (1988). Diplomacy and domestic politics: The logic of two-level games. *International Organization, 42*(3), 427–60.

Smith, K. E. (2014). *European Union foreign policy in a changing world*. Cambridge: Polity Press.

Uçarer, E. M. (2018). NGOs go to Brussels: Challenges and opportunities for research and practice in the area of freedom, security and justice. In A. Ripoll Servent & F. Trauner (Eds.). *The Routledge Handbook of Justice and Home Affairs Research* (458–67). Abingdon: Routledge.

Van Schaik, L. G. (2013). *EU effectiveness and unity in multilateral negotiations: More than the sum of its parts?* London: Palgrave Macmillan.

Wouters, J., & Van Kerckhoven, S. (2013). The International Monetary Fund. In K. E. Jørgensen & K. V. Laatikainen (Eds.), *Routledge handbook on the European Union and international institutions: Performance, policy, power* (221–33). Abingdon: Routledge.

Zürn, M. (2004). Global governance and legitimacy problems. *Government and Opposition, 39*(2), 260–87.

Zürn, M., Binder, M., Ecker-Ehrhardt, M., & Radtke, K. (2007). Politische Ordnungsbildung wider Willen. *Zeitschrift für Internationale Beziehungen, 14*(1), 129–64.

Chapter Five

Representing Persons: Evocative Representation

Mihnea Tănăsescu

As the first part of this volume has argued, there are several tension points around which the concept of representation is being challenged. First, it is no longer elected politicians alone that represent constituencies; indeed, it is no longer constituencies alone that are being represented. Second, social heterogeneity, which has been identified in the previous chapters as one of the most salient challenges to representative politics today, suggests that the individual person is itself an important target of representation. Persons are the basic unit of diversity and as such are in need of representation in a diverse society. But is it possible to represent persons? And if so, what would that mean?

This chapter begins to discuss these questions by analyzing the multiplicity of persons and the implications that this might have for a concept of representation. What is meant by *person* is not the actual physical human being, but rather a particular conceptual constellation that unifies the multiplicity of beings within the confines of a subject-position (see "The Subject-Position" and "The Person" below). What I hope to show is that, in order for representation to be responsive to the fact of diversity, it needs to anchor itself in the fundamental similarities of being a person.[1] What I mean by the fact of diversity is twofold: on the one hand, it signifies the heterogeneity of contemporary societies; on the other, I will argue that persons themselves are characterized by heterogeneity. In other words, the fact of diversity puts front and centre both social and individual multiplicity (also see Tănăsescu, 2014) and tries to take it seriously in theorizing what it might mean to politically represent.

The concept of a person has been understood from a variety of angles throughout its long and illustrious career. One particularly important way in which the person comes through in political discourse is in terms of legal personality. "A legal person is any subject-matter to which the law attributes a merely legal or fictitious personality" (Salmond, 1924). In other words, anything that the law deems to have legal personality, has it; it need not coincide with a living being at all. This is not the sense with which I am concerned here, important though it may be in the history of the person more widely. Instead, and as the chapter will develop at length, I am interested in a philosophical moral conception of the person, understood as the delimitation of a subject-position in light of morally relevant characteristics that are given expression through a network of representative claims.

Political representation is more traditionally thought of as being reliant on individuals or citizens. However, the constructivist turn in political theory, as well as the development of increasing contestation from the grass roots in representation practice, suggests that, at least implicitly, we are already exploring what it would mean for the basis of representation to be in the person (as a primarily moral category). For example, civic campaigns that are disillusioned with how subjects (women, people of colour, immigrants, nongender conforming, and so on) are represented predicate part of the claim of disillusionment on the misrepresentation of the person understood in moral terms. Citizenship as a basic unit systematically leaves out those that do not enjoy its perks (for reasons of provenance but also for lack of power), and individuals are all too often framed as responsible (a basic concept for individuality) for systemic issues. Contesting the representation of women, for example, implicitly contests their representation as individuals or citizens. The claim already implicit in much activism is that the person is the ultimate unit of representation, and in this chapter I want to explicitly explore what this might entail for representation theory more generally. The chapter is, in this sense, an experiment.

The argument will proceed as follows: First, I will specify the general outlines of a theory of representation that situates later reflections on the meaning and importance of the person for political representation; this will provide the context of the present arguments and relate them to current developments in representation theory. Then, I will unpack the notion of the person in terms of the subject-position. After explaining this notion and how it relates to the general theory of representation, I will introduce the idea of commonality and argue that it is through it that we can start to see how representation can occur in a world of diversity. The argument will treat electoral and non-electoral forms of representation together because it focuses on the structure of representative claims, which can be advanced both in electoral and non-electoral settings.

REPRESENTATION AS RELATIONAL

What has come to be known as the claim-making framework started with an attempt to think of representation outside the confines of electoral politics (Saward, 2006). This is not to deny the usefulness of theorizing representation in terms of its forms, but rather to point out the limitations of that approach. Saward (2014) makes this clear in developing the idea of the shape-shifting representative and arguing that changing representative roles is of the essence of representation, and not an exception to the rule. From the point of view of representation's norm, the importance of recognizing shape-shifting as fundamental to the activity of representation is as resistance to the tendency of "contemporary normative frames [to] stress singular and consistent roles of political actors or leaders" (2014, p. 724). In other words, conceiving of representation as shape-shifting allows us to see that different roles (trustee, delegate, surrogate, and so on) are part of the repertoire of representation, but not identical to it. Furthermore, Saward argues that another pernicious effect of identifying representation with roles is the implied 'normativity' of the role. So usually the performance of shape-shifting is seen pejoratively because we expect representatives to conform to one role. This is what Saward calls 'normative prejudgment' (p.725) and, rightly, points out that it is not the same as the norm of representation.

Representation conceived of as an activity of making claims has two important characteristics: it is a dynamic relation, and this relation is constitutive of the subjects on either side of it. What this means is that a representative *does* representation *by* advancing claims to represent. Within this broad framework, she is free to shape-shift at will, but every time she presents a claim, she also at the same time creates the political subjectivity of the represented that she claims to speak for. Furthermore, she creates her own political persona as representative, highlighting certain features here, others there, in order to substantiate the claim that she can speak in the name of another. So, the activity of representing, though not identical to inhabiting a role, does involve the creation of subjectivities. To stress this, Saward proposes to replace *role* with *subject-position*. When speaking of subject-position being better than 'role', he says that "the 'role' of the shape-shifting representative is not just one more role character alongside (e.g.) the trustee, the delegate, the surrogate, or the gyroscopic representative. The 'role' of the shape-shifting representative is highly distinct; in theory and in practice it disrupts, conjoins, de- and re-attaches other, more familiar, roles".

The basic point of this development in representation theory (for more on the context of this development, see Severs, this volume) could be summarized thus: representation is not about setting up a conveyor belt on which interests can pass from constituencies to representatives, but rather about the very formation of constituencies themselves. This insight can be expressed as representation being about relations, because the notion of relation points toward the back and forth which forms the political being of the participants in representative politics (Tănăsescu, 2014, 2016). How exactly political participants are formed, and what implications this has for how representation should work, remain very contentious points. The rest of this chapter will try to offer some ways forward in this debate.

One way of discerning what it means for representation to form persons, and what implications this has, is to describe in greater detail this fundamental process of creation. The relational, constitutive nature of representation can also be gauged through empirical political science. Within the domain of policy analysis, an empirically grounded but critically astute current has been consistently showing that constituencies are formed by policies. The policy feedback literature, through an examination of cases ranging from pensions (Campbell, 2002, 2003) to education (Mettler & Soss, 2004), shows that the design and implementation of policy creates the groups that policy supposedly responds to. This literature is starting to shed some light on the exact mechanisms that are responsible for the creation of constituencies (Campbell, 2011, 2012), though much work remains ahead. What can already be said is that the usual understanding of policy as responding to people's interests formulated as demands is misleading, for several reasons. The instigation of policy, both in terms of agenda setting and policy formulation, is usually the work of policy entrepreneurs or advocacy networks, which indicates that the interests baked into policy do not originate in the people as such. Second, once an issue is on the policy agenda, it might or might not create its own constituency, depending on how widely and successfully it is publicized and communicated, and on whether it is an entirely new policy, an incremental or a radical change from the status quo. And finally, it is only after a policy has become the new status quo that we can clearly trace the political activity of a constituency around the interests encompassed within the relevant policy.

For example, Campbell shows that social security in the United States (elsewhere known as pension policy) was responsible for the creation of the group now known as senior citizens. She demonstrates that the level of political activity of senior citizens can only be registered *after* the implementation of a pension policy. Similarly, welfare recipients come into being with the implementation of welfare policy. The exact manner of implementation then largely determines how the newly constituted welfare recipients engage with the political process (Hacker, 2004; Soss, Fording, & Schram, 2011; Soss & Schram, 2007).

Disch (2012b) takes this phenomenon and analyzes it in terms of what she calls 'constitutive effects'. Drawing on the policy feedback literature, she makes the point that representation (here widened to include policy as well as politics) "neither simply reflects nor transmits demands; it creates them as it actively recruits constituencies". This way of phrasing the issue has the benefit of making it clear that 'preferences' and 'interests' are themselves a product of the representative activity and not simple givens read off the existence of people. Disch's (2011) mobilization conception of representation therefore understands this activity as one which creates the subject-positions *and* the preferences and identities that are retrospectively associated with them. These arguments are usually taken to mean that constituencies are coalesced around issues in the process of representation. But the fact of diversity further suggests that, within constituencies themselves, there are a multiplicity of subjects. In other words, the class of senior citizens cannot correspond to any one person called a senior citizen but is itself an abstraction that risks hiding inter-group diversity and therefore legitimizing mechanisms of exclusion. As Spivak (1988) reminds us, critical engagement does not allow the theorist to assume either the homogeneity of a group, nor the authenticity of the physical individual. In other words, heterogeneity thought through does not allow a final fixed point at all[2] (whether groups, classes, or individual people).

Even though the policy feedback literature and its uses in political theory so far point in the right direction, we need other resources to understand how the diversity of persons risks being smoothed over in the process of creating constituencies. I will now turn to a different set of authors which give us the resources to think about how exclusion is part and parcel of representation, and what can be done about it. This will also take us one step closer to the importance of the person for representative politics.

THE SUBJECT-POSITION

Following the arguments of the previous section, I want to detail further and by using other resources the ways in which subjects are coalesced in the process of speaking. I want to employ here J. L. Austin's theory of language as well as Judith Butler's use of it. The choice of Austin is given by the simple observation that, inasmuch as representation is characterized as an activity of advancing claims, it is the workings of language that will reveal much of what representation is about. If the key to representation is the act of speaking, then we must begin with speaking itself.

In *How to Do Things with Words* (1975), Austin conceptualized the working of language in terms of *speech acts*. The idea of a speech act emphasizes the way in which language is often—if not always—about action and worldly engagement (and not, as the positivists would have it, about truth values). It is what one *does* with language that is of primary importance for the way we understand speaking itself. He then proceeds to classify different speech acts—different ways of doing things with language. It is not important to recall his entire classification here, as I am mostly interested in one type of utterance: the illocutionary speech act. These are parts of speech that inaugurate something new as opposed to simply representing a state of affairs. Let me illustrate this negatively at first, through language that does merely describe. So, for example, "it is snowing out" is a *constative* speech act, because it simply reports on a verifiable, factual state of affairs. This kind of speech can be either true or false. If it is indeed snowing out, it is true; otherwise, it is false. An *illocutionary* act on the other hand does something *through* saying it, and hence is qualified as a performative. "I now pronounce you husband and wife" is an illocutionary speech act because it modifies the terrain on which any constative can function: it inaugurates a new relationship by mere stating. This kind of act cannot be true or false, but rather, following Austin, happy or unhappy. So, a happy illocutionary in the above example would be one where the statement of the authority does bring about a new state of affairs: a married couple. An unhappy utterance of the kind would be one that fails to bring about the desired state of affairs. The relevant authority might for some reason not be able to produce the utterance that ritually counts as bringing about a new state, therefore resulting in an unhappy illocutionary—an unsuccessful inauguration.

Butler takes this basic structure of illocutionary speech acts and generalizes it to social norms. Austin was really only interested in the philosophy of language and the way language manages to achieve results in the world. Butler generalizes his classification, and particularly the illocutionary, to understand how much of what is considered social reality is constantly renewed through this performative use of language. Of utmost importance here is the entire culture that surrounds speech acts because it is through that culture that they can count as happy or unhappy, that they can do or fail to do what they intend. To come back to the above example, there are as many ways to respond to the authority's pronouncement as there are cultures. The point is that the pronouncement and the behaviour have to be in sync for the utterance to be happy. Butler uses this insight to analyze, for instance, hate speech. The fact that hate speech literally hurts its victims derives exactly from its having an illocutionary vigor that is supported by a culture of hate that wants to normalize the deviant.

In line with this reasoning and the arguments presented in the previous section, I want to suggest that the representative claim is best understood as an illocutionary speech act, because it does not simply describe what is the case, but rather summons a new state of affairs into being *through* the act of speaking. For example, if nature advocates present a claim on behalf of nature of the form "we need to protect nature because it is our home", they are creating a state of affairs where there is a privileged relationship between the representatives and nature-as-home. I think that the best way to understand what is being *done* through this claim is to consider that the claim itself inaugurates nature-as-home. Of course, as far as the claim makers are concerned, nature has always been our home and merely awaited someone to speak for it. But far from that being the case, nature-as-home becomes a concept through its very presentation. It is in saying "nature is our home" that a particular cultural apparatus is engaged in the production of that which has been stated. The interesting thing to note here is that, in representative claims, the claim maker wants to disguise the claim as a constative. In other words, advocates would insist that they are merely reading off the homeliness of nature from nature itself; they will insist that their utterance is amenable to factual checking. Similarly, Islamophobic hate speech insists that it is merely presenting what is the case, while advocates for the rights of Muslims will themselves insist that they are merely describing a state of affairs. The point is that the illocutionary character of representative claims is constantly disguised, so as to veil the ways in which the subject is summoned into being by and through the claim.

The illocutionary force of the representative claim works together with the relationality that was presented earlier. Said differently, advancing a claim consolidates the representative and the represented as *subject-positions*. To be precise, a subject-position is the delimitation of an area, through the performative use of language, where similarly situated subjects can exist. So, in speaking for nature, the representative inaugurates her subject-position as the area of discourse consisting of certain kinds of claims on behalf of nature. No single claim on behalf of nature is exhaustive but is rather part of a family of possible claims that allow the representative process to evolve while maintaining a moral grounding. Nature as home is compatible with nature as mother, nature as subject, and so on. Similarly, the represented is inaugurated as a subject-position because she is also part of a dynamic multiplicity of possible political subjectivities that enter the political arena through the representative claim. But the representative subject-position has, as it were, the upper hand. Through speaking on behalf of another, the choice of *their* subject-position is made by the representative. This is most obviously clear in the representation of non-humans, but it functions just as well with human beings. Speaking for another appropriates the power of voicing to the representative. It is only through vigorous contestation that this inequality in the representative relation can be remedied; it is only through the represented becoming representatives of themselves that they can use the force of speech to their advantage.[3]

Let us take another example.[4] A minister for integration says, "The Roma are reluctant to integrate into our societies; their ways are such that we will never manage to live together without conflict." This kind of statement is not amenable to any kind of factual checking. It is not, in any way, constative, though it is presented as such (the Roma *are*). Seen through its illocutionary, performative character, there are two separate subject-positions inaugurated by the statement: that of the minister, and that of the Roma. Now, the minister does not speak in his name. He uses 'we' to denote the area of discourse where his subjectivity can coalesce around the moral indignation felt at foreign ways and the moral certainty of his group's superiority. Similarly, the Roma are a category that in this statement only functions to bolster the minister's subject-position, but that, in order to do that, itself lays claim to a subject-position, namely that of the subaltern alien. Note that the process that I am describing can work to chastise and control (also consult Butler, 1997, on hate speech), as well as to elevate and emancipate. The Roma can themselves counter this kind of claim with their own representative claims, but the dangers of exclusion and denormalization lurk within the structure of representation no matter who speaks.

The formation of subject-positions, I have argued, is part of the structure of representation. Whether one wants to engage in this performance does not matter; inasmuch as representative claims are presented, subject-positions and relations between them are being inaugurated. This structure, which begins to reveal the importance of a notion of the person for an understanding of political representation, can be co-opted for emancipatory politics or else used to reinforce subaltern positions. The area of discourse that the subject-position delimits allows for multiple articulations of interests and identities. But the important point for the present purposes is that through delimiting subject-positions, representative speech is always also disciplinary and exclusionary; it specifies what the correct, normal subject-position is and does so to the exclusion of other possible ways of being. When speaking of 'the Roma' as incapable of 'integration', a subject-position is delimited which a priori excludes the heterogeneity of being Roma. In other words, the diversity of persons always risks being sacrificed, and this risk is part and parcel of what it means to speak for others, and hence of representation. We have seen it function at the level of groups, through the discussion of constitutive effects. Here, I have argued it also functions within groups, because of the nature of representative speech itself. I now want to specify further how the person is coalesced within the framework presented so far, and what this means for how representation should be done in order to safeguard against its internal dangers.

THE PERSON

As I argued above, the delimitation of the subject-position is an operation which opens up various possibilities for subjectivities to coalesce, but always within the field delineated by a claim. It is in the nature of speaking for others in representative terms that we find both the possibility of diverse persons, and the restriction of diversity to a normalized type. All too often, when speaking for women's rights, for instance, the figure that is actually being summoned is that of a particular woman of a particular socio-economic status and of a particular ethnicity. To marry this example with the one about the representation of Roma, when speaking for women's rights it is precisely *not* the Roma that we have in mind. If we do, then we speak of Roma women, which in fact demonstrates the ways in which the representative claim binds the person to certain pre-given characteristics. The person, the ultimate unit of representation, is nowhere given the freedom to determine itself.

I do not want to suggest that the person somehow knows exactly what its interests and preferences are and can specify its own identity in great detail. However, the person is also not merely an intersection of extra-personal forces but exists as a constant supplement to this interaction (Badiou 2002, 2007; Spivak, 1988); this is whence its moral universal claim is derived. The fact that this supplement is not exactly specified does not speak against the person, but rather shows that heterogeneity goes all the way down, to the nature of the individual person itself. If this is the case, then here we reach an impasse: the person cannot be properly represented, because it is both delimited by the subject-position made available for it, and it cannot itself provide a solid foundation which would settle its representation once and for all. It would seem that representation cannot be responsive to the diversity of persons; if the person is itself multiple *and* created, then representation becomes impossible, or else a perpetual clash of fictitious solidities.

One way out of this impasse, and forward in thinking about the nature of political representation, is to more specifically attend to the normative implications of this argument. In other words, we need to ask what it might be to represent a person well. Given the radical diversity that I have so far described, what *could* it mean to represent persons well? The question of 'well' is necessary for asking what it is to represent at all, in the case of the person, because otherwise we cannot discern between a mere claim and a representative claim. In other words, without an understanding of what it is to represent well, we can make no progress on the question of how to overcome the structural deficit of representation.

The way forward is already indicated by the choice of the term *person* to designate the final, though by no means stable, unit of representation. Throughout the history of philosophy, what counted as a person was the crucial battleground for moral considerability. The person is not equivalent to the biological human but is rather the reflection of a (set of) characteristic(s) that, if present, demand moral consideration. The list of such characteristics is both long (language, free will, abstract thought, and so on) and contentious. The history of the 20th century could be rewritten as a continuous toppling of previously 'uniquely human' characteristics (see Bourke, 2011). In fact, the non-coincidence of a person with the biological body of a species means that persons need not be human, and that inasmuch as someone is considered a person, based on whatever salient characteristics, it is owed moral consideration.

So inasmuch as representation is ultimately reliant on the person, it means that at the heart of any representative relationship is a binding moral consideration for the other. If we accept a relational view of representation, then the moral consideration embedded in the concept of person is due not only to the represented, but also to the representative herself and to the collateral represented involved in the act of claim making. Even though the earlier invoked minister for integration spoke on behalf of a particular constituency, she also at the same time invoked the image of the Roma, which in this sense (and through the subject-formation explored earlier) become collaterally represented. Presenting representative claims that a priori excludes these persons from moral consideration should, on this account, be highly suspect.

As we have seen via the discussion of Austin and Butler's work, one way to heed the importance of naming and voicing in political representation is to think about the nature of sentences. There, we saw that representative claims can be characterized as illocutionary sentences disguised as constative. This implies that we cannot ascertain whether a claim is made well based on form alone, but rather only on content. In other words, we cannot decide procedurally whether claims are representative, but only through attending to their meaning. This is one of the central insights at the root of theorizing political representation away from its electoral forms alone. Disch (2015), in an analysis of Saward's contributions to political theory, develops the idea of the 'citizen standpoint' as a possible way of making progress in describing the norm of representation without betraying the constructivist underpinning of representation as claim making. She argues that "to assess representative claims from the 'citizen standpoint' does not mean taking at face value whomever or whatever citizens regard as representing them" (2015, p. 493). Similarly, we cannot assess the representativeness and the value of representative claims by simply taking at face value what representatives themselves say. Instead, we should understand "a standpoint [as] an epistemological and political achievement that does not exist spontaneously but develops out of the activism of political movements together with the critical theories and transformative empirical research to which they give rise". In other words, the citizen standpoint is the critical space in which claims can be both assessed, and 'taken up' (Disch, 2015, p. 495) or rejected as illegitimate. This allows a claim to be successful yet wrongheaded, illegitimate, and suspicious, on ethical grounds.

Disch makes the point thus: "It is up to the constituency—both intended and actual—to accept the claim, by deciding whether the claimant represents them in the twofold sense of standing/acting for them and depicting them in terms they recognize and want to own" (2015, p. 494). Importantly, this does not mean that the audience is the ultimate guide in the legitimacy of a claim, because audience and constituency can, but need not, overlap. In this sense, the citizen standpoint that she extracts from the work of Saward can do the job of specifying whether a claim is normatively sound without insisting on a procedure of representation. To this end, she uses the well-known example of Bono, the front man of the rock group U2, speaking on behalf of Africans. There, the audience was made up of diverse groups of people that the clai-mant was directly targeting for action: charitable organizations, Western governments, and so on. However, the intended constituency, namely the African 'voiceless' that Bono ostensibly spoke on behalf of, could not 'take up' the claim because they were a priori excluded from doing so. In Disch's terms, echoing Saward's, the claim "was not democratically legitimate be-cause it was not made to be taken up. . . . It did not need the approbation of the constituency and in fact portrayed that constituency as incapable of speaking for itself" (2015, p. 494). Indeed, it is hard to argue for the demo-cratic legitimacy of a claim that does not need the approbation of its intended constituency. Let us assume, then, that the 'African voiceless' that Bono ostensibly spoke on behalf of could themselves weigh in on the legitimacy of the claim. Following the idea that it is up to the constituency to critically assess the claim, it would then be possible for Bono's claim to be legitimate. So perhaps instead of speaking on behalf of the Africans that cannot them-selves speak, as he claimed, he could have said that he was speaking on behalf of Africans living under one dollar a day, and he could have also said that they themselves had asked him to do so. Assuming that to be true, the modified claim would then be something like this: "I, Bono, represent people in Africa that live in poverty, and I do so because they asked me to".

In this modified hypothetical claim, the constituency is included and can weigh in on the claim. We can also imagine that many in Africa who live in poverty would indeed take up the claim. Would it then follow that it is legitimate? According to the discussion in this chapter, this conclusion is not immediately warranted, because the notion of constituency itself hides the diversity of persons. The 'African poor' are not a constituency of one, but rather a subject-position delineated by the claimant. In the terms of the present discussion, the constituency is summoned into being by the claim, and it therefore becomes important for ascertaining its legitimacy to know which members of the constituency are taking the claim up, and which are barred from doing so. It could be argued that this line of reasoning leads to a reductio ad absurdum, where *everyone* would need to take up a claim in order for it to be legitimate. The point is rather that, given the logical impossibility of everyone's assent, the possibility of objecting should be, as it were, writ-ten into the claim.

The notion of 'citizen standpoint', though important for thinking the nor-mative commitments of a constructivist theory of representation, does not take fully into account the heterogeneity that is hidden away by the concept of constituency. In order to remedy that problem, I suggested that one way to allow for the fact of diversity is, precisely, to treat it as a fact, and not a norm. The fact of diversity means that no representative claim on behalf of constituencies can be fully legitimate, but only partially so, inasmuch as it is taken up by those within the constituency that best fit the subject-position delineated by the claim. This, what I called earlier the deficit of representation, stubbornly remains even when we suppose an enlightened, critically engaged constituency, because of the very structure of making claims. So, what can specify further the norm of representation such that it can supplement the acceptance of a constituency without compromising the position of subaltern persons?

Representation's norm is absolutely tied to the *content* of claims, to what they say. In the case of conceiving representation as naming, the act of speaking counts as naming because of how it is embedded in a set of practices, including linguistic practices. Here, things like venue, time, audience, the claims of others, and so on are important for a sentence to count as a representative claim, as naming, or as speaking for someone. However, none of those elements that make a sentence a sentence of the representative type can also tell me whether naming has been accomplished well. For example, if Bono speaks on behalf of the 'African poor', his claim must first and foremost be accepted *and* taken up, but it must also allow for the fact of diversity to destabilize the subject-position of 'African poor'. It is, in other words, axiomatically true that the subject-position invoked by Bono is itself multiple, and therefore the legitimacy of the claim also hangs on the claimant allowing for that diversity. Of course, there is no formula that Bono, to run with the example, could use to allow for the multiplicity of persons bunched together under the constituency. He could say something like, "I represent some people living in poverty from certain regions of Africa that have struck me as being voiceless and in need of representation; some of them asked me to help", but that doesn't exactly fit the fund-raising language that his claim was geared to. It does, however, strike one as infinitely more accurate, precisely because it is conscious of the empirical multiplicity washed over by the sweeping category of 'African poor'.

VISIBILITY, VULNERABILITY AND COMMONALITY

The exclusionary tendencies at the heart of representative claims cannot be avoided. I have argued that they are part and parcel of what it is to represent, and in this sense constitute an enduring conceptual and practical edge. Recognizing this deficit of representation therefore becomes crucial for doing representation as well as it can be done. So how can the concept and practice of representation approach as faithfully as possible the infinite and irreducible multiplicity of being a person?

I have argued that, inasmuch as we hold fast to the multiplicity of persons, we must also consider them the ultimate unit of representation. If this is so, then at the heart of any representative claim is a binding moral consideration for the other, rooted in the ultimate indeterminacy of being a person. This indeterminacy, or what I also called infinite multiplicity, is only a mortal threat to representation inasmuch as we conceive of the process of representation as a transfer of something solid (for example, interests) from the represented to the representative. But if representation is no longer conceived of in these terms, then there are no barriers to accepting that processes of representation can operate without final solidities. Inasmuch as representation is understood as a process of creating relations, rather than translating interests, then the representative relation must fall under the sign of the moral imagination—it must first and foremost build a relation of mutual recognition. One way forward then in thinking about the norm of representation conceived thus is to further attend to the duty of representative claims to place the figure of the other at their centre. In other words, representative claims must engage the moral imagination of both audience and constituency such that the constituent vulnerability of being a person is evident for all to see.

The irreducible multiplicity of persons can existentially be interpreted as constituent vulnerability. Whereas irreducible multiplicity is a logical and ontological category (see Badiou, 2007), its existential expression is the feeling of vulnerability, of perpetual change with no guarantee of need fulfillment. Even if we very precisely spell out what would be needed for a fulfilling human life, as Sen (1993, 2005) and Nussbaum (2003, 2006) do in advancing capabilities, these still exist on the background of multiplicity and are therefore perpetually threatened by the shifting ground of being. Politics then becomes a communal response to the vulnerabilities of being a person, and representative politics can do no better than inscribing this basic vulnerability in its very core.

Representative claims that focus on commonality engage the audience in an exercise of moral imagination. They open the possibility of understanding the position of the other based on features shared universally in virtue of being a person. One such feature I have referred to as vulnerability (for more on this in moral philosophy, see Diamond, 1978, 1991). I would like to call the kind of representation that anchors itself in personal vulnerability *evocative*, in order to hint toward the fact that part of what it is to represent well is to evoke that which you are speaking of in an imaginatively stimulating way. One complementary way to make the point is to say that there is something powerful in the deep realization that an other *has a life*[5] (Diamond, 1978). The power of the realization comes from anchoring the person in its constitu-

ent vulnerability, which existentially means regarding others as equal participants in the trials and tribulations, the joys and hopes, that qualify being
vulnerable. Part of what it takes to represent a person conceived thus can also
be interest advocacy, but it becomes secondary to the simple evocation of the
person as an undisputed equal.

The idea that being touched by the common vulnerability of the other is
important for accurately representing, though well exemplified in literature,
seems absent from thinking about political representation. Its importance for
morality has been extensively argued for by Diamond (1978, 1988a, 1988b,
1991) and Cavell (2002) (see also Crary, 2007). In literature, what it means
to represent a character well is to allow imaginative identification. So, part of
the norm of literary representation is crucially tied to moral imagination. So
is the norm for other kinds of activities that might come under the heading
representation. The subjective feeling of being well represented by another,
whether in political terms or not, is usually tied to how well your very
subjectivity shines through the claims of your representative. What I want to
underline here is that this way of thinking about the normative aspects of
representation allows for the diversity of persons to persist despite the tendency of claims to collapse it into mere sameness. The vulnerability of being
a person is not merely the same across the board; rather, it is a common
feature that can therefore act—and in fact does act—as the background of
normative relations.

To evoke something is also at the same time to make it visible, and in this
sense the task of representative claims is to make visible those that are
hidden. I have argued elsewhere (2014) that representing an object in a
painting similarly involves an imaginative effort of making visible, as opposed to mere presenting, again. This account of representation as fundamentally tied to visibility need not be restricted to the representation of human
beings alone. The person, as argued earlier, can incorporate any kind of being
in virtue of certain relationships deemed morally necessary. Evocative representation can therefore function equally well for human and non-human persons. The norm of the evocative representation of persons (human or otherwise) is the imaginative moral stimulation of common vulnerability. When
campaigners for animal rights represent polar bears well, they do so precisely
in virtue of the commonality of having a life in a changing world. We relate
to the bear, and therefore personify it, inasmuch as our moral imagination
manages to live through its eyes.

The above discussion could be summed up by saying that representation
must first of all count and make visible the other. This means that representative claims can be judged as good, competent, and well made inasmuch as
they evoke the other as an equal, and therefore as someone that cannot be a
priori discounted. Referring to others, for example, as 'illegal aliens' already
forfeits the possibility of good representation, because those terms do not

allow for an empathic identification. And outside of such identification, the diversity of persons and their equal dignity cannot be guaranteed in the making of representative claims. In other words, the norm of representation is crucially tied to the evocation of the fundamental commonality of persons.[6] What it means to represent well is, on the one hand, allowing for the claim to be accepted and taken up by a constituency and, on the other, evoking the constituency based on the generic personhood that counts all as potential members of a moral community.

We see the perils of the dominance of groups for representation every day, especially in our hyper-polarized world. Deafness to each other, which I have explained as part of the structure of speaking for another, cannot be countered with more group identification. Instead, we need to recognize that behind every claim there is infinite multiplicity, and that in order to safeguard it while not allowing it to annul political debate, we must search for the commonality that lies behind claims and that, in the final analysis, imparts on them moral force. Commonality is itself implied in the irreducible multiplicity of being a person: the perpetually shifting ground of being gives rise to a shared sense of vulnerability. Commonality here does not mean unity, and conflict can meaningfully exist, as it should, in a representative environment geared towards the person. But inasmuch as the person is the ultimate unit of representation, conflict can only be about ideas in a common project, and not about the being of the other.

NOTES

1. For an argument developing the view that representation cannot escape being primarily concerned with groups, see Chapter 6.

2. For an ontological argumentation of this position, see Badiou (2002, 2007).

3. Note that, at this point, the structure that I am describing is engaged all over again. Whether I speak for myself or for another does not change the argument, but only its repercussions.

4. Chapter 8, discussing the cases of Black Pete, can also be read from this perspective.

5. This expression of Diamond's is contrasted with the idea that having a life is a biological fact. As a biological fact, it is morally meaningless; it acquires moral weight, as it were, when understood as an expression that signals a certain kind of fellowship, allows the listener to contemplate the mystery of another's life, to be touched by someone else having a life to lead.

6. It is an apparent paradox that commonality is the only way to safeguard diversity: without the idea of a fundamental equality given by the fact of being alive, diversity cannot but hide the exclusion and disciplinary practices that were detailed earlier in the chapter.

REFERENCES

Austin, J. L. (1975). *How to do things with words.* Oxford: Oxford University Press. (Original work published in 1962)

Badiou, A. (2002). *Ethics: An essay on the understanding of evil* (P. Hallward, Trans.). London: Verso.

Badiou, A. (2007). *Being and event* (O. Feltham, Trans.). London: Continuum.

Bourke, J. (2011). *What it means to be human: Reflections from 1971 to the present*. London: Virago.

Butler, J. (1997). *Excitable speech: A politics of the performative*. New York: Routledge.

Campbell, A. L. (2002). Self-interest, social security, and the distinctive participation patterns of senior citizens. *American Political Science Review, 96*(3), 565–74.

Campbell, A. L. (2003). *How policies make citizens: Senior political activism and the American welfare state*. Princeton, NJ: Princeton University Press.

Campbell, A. L. (2011). Policy feedbacks and the impact of policy designs on public opinion. *Journal of Health Politics, Policy and Law, 36*(6), 961–73.

Campbell, A. L. (2012). Policy makes mass politics. *Annual Review of Political Science , 15*, 333–51.

Cavell, S. (2002). *Must we mean what we say? A book of essays*. Cambridge: Cambridge University Press. (Original work published 1969)

Crary, A. (2007). *Beyond moral judgment*. Cambridge, MA: Harvard University Press.

Diamond, C. (1978). Eating meat and eating people. *Philosophy, 53*(206), 465–79.

Diamond, C. (1988a). Throwing away the ladder. *Philosophy, 63*(243), 5–27.

Diamond, C. (1988b). Losing your concepts. *Ethics, 9*(2), 255–77.

Diamond, C. (1991). The importance of being human. *Human Beings, 29*, 35–62.

Disch, L. (2011). Toward a mobilization conception of democratic representation. *American Political Science Review, 105*(1), 100–114.

Disch, L. (2012a). The impurity of representation and the vitality of democracy. *Cultural Studies, 26*(2–3), 207–22.

Disch, L. (2012b). When is representation democratic? Analyzing the constituent effects of public policy. In *Annual Meeting of the Western Political Science Association*, March (pp. 1–38).

Disch, L. (2015). The "constructivist turn" in democratic representation: A normative dead-end? *Constellations, 22*(4), 487–99.

Hacker, J. S. (2004). Privatizing risk without privatizing the welfare state: The hidden politics of social policy retrenchment in the United States. *American Political Science Review, 98*(2), 243–60.

Mettler, S., & Soss, J. (2004). The consequences of public policy for democratic citizenship: Bridging policy studies and mass politics. *Perspectives on Politics, 2*(1), 55–73.

Nussbaum, M. (2003). Capabilities as fundamental entitlements: Sen and social justice. *Feminist Economics, 9*(2/3), 33–59.

Nussbaum, M. (2006). *Frontiers of justice: Disability, nationality, species membership*. Cambridge, MA: Harvard University Press.

Salmond, J. (1924). *Jurisprudence* (7th ed.). London: Sweet & Maxwell.

Saward, M. (2006). The representative claim. *Contemporary Political Theory, 5*(3), 297–318.

Saward, M. (2014). Shape-shifting representation. *American Political Science Review, 108*(4), 723–36.

Sen, A. (1993). Capability and well-being. In M. Nussbaum & A. Sen (Eds.), *The quality of life*. Oxford: Clarendon Press.

Sen, A. (2005). Human rights and capabilities. *Journal of Human Development, 2*, 151–66.

Soss, J., Fording, R. C., & Schram, S. (2011). *Disciplining the poor: Neoliberal paternalism and the persistent power of race*. Chicago: University of Chicago Press.

Soss, J., & Schram, S. F. (2007). A public transformed? Welfare reform as policy feedback. *American Political Science Review, 101*(1), 111–27.

Spivak, G. Chakravorty. (1988). Can the subaltern speak? In C. Nelson & L. Grossber (Eds.), *Marxism and the Interpretation of Culture* (pp. 271–313). Bassingstoke: Macmillan Education.

Tănăsescu, M. (2014). Rethinking representation: The challenge of non-humans. *Australian Journal of Political Science, 49*(1), 40–53.

Tănăsescu, M. (2016). *Environment, political representation, and the challenge of rights*. London: Palgrave Macmillan.

Chapter Six

Theorizing Representation Fairness

Why We Need to Account for Social Groups

Eline Severs

This chapter starts with the assumption that without a conception of social groups we are unable to theorize the conditions of just or fair political representation. Without a conception of social groups and the systems of domination (related, but not exclusive to, gender, 'race'/ethnicity, [1] sexuality, age and class) that structure people's lived experiences, we can only describe patterns of inequality between aggregate sets of individuals. We cannot, however, evaluate whether there is something problematic or wrong about such patterns. The reason is simple: patterns of inequality are never in themselves good or bad. While some may result from what we consider unjust treatment, other types of inequalities may be attributable to individuals' choices or sheer bad luck (cf. Young 2001).

We seldom problematize differences when these can readily be attributed to individuals' personal tastes or preferred lifestyles. When we problematize patterns of inequality we do so because we judge the causes of such patterns to be unfair. This is, for instance, the case when we consider the reasons for adopting a particular lifestyle as being beyond individuals' control and, therefore, not reflecting their consciously held choices. We, however, also problematize individuals' consciously held preferences when we believe these preferences originate in dire life circumstances that reduce the range of *real* choices available to individuals. For this reason, we are indifferent to the middle class's appreciation for food truck cuisine but problematize poor people's preference for fast food.

"If we simply identify some inequality of condition or situation between individuals at a particular time," Iris Marion Young (2001, p. 8) aptly stated, "we have no account of the causes of this unequal condition. It is the causes and consequences of some pattern of inequality, rather than the pattern itself, that raises issues of justice". What constitutes the injustice of patterns of inequality is the ways in which they align with other patterns of inequality and how this concurrence offers evidence of generalized social processes which negatively affect some people, and positively affect others. To identify such generalized patterns of inequality, we need a conception of social groups. Only a conception of social groups allows for linking patterns of inequality in one realm (such as political representation) to patterns of inequalities elsewhere (such as the household, education) and the broader systems of domination that structurally affect the opportunities available to people (Young, 2001, p. 16).

This insight has been central to the development of group-based approaches to fair representation (e.g. Kymlicka, 1993; Phillips, 1995; Williams, 1998). Increasingly, however, the relevance and adequacy of situating social groups at the centre of theories of representation fairness is called into question. Intersectionality theory—or the understanding that systems of domination are interdependent and mutually constitutive—has sensitized scholars to biases in their definitions of social groups. Scholarly definitions have often prioritized the experiences of more privileged group members, rendering the experiences of marginalized subgroups invisible or causing these to be seen as deviating from the standard group members (Beckwith & Cowell-Meyers, 2007; Strolovitch, 2006). The growing influence of socio-constructivism on representation theory has intensified scholars' suspicion towards coherent collective identities, such as 'the people' or 'women'. The insight that political representation helps constitute the very reality it describes has robbed representation theory of objective benchmarks (Disch, 2011): it is logically impossible to justify social practices, such as political representation, by referring to the groups and preferences they have helped to produce (Severs, Celis, & Meier, 2015; Sunstein, 1991).

The literature on political representation, thus, seems characterized by a catch-22: [2] although we know that a conception of social groups is needed for adequately theorizing the conditions of fair political representation, it appears impossible to study and, hence, refine these conditions without also introducing a sense of collective identity which we consider suspect in the first place (Severs, 2016). Given this challenge, it is not surprising to find that contemporary contributions to representation theory predominantly refer to the subjects of political representation in terms of individuals[3] or 'those affected' (e.g. Disch, 2011; Runciman, 2007; Saward, 2010). Although these concepts have their merit for theorizing fairness, neither performs the normative work that a conception of social groups can. While the concept of 'those affected' emphasizes the notion that individuals rightly have a stake in the representation processes that affect them, it is not premised, unlike the concept of social groups, on the insight that the opportunities for political representation are unevenly distributed among sets of individuals. The concept of 'those affected' may even downplay the structural character of interest conflicts in that it considers those affected as dependent on the issues that are represented.

The need to underline the centrality of structural inequalities in representation theory forms the motivation of this chapter. First, it seeks to argue for the continued role and relevance of social groups in representation theory. To this end, I review liberal accounts of political representation and feminist critiques of liberal individualism. Following that, I clarify the commonalities and differences between liberal democratic theories and contemporary constructivist accounts and argue that feminist critiques still hold. If we seek to theorize representation fairness, we must account for the social conditions that hinder or enable effective types of political agency. To this end, a conception of social groups remains needed. The chapter, second, invalidates the described catch-22 by elaborating on the conception of social groups that underpins group-based theories of representation fairness. Their contextualized accounts of representative democracy locate the origin of social groups—much like constructivist representation theories—within processes of naming, ordering and presenting political reality. But, as opposed to contemporary constructivist accounts, they underscore how the routinization of such processes locks individuals into social positions that unequally shape their capacity to effectively contest the claims made on their behalf.

LIBERAL DEMOCRATIC THEORY: INTEREST GROUPS

Scholars' conceptualizations of the fairness of political representation typically reflect their understanding of the function that representation is expected to fulfil in contemporary democracies. Stated differently, how scholars define representation fairness follows their understanding of the problems that representation is expected to solve (Rogowski, 1981). For liberal democratic theorists, political representation mainly serves as a means to generate legitimacy in government. As a mode of linking the people to government, representation rendered the elitist model of elections compatible with the democratic principle of self-rule (also see Chapter 2).

To understand why liberal democrats defined political representation in terms of linkage, it makes sense to first explore their arguments for separating citizens from decision-making. Finding their origin in 18th-century Enlightenment ideals, liberal democratic theories identified the heterogeneous body of the people, as opposed to some monarch or deity, as the ultimate source of legitimacy. The heterogeneity of the people, however, raised important challenges to the stability and legitimacy of political rule. As an unruly body of individuals, the people lacks unity, and therefore agreement among its members needed to be created. The possibility of conflict suggested the need for institutions that would allow citizens to mediate interests in democratically defensible ways, that is, based on respect for citizens' equal moral standing. However, liberal democrats were wary of citizens' democratic competences. They conceived of citizens as rational maximizers of preferences whose political judgements closely follow their self-interest, and considered it likely that individuals would pursue their interests in ways that threaten the rights and liberties of other individuals. To protect individuals from oppression, liberal democrats concluded, institutions should be designed to separate political judgement from the judgements of individuals themselves (Warren, 1992, p. 9). Only such a separation would safeguard the general interest from the tyrannical passions of the majority and the particular interests of factions (Urbinati, 2005, p. 196).

Elections, in this regard, became a mechanism by which the bulk of the demos could self-exclude or opt out of systematic involvement in decision-making, yet without making such exclusion definitive or irreparable (Judge, 1999, p. 8). While competitive and regular elections provided citizens opportunities to delegate the choice of determining what is in their interest to others ('authorization'), they retained the right to judge the decisions made in their name ('accountability') (Dahl, 1989, p. 99). Elections, however, do not in themselves suffice to speak of democratic self-rule. Only the representative relationships brought about by elections allow for conceiving of the people as giving, through their representatives, laws to themselves.

Because mediation of citizens' interests is needed, liberal democrats generally refrained from defining fair representation in terms of the equal satisfaction of individual preferences (cf. Williams, 1998). Because of the incommensurability of individual preferences, it is impossible to satisfy all individuals all the time. The requirement of unanimity would give almost total power to those who benefit most from the status quo (Mansbridge, 1994, p. 57). However, no group of citizens should systematically come out on the losing end, either. A member of the demos that can never affect the outcomes of representation, Rogowski (1981, p. 398) argued, "cannot be distinguished analytically from a non-member". As members of the demos, citizens hold equal moral standing, making it reasonable to demand that their preferences would, at least sometimes, shape political decisions. For this reason, liberal democrats defined the fairness of representation in terms of the procedures we may expect to produce fair outcomes on the basis of their equal respect for the agency of each member of the demos (Saunders, 2010, p. 158).

As Melissa Williams (1998) demonstrated, the design of such procedures generally centred on two distinct yet mutually reinforcing principles of political equality, namely the principle of *equally weighted representation* and that of *equally powerful representation*. The first principle, generally conceived in terms of universal suffrage ('one citizen, one vote'), seeks to fulfil individuals' fundamental equality by granting them an equal chance to affect the outcomes of representation. By attributing equal standing to those who may otherwise be conceived unequal (Bickford, 1996, p. 57), universal suffrage offers a correction for natural or social contingencies (such as those related to education, class, luck, or innate cognitive capabilities). The second principle, equally powerful representation, refers to a fair method of aggregating citizens' preferences and seeks to ensure that the preferences of each citizen count the same as everyone else's (Williams, 1998, p. 69). Liberal democrats generally favoured majority rule as a method of aggregation: it ensures that individual preferences have, in the abstract, an equal chance to affect the outcomes of decision-making ('anonymity') and that any two policy proposals supported by equally large subgroups have the same power ('neutrality') (cf. Mayo, 1960). Majority rule, put differently, expresses a social decision function in which individuals' preferences are weighted in proportion to the number of allies one has on an issue (Mansbridge, 1994, p. 61).

Post-war liberal theorists expanded upon the conditions under which majority rule may be considered fair. In contrast to 18th-century constitutionalist theorists, they argued that the fairness of majority rule (and with it, citizens' willingness to abide by majoritarian decisions) cannot be ensured by constitutional measures alone. Constitutional restraints upon majority action, such as institutional checks and balances, fail to cover the entire range of political activities that set the process of decision-making in motion. "In the absence of certain social prerequisites," Robert Dahl (1956, p. 83) stated, "no constitutional arrangements can produce a non-tyrannical republic". The fairness of majority rule also requires a fair distribution of opportunities for mobilizing others and forming majority coalitions. Only when citizens have had a real chance to exert influence on the processes of political representation will they accept its outcomes.

This insight forms the starting premise of post-war pluralist theories. They advanced open and free interest competition as the basic condition for a system of democratic counterbalance whereby the powers of competing interest groups have the capacity to cancel each other out and reduce the risk of majority domination. Systems of open and free interest competition, Robert Dahl (1956) argued, promote a decentralization of power: the possibility of mobilizing others and joining or endorsing a diversity of interest groups creates multiple centres of power that hold each other in check. Individuals' cross-cutting group memberships both reduce the intensity of societal conflicts and promote a minoritarian sensibility. Because majorities are nothing more than temporal and unstable coalitions of minorities, it is in the interest of majorities to promote minority rights. Once the majority coalition has accomplished its limited purpose, it is likely to break apart and its members may enter new coalitions for different purposes. The temporal and unstable character of interest coalitions makes members of the majority considerate of the possibility that one day they too may find themselves in the minority. This insight is expected to heighten their willingness to endorse respect for and tolerance of minorities (Eisenberg, 2001, p. 153). Based on this view, democracy is not rule by the majority but, rather, rule by minorities (Dahl, 1956, p. 128).

The group in liberal democratic theory, thus, mainly serves as a vehicle for creating agreement and forging unity in democratically defensible ways. Groups, furthermore, are ephemeral in that they stem from individuals' purposive yet invariably temporal alignments with others. Liberal democratic theorists conceive of individuals as bearers of unique interest constellations. Because of their uniqueness, it is unlikely that the distinct interest constellation of one individual will ever completely map onto that of others, let alone be adequately represented by others. For this reason, individuals' alignments with others are bound to be topical rather than structural and will be characterized by a sense of unpredictability arising out of the individual's uniqueness (cf. Eulau, 1967, p. 69; Pennock, 1979, p. 353).

THE SHORTCOMINGS OF LIBERAL INDIVIDUALISM

Many have challenged liberal individualism as a neutral vantage point for theorizing fairness in political representation. The critiques mainly centre on three axes. Scholars have, first, contested liberal theorists' conception of the individual as an unencumbered self. Such a conception ignores the fact that some of individuals' interests are integral to their identity. As members of a family, community or people, individuals become bearers of common histories, allegiances and sentiments. As Michael Sandel (1984, p. 90) has argued, individuals often find themselves bound to others not because of agreements they have entered into freely but, instead, by the enduring attachments and commitments that, taken together, partly define the person that they are.

The liberal conception that individuals' self-identifications are wholly voluntary and, perhaps, even reversible ignores, as Iris Marion Young (1989, p. 260) aptly argued, that social groups have an element of *thrownness* to them: there is no act of 'joining' a social group. Instead, individuals find themselves together as members of a group whose existence and relations to others are experienced as prior to themselves. Contrary to interest groups, leaving a social group is difficult if not impossible. It would not only require a transformation of self but also others' recognition thereof (cf. Young, 1997, p. 385). This signals that, to the extent to which our interests derive from our social identities, they have a structural as opposed to a purely individual and ephemeral character.

Drawing upon the foregoing, scholars have, secondly, challenged the liberal assumption that open and free interest competition will reduce the intensity of societal conflicts and the likelihood of structural exclusion. This assumption only holds when we treat the individual as an 'unencumbered self', or as the bearer of a unique interest constellation whose alignments with others are unpredictable. Under such circumstances, it becomes possible to see how individuals may benefit from joining or endorsing a diversity of cross-cutting interest groups, thus preventing interest conflict from crystallizing into sharp fault lines or cleavages. However, when we view individuals as socially embedded selves—as defined, at least in part, by their relations with others—we can no longer claim that their political preferences and alignments are unpredictable. If we accept this, it becomes less plausible to argue that interest group competition will diffuse societal conflicts and prevent structural exclusion: when individuals' interests are rooted, at least in part, in their belonging to social groups, interest conflicts are likely to overlap to a significant extent, and majority rule may produce structural, as opposed to alternating, winners and losers.

Feminist theorists have, thirdly and most extensively, demonstrated that the liberal model of interest group pluralism reproduces categorical inequalities. As Melissa Williams (1998, p. 57) has argued, the model of interest group pluralism advances a market-based approach to determining which preferences should prevail in decision-making: rather than decide a priori what kind of preferences should prevail (for instance, the preferences of those most affected by a political decision, the preferences of experts, etc.), the model of interest group pluralism weighs individual preferences according to the extent to which they mobilize others and are endorsed by them. The weight of citizens' preferences on decision-making is, put differently, dependent on the organizational effort they expend. Under conditions of free interest competition, any outcome that aggregates citizens' preferences according to their number and intensity is considered fair (Williams, 1998, p. 57).

Although much may be said in favour of an approach that leaves it to the people to decide which interest constellations should prevail (see infra), the fairness of such an approach calls for more proof of citizens' equal opportunities for mobilizing others than liberal democrats have generally provided. In *The Semi-Sovereign People* (1960), Schattschneider formulated a first critique on the elitist character of interest group pluralism. According to Schattschneider, interest group pluralism produces outcomes that are biased towards the most educated and highest-income members of society. More affluent groups of citizens have greater means to mobilize politically and, as a result, their preferences have a greater chance of being considered relevant to collective decision-making. Elites, furthermore, need not necessarily mobilize a genuine majority of the people, as the perceived intensity of their preferences often trumps the reality of numerical distribution or support for these preferences (Forrest & Hindman, 2015). The flaw in the pluralist heaven of liberal democrats, Schattschneider (1960, p. 35) argued, is "that the heavenly chorus sings with a strong upper-class accent".

Feminist theorists have expanded upon this critique and have demonstrated that a political system is never fully neutral or bereft of cultural ethos (Benhabib, 2004, p. 3; Young, 1990). Even in the absence of formal exclusions, informal pressures that marginalize the contributions of subordinate groups persist, rendering their preferences less comprehensible or acceptable to wider audiences. Because members of historically marginalized groups often apply different stylistic registers, they find it more difficult to convey their messages to others and are sometimes even encouraged to keep their wants inchoate when these appear to conflict with majority interests (Mansbridge, 1990, p. 127; Young, 2000, p. 23).

Because it fails to consider these structural constraints, the model of interest group pluralism risks holding historically marginalized groups responsible for their own under-representation (cf. Lukes, 1974; Severs, Celis, & Erzeel, 2016). Rather than examine the reasons for marginalized groups' lower participation in interest group politics, liberal theorists tend to attribute non-participation to people's ignorance, indifference or quiescence (Gaventa, 1980, pp. 8–9). This conclusion, however, fails to consider the large body of empirical evidence that demonstrates that citizens are not disaffected by nature, but largely by brute force of socio-economic circumstance (Krouse, 1982, p. 449). Attributing marginalized groups' absenteeism to their disinterest in politics, Schattschneider (1960, p. 105) argued, also misses the point that their absence "often reflects the suppression of the options and alternatives that reflect the needs of the non-participants". Similarly, when minorities fail to elect candidates who share their identities, such outcomes cannot simply be considered as reflecting the lack of salience of those identities (Williams, 1998, pp. 10–11). Such an explanation downplays the ways in which systems of domination (related to, but not exclusively, gender, 'race'/ ethnicity, sexuality, age and class) negatively affect the opportunities of some people.

FEMINIST THEORIES: ENTER THE SOCIAL GROUP

The main problem of feminist theorists with liberal accounts is their failure to extend considerations of domination to civil society and to the relations between individuals and groups. Liberal democrats wrongly presume that political struggle is primarily about the state and its coercive capacities. As a result, their conception of representation fairness fails to consider how legacies of historical marginalization restrain the capacity to exercise self-determination and the development of marked individuals (Bickford, 1997, pp. 117–21).

Feminists' critiques of a 'difference-blind' liberalism therefore need to be understood as an attempt to extend considerations of injustice from state-society relations to the durable inequalities among citizens. Feminists' accounts of representation fairness do not reject or contest the individual as the primary bearer of rights but, instead, call attention to the group-related vulnerabilities that individuals experience based on their social position. Social relations and processes, Iris Marion Young (2008, p. 95) argued,

> put people in differing categorical social positions in relation to one another in ways that privilege those in one category in relation to another or others, both in the range of opportunities for self-development available to them, the resources they have or can access, the power they have over others or over the conditions of the lives of others, and the degree of status they have as indexed by others' willingness to treat them with deference or special respect.

This positional conception does not define social groups based on intrinsic or internal characteristics such as, for instance, culture.[4] It does not tie social groups' identity down to some ingrained set of characteristics that are passed on from generation to generation. On the contrary, it makes groups' identity relative to a constantly shifting context shaped by their interactions with others, the economy, cultural and political institutions and prevailing discourses (Alcoff, 1988, p. 434). This positional conception of group difference steers clear of essentialism. It does not presuppose a fixed set of attributes or objective group interests but, instead, conceives of groups as emergent from a historical experience. What defines the group and sets it apart from others is, in this regard, both contingent on socio-political and cultural contexts, and open to change.

Although it is impossible to account here for the divergent and oppositional perspectives on theorizing identity and subjectivity,[5] I want to underscore that a positional conception does not treat groups as fully indeterminate. While the position of 'women' is relative to context and thus subject to change, historical processes of marginalization have attributed a certain stability to social locations of privilege and disadvantage that materialize in group members' lives. As Linda Alcoff (1988, p. 435) argued, "It is simply not possible to interpret our society in such a way that women have more power or equal power relative to men". As the result of historical legacies of patriarchy, women today share a vulnerability to sexism. This notion of vulnerability does not bring about a politics of sameness: not all women experience sexism, nor attribute meaning to these experiences in a uniform way. Women's vulnerability to sexism does, however, provide a commonality based on which women can start to interpret and construct shared values, norms and interests (cf. Alcoff, 1988, p. 434).

This emphasis on commonality—as opposed to sameness—is crucial.[6] It allows those applying a positional conception of social groups to successfully navigate, as Fraser (1992, p. 68) stated, "between the twin shoals of essentialism and nominalism, between reifying essentialist conceptions of social groups and dissolving social identities into sheer nullity or meaninglessness." Although I do not wish to rehearse the arguments here, it must be clear that a conception of positional difference actively rejects the post-identity claim that social groups are nothing more than discursive constructs that restrain individuals' agency and should, thus, be resisted. A conception of positional difference, instead, treats individuals' ability to act— including their ability to resist dominant discourses—as mediated by extant power relations. Individuals' social locations do not only shape, restrain and enable the effectiveness of their agency. They equally inform individuals' perspective on politics to the extent to which their identities, as linked to hierarchical relations of power, may form a resource for mobilizing political action (Alcoff, 2006, pp. 38–40; McNay, 2010, pp. 514–15). The very coercion that lumped sets of individuals together into social groups is also the coercion that allows them to act in a meaningful manner: being 'like' others, and exchanging experiences with others, is what allows individuals to identify patterns of inequality that qualify as injustices (Mansbridge, 1994, p. 66). Stated differently, group identities (however constructed) matter: the result of systems of domination, they equally form a powerful resource for dismantling these systems.

Stated differently, although integral to what it means to act, the attention of post-feminist theories to individuals' resistance against restrictive group identities should not reduce conceptions of individual agency to acts of resistance. "Resistance and subversion", Lois McNay (2017) argues, "are limited modes of action because their displacements remain within the parameters of the given, within the existing rules of the game rather than challenging the game itself". Individuals' social locations, structured by hierarchical relations of power, give direction to resistance, allowing individuals to identify which injustices require political action. Individuals' social locations, put differently, form a powerful base for their ability to construct positive alternatives to extant power relations. It is individuals' ability for constructing societal alternatives, and not their ability for undirected or 'blind' resistance, that brings about radical transformation (cf. Collins, 1998).

These insights underpin group-based approaches to theorizing representation fairness. Scholars (e.g. Mansbridge, 1999; Phillips, 1995; Williams, 1998; Young, 1990) have invoked the epistemically significant impact of representatives' social location to advocate an institutionalized presence of historically marginalized groups in democracies' central decision-making institutions. As the result of their history, experiences with structural inequalities, and relationships with other group members, individuals of historically disadvantaged groups are likely to understand social events in a different way than members of privileged groups. In a similar vein, restricted by their proper social locations, privileged actors are less likely to understand and acknowledge the relevance of minority perspectives (Alcoff, 1991, p. 7; Young, 1989, p. 264).

The impact of representatives' social locations reveals the limitations of traditional mechanisms of accountability that are rooted in representatives' relations to an anonymous electorate. Trusting "some groups to protect another group's interests (e.g. letting husbands take care of their wives' interests) has, more often than not, produced unsatisfactory outcomes for disadvantaged groups" (Dovi, 2002, p. 730). Contrary to liberal beliefs, the social identities of representatives are politically relevant: their social locations and related knowledge affect the kind of social perspectives judged relevant for collective decision-making. In contexts of historical marginalization, Dovi (2002) argued, "democratic representation sometimes requires descriptive representation".

Feminists' arguments for an institutionalized presence of historically disadvantaged groups (also see Chapter 3, this volume) oppose the liberal belief that the political under-representation of historically disadvantaged groups reflects the lack of salience of those identities (Williams, 1998, pp. 10–11). Instead, feminist scholars treat systemic disparities in representation outcomes as evidence of the different positionality of social groups and the unequal opportunities linked to these positions. Presenting representation outcomes as a measure of procedural fairness, Anne Phillips (2004, p. 10) argued,

> Either we are sufficiently similar in our concerns and interests and experiences for the sex or ethnicity of our representative to be irrelevant—in which case, the similarities in our lives would already throw up a rough parity in representation. Or we are in truth very differently situated, in which case there is a compelling argument for ensuring not just a formal equality of chances but equal outcomes as well.

When representation outcomes vary distinctively across social groups, the only plausible explanation is that they must be differently positioned within society. When all formal conditions are equal (e.g. the right to vote, speak, meet and mobilize politically), it must be that certain groups have less resources (such as education, or time—because working three jobs or raising kids) to take an interest in politics and go to meetings, or are not judged worthy or competent enough to serve as representatives of the people. The fact that such differences are large enough to explain under-representation testifies to their political relevance. This, in turn, qualifies the dominance of political life by some of a variety of social groups as a form of injustice: unequal representation reflects patterns of socio-economic, political and cultural inequality and inhibits a collective's ability for dismantling such patterns (Phillips, 2004, p. 10).

While advocating an institutionalized presence of historically disadvantaged groups in political institutions,[7] feminist accounts of representation fairness have rejected a strict notion of accountability on the part of descriptive representatives. Melissa Williams (1998, p. 6), for instance, states that "it would be absurd to claim that a representative, simply because she is a woman, therefore represents the interests or perspectives of women generally". Women's shared social location only figures, as Phillips (1995, p. 156) put it, "as a promise of shared concerns". The difference that descriptive representatives make to representative democracy, Jane Mansbridge (1999) succinctly stated, mainly consists in their capacity to demonstrate the 'ability to rule' of disadvantaged group members, and their potential for mobilizing disadvantaged group members. In contexts of group mistrust and uncrystallized, not fully articulated, interests, the experiential knowledge and better communication of descriptive representatives may empower group members that kept silent before.

This emphasis on communication and mobilization also characterizes Suzanne Dovi's (2002) conception of *preferable* descriptive representatives. Accounting for within-group power differentials, Dovi defines preferable descriptive representatives as having "strong *mutual* relationships with *dispossessed* subgroups" (p. 729, emphasis in original). The requisite of mutual recognition underscores the insight that the gender of female representatives forms but a precarious basis for grounding claims to speak on behalf of 'women'. The latter also requires consultation of other women, especially those situated at the intersection of systems of domination (such as, for instance, racism and sexism).

It should be clear by now that the arguments for group representation do not centre on a politics built around 'what' a group is about (i.e. on identity). Instead, they draw upon 'who' the group is or how its members stand in contextualized relations to others (Bickford, 1997, p. 117; Zerilli, 2017, p. 13). This focus allows one to conceive that in contexts of historical marginalization, descriptive representatives offer new ways of communicating that may open politics and potentially make democratic systems truly competitive marketplaces of interests (Mansbridge, 1999; Shapiro, 2015). In this regard, an institutionalized presence of historically disadvantaged groups predominantly seeks to mobilize differently situated others and draw them into the political debate as moral equals.

THE CONSTRUCTIVIST TURN: ALL GROUPS SUSPECT?

Recent contributions to theorizing political representation have challenged long-standing understandings that define representation in terms of *mimesis*. Increasingly, the belief that representation serves as a vehicle for linking citizens' preferences to decision-making processes is found lacking. The idea that representation merely reflects, mirrors or copies citizens' preferences ignores the *constitutive* character of representation: like other acts of naming, representations select particular features of political reality and organize them in comprehensive ways (for more on representation as naming, consult Chapter 5, this volume). In doing so, representations contribute to how we perceive and understand political reality. Representation, in this regard, helps people come to terms with their political environments and allows them to find themselves together as political subjects ('the people') capable of making enforceable demands on their leaders (Näsström, 2006, p. 330).

The insight that "the people, as a totality, taken in the singular" is not absent but nowhere to be found (Rosanvallon, 2008, p. 206; Young, 2000, p. 84) greatly affected theorizing on representative democracy. Scholars' appreciation of the constitutive qualities of political representation radically upgraded the status of political representation in democratic theory. Once cast aside as but a second-best alternative for the desired yet unattainable ideal of direct democracy, representation is now considered quintessential to democratic politics (cf. Ankersmit, 1996; Plotke, 1997). Without representation, the people is nothing but a dispersed, fragmented and unruly set of individuals. Representation, however, has the capacity to mobilize individuals: while inviting them to consider themselves affected by the representations offered to them, representation beckons individuals to rise above their immediate experiences and find themselves together with others. This mobilizing force makes representation a necessary condition for peoplehood (Disch, 2011). Because representational relationships foster unity, they enable what is a naturally inarticulate and dispersed public to "speak and act of their own accord, that is, the democratic public" (Brito Vieira, 2015, p. 506).

Scholars' appreciation for the constitutive and mobilizing force of representation transforms the people from something hard, given or fixed "into something more fuzzy and coterminous with their representative" (Ankersmit, 2002, p. 350). This reconceptualization of popular sovereignty exposes the limitations of traditional 'linkage' conceptions of representation that separated an extra-institutional constituent power ('the people') and constituted power (government). If we accept that 'the people' gains its face and value only after and through representation, it is no longer possible to define the quality of representation in terms of preference satisfaction. It is logically impossible to justify representation practices by making reference to the groups and preferences they have helped to produce (Severs et al., 2015, p. 619; Sunstein, 1991, p. 8).

Instead, political representation is increasingly conceived as a means for democratic self-actualization. Its main function or contribution to democracy consists in enabling individuals to conceive of themselves as affected by decision-making processes and claim a stake in these processes. This defines the democratic function of representation as an act of balancing: representation should create a sense of generality needed for collective decision-making but, at the same time, should resist unyielding discourses of unity that inordinately subject and confine the power of would-be members of the demos. While it is the case that decision-making requires closures, these closures should be provisional at best and safeguard the multitude's right to disagree. Representation should, as Nadia Urbinati (2006, pp. 35, 177) argued, facilitate a continuous circular movement between constituent power ('the people' as an unruly body of individuals) and constituted power ('the people' as a coercive agent).

Because they treat 'the people' as something fuzzy or coterminous with political representation, contemporary constructivist accounts have abandoned prior conceptions of the people and refrain from articulating the type of individuals (e.g. citizens) and groups that can formulate, on the basis of their membership in the demos, claims for inclusion in decision-making processes. Abandoning a priori considerations of the parts that constitute the people, scholars have reverted to the language of 'individuals', 'those (potentially) affected', or 'would-be members of the demos'. This language of unencumbered selves echoes the tradition of liberal individualism and signals the need for closer investigation of the commonalities and differences between contemporary constructivist theories and liberal accounts of representation.

Although it is beyond the scope of this chapter to offer a full comparison, I want to indicate two points on which constructivist accounts differ from liberal democratic theories of representation. These points of difference are crucial to understanding the nature of the so-called 'constructivist turn' and may bring deeper understanding of what it is we are turning away from (cf. Disch, 2015; Näsström, 2011). Constructivists' accounts of power, first, greatly differ from liberal democratic ones. As demonstrated in the previous sections, liberal democrats' focus on individuals and the uniqueness of their interest constellations caused them to underplay structural inequalities that affect the political agency of social groups differently. Constructivist approaches to theorizing representation, in contrast, give a much fuller account of the structural inequalities of contemporary democracies.

The attention of constructivist theorists on power relations follows directly from their understanding of political representation as a relationship between a representative, or claim maker, and the audiences to whom a claim to represent is offered. While the interplay between claim maker and audience reveals that both hold power (cf. Severs, 2010), it equally points to the important ways in which context shapes and restrains political representation or the range of representative claims that can plausibly be made. In *The Representative Claim*, Michael Saward (2010) elaborated on the contextual limits to representatives' creativity and the need for an aesthetic fit between a claim to represent the people and the audiences to whom such a claim is offered. The credibility of a claim, Saward argued, depends both on the power and resources of a representative (her descriptive identity, election, appointment, etc.) and the claim's alignment with the audience's familiar contextual, discursive and habitual repertoires. When a claim strays too far from the audience's familiar conception of 'the people', it is unlikely that the audience will recognize such a claim as 'standing for' or 'being about' the people (cf. Saward, 2010, p. 56).

The same holds for a representative's stylistic repertoires: when these differ too much from so-called standard modes of expression, the claim maker will experience greater difficulty to convey her claims to others. The style and language in which a claim is stated greatly affects its perceived significance (cf. Mansbridge, 1990, p. 127). These contextual repertoires not only restrain the creativity of political representation but also serve those who benefit from the status quo. Echoing Schattschneider's (1960) critique of interest group pluralism, Lisa Disch (2012, p. 610) problematized the ways in which powerful groups set the terms of the debate and manage to keep certain conflicts off the table.

The insight that privileged actors (such as the rich, the higher-educated, citizens who hold nationality status, etc.) have the ability to narrow the scope of political conflict explains constructivist theorists' appreciation of contestation. At this point, constructivist accounts again differ greatly from liberal democratic theories. Although both strands of literature take an unruly and disorderly multitude of individuals (the citizens versus those affected) as their starting point, they ascribe different meaning to the potential for conflict stemming from individuals' diverging interests. Liberal democratic theories greatly problematized the implications of conflict for political rule: the divisiveness of the people signals that unification can only be attained through coercion (allowing the majority to stand for the whole) and calls for reasons that could legitimate such coercion. Liberal democrats, therefore, predominantly invested in defining procedures that could legitimate control over the unruly body of the people (Grant, 2014, p. 582). Constructivist theories, in contrast, no longer conceive of conflict as an empirical reality that should be overcome or pacified. For constructivist theorists, contestation holds normative value: it exposes the selectivity of any actor's claim to speak on behalf of the people and, in doing so, facilitates "a destabilization of institutions and authority and the repeated revision of norms" (Hayward, 2009, p. 125).

The indeterminacy of democratic constituents together with scholars' acknowledgement of the structural inequalities in representative systems generated a shift in our normative assessment of political representation. Although representation continues to be conceived of as a unifying practice, its democratic quality is increasingly defined by the extent to which it achieves a decentring of power or prevents any one interpretation of 'the people' from claiming final authority (cf. Garsten, 2009, p. 94). Such a decentring is needed for all affected to participate and be able to claim a stake in the processes that define the terms of their living together. The central normative question, Disch (2015, p. 495) argues, no longer centres on whether decision-makers were right in taking up a particular claim. Such evaluation would imply reinscribing a prior, scholarly conception of peoplehood on the basis of which rights to a certain outcome can be evaluated. The real normative issue revolves, instead, around the question of whether a representative system provides sufficient opportunities for those affected by processes of representation to recognize themselves as such, cast judgement on the claims made on their behalf, and give their judgement a public voice that is strong enough to elicit response (cf. Disch, 2012, p. 611; Urbinati, 2000, p. 760).

Evidence of this shift in normative thinking can be found in scholars' growing emphasis on individuals' capacity for objection. Although they call representative relationships into question,[8] individuals' objections to the claims formulated on their behalf offer proof of power sharing between those represented and their (would-be) representatives. This notion of power-sharing inspired some scholars to reconceptualize the normative standards or ethical principles to which individual representatives should adhere (e.g. Mansbridge, 2003; Montanaro, 2012; Severs, 2010; Severs & Dovi, 2018). The majority of recent theorizing, however, focuses on the representative system as a whole and specifies structures, mechanisms and conditions that empower those affected (Disch, 2011; Geenens et al., 2015; Mansbridge, 2011; Saward, 2010, 2014).

While specifying the conditions that promote individuals' agency (understood as their capacity for judgement and objection), contemporary constructivist accounts have attributed but little attention to social structures. This blind spot is somewhat puzzling as constructivist accounts extended considerations on domination from state-society relations to the broader set of relations among individuals in civil society (cf. Young, 2000, p. 38). Contrary to liberal-democratic theorists, social constructivists of political representation conceive of individuals as socially embedded, as defined, at least in part, by their social positions and relations with others. However, in their attempt to de-naturalize social and political identities, these constructivist accounts have omitted that social identities may form a basis for effective mobilization and political agency. Constructivist accounts of political representation have mainly underscored the relevance of reflexivity, or individuals' capacity to cast critical judgement on—and, in this sense, become increasingly free from—the social structures that define them. The argument that individuals should become (more) free from social structures has, in a sense, prevented scholars from articulating how these structures still affect processes of representation and unevenly shape individuals' political opportunities.

The deferral of issues of equity also follows from constructivists' suspicion toward prior notions of 'the people'. It is impossible to attribute individuals a right to a fair share in the outcomes of representation processes without also re-inscribing a notion of peoplehood on the basis of which individuals hold such a right. This would make scholars, as Nadia Urbinati (2016, p. 378) critiqued, accessories of particular, invariably selective, conceptions of peoplehood:

> Some contemporary political theorists seem to exalt the value of the outcome over and above procedures, or, to put it another way, they evaluate the goodness of the democratic procedures based on a consequentialist approach, thus subordinating the principle of equal liberty to some desired outcome.

Because constructivist theorists treat 'the people' as coterminous with political representation, they are reluctant to identify bearers of rights. Identifying a set of individuals or a social group as entitled to a stake in representation *outcomes* requires a conception of 'the people' as a whole, and an account of the standards by which that people seeks to govern itself. Only a conception of 'the people' allows individuals and groups to claim, as members, a right to a stake. But because constructivists' accounts treat 'the people' and the standards by which it seeks to govern itself as indeterminate (a work that remains forever 'in the making'), scholarly assertions that particular groups hold rights to a stake in determining the outcomes of representation are often conceived as privileging this or that group and as trumping individuals' equal liberty to (re)define 'the people'.

Scholars' concerns for individual freedom, and their accounts of political representation as a means for maximizing freedom (allowing the people to define itself) should, however, not divert attention from political realities. As David Runciman (2007, p. 26) argued, individuals cannot readily opt out of the consequences of political decisions. Although we pass judgement on our representatives as individuals, they act not in our names as individuals but in the name of larger political collectives (such as, 'the people', the European Union; also see Oberthür in this volume). As a consequence, our objections to representatives' claims ('not in my name') do not provide us an opt-out: as citizens, we are bound to the decisions made on our behalf. Members of a social group, similarly, cannot escape the impact of stereotyping by simply claiming not to identify themselves with the group. Stated differently, while processes of political representation may enhance the freedom of individuals, realities of governance, themselves facilitated by representation, continue to circumvent and restrain individuals' freedom. Our recognition of the socially constructed character of 'the political' may not prevent us from calling out structural inequalities and incorporating critical reflection on these inequalities in our theories of what makes a good representative system.

DISCUSSION AND CONCLUSION

This chapter has attempted to trace the theoretical edges to theorizing representation fairness. Drawing on Iris Marion Young's (2001) work, it has taken structural inequalities as its point of departure and has sought to clarify the contemporary relevance of social groups to theorizing representation fairness. To this end, it compared contemporary constructivist accounts to both liberal democratic theories (that is also suspicious of coherent, collective identities) and group-based accounts of representation fairness. The comparison reveals that many of the criticisms of liberal individualism can also be applied to contemporary constructivist accounts: although the latter offers a conception of the individual that is socially embedded, its emphasis on reflexivity (or individuals' ability to call into question the social structures that partly define them) allows for but little attention to the ways in which social identities also function as effective means for mobilization and political agency. As a result, their accounts of political representation begin to closely resemble those of liberal-democratic theorists. There is but little recognition that a fair representative system not only depends on mechanisms for contestation but also relies on the identification of power relations against which contestation should be directed (such as racism, sexism, homophobia, etc.). Only the latter, I argue, gives meaning or direction to contestation and helps us understand what a fair model of representative democracy requires.

Contemporary theorists' attentiveness to the constitutive character of political representation explains their suspicion toward coherent collective identities, and their confinement to a theoretical language centred on 'individuals', 'those affected', or 'would-be members'. However, by reverting to these terms, scholars inadvertently risk replicating the biases of liberal individualism. The focus on individuals sidesteps the ways in which systems of domination structurally affect, shape and restrain the abilities and opportunities of historically disadvantaged groups to participate in public debate. Because it makes the groups of people that have a right to a stake dependent on the issues that are represented, the concept of 'those affected' similarly risks obfuscating the structural character of political conflict.

The understanding of political representation as a mechanism for 'people making' and establishing freedom may, furthermore, not divert attention from the ways in which citizens are bound by governance structures. When we accept this reality, we cannot limit our accounts of fairness to processes of representation, but we should extend our normative attention to the outcomes of representation. Not because individuals have an objective right to a particular outcome but because the ways in which outcomes are structurally dispersed across groups of individuals informs us on the political opportunities available to people (cf. Phillips, 2004).

Finally, theories of representation must not overstate the free-floating, open-ended nature of political representation. Representation remains closely linked to forms of decision-making and coercion. The statement 'not in my name' does not free citizens of their duty to pay taxes. Similarly, we cannot by simple assertion escape the consequences of claims to speak on behalf of 'our' social groups. As women, irrespective of the fierceness of our nature, and the range of our competences, we undergo the impact of sexism and gender stereotyping. Stated differently, there exists a political world outside of discourse. The indeterminacy of democratic constituents, however correct, may not lead to a fetishization of the inchoate (Deveaux, 1999, p. 14). Just as processes of state formation have rendered the impact of state membership real, historical processes of marginalization, consisting of a reiteration of power relations, structurally shape the political opportunities of social groups. Closer attention to the social conditions for effective agency (i.e. how social groups are differently situated) should, in this regard, be understood as a contextualized application of the general normative principles outlined by contemporary constructivist theories.

Although it is beyond the aims and scope of this chapter, the coherence between contemporary constructivist theories of political representation and group-based accounts of fairness hinges upon scholars' conceptualizations of social groups. This has far-reaching implications for empirical research: no longer can scholars take preconceived conceptions of social groups as their point of departure and judge the fairness of representation outcomes by the extent to which a particular set of, for instance, women's interests are advocated by representatives. Instead, and drawing upon Young's (1989, 2001) politics of positional difference, scholars should root their evaluations in deeply contextualized understandings of power relations and should ground their normative evaluations in reflections on what it would take to transform relations between historically advantaged and disadvantaged groups and make them more equal.

NOTES

1. I place the term *race* in between inverted commas to indicate that it is socially constructed, as opposed to being an objective biological marker. Like Lutz, Herrera Vivar, & Supik (2011, p. 3), I find the concept problematic but consider it key to studying, explaining, and thereby rendering less powerful, processes of racialization (Severs, 2016).

2. The term *catch-22* finds its origin in Joseph Heller's (1961) novel that describes the fictive story of an air force base during the Second World War. Since the publication of Heller's novel, the term is used to refer to a set of contradictory rules that prevent individuals from solving a problem.

3. For a complementary approach, based on the concept of person, see Chapter 5, this volume.

4. For a fuller account on the conceptualization of culture, see Young's (1990) discussion of the politics of 'cultural difference' and 'positional difference' and Phillips's (2004) rejection of a strong notion of culture.

5. For excellent overviews of these debates, see Dietz (2003) and Bernstein (2005).

6. For a complementary account of commonality and its importance in political representation, see Chapter 5, this volume.

7. For a fuller account of the arguments for an institutionalized presence of historically disadvantaged groups, see Phillips (1995) and Mansbridge (1999), or Chapter 3 in this volume.

8. For a thorough discussion on representative relationships between a claim maker and the groups she claims to stand for, and whether such relationships can be re-invoked by individual objections, see David Runciman (2007).

REFERENCES

Alcoff, L. (1988). Cultural feminism versus post-structuralism: The identity crisis in feminist theory. *Signs, 13* (3), 405–36.

Alcoff, L. (1991). The problem of speaking for others. *Cultural Critique , 20*, 5–32.

Alcoff, L. (2006). *Visible identities: Race, gender and the self.* Oxford: Oxford University Press.

Ankersmit, F. R. (1996). *Aesthetic politics: Political philosophy beyond fact and value.* Stanford, CA: Stanford University Press.

Ankersmit, F. R. (2002). Representational democracy. An aesthetic approach to conflict and compromise. *Common Knowledge, 8*(1), 24–46.

Beckwith, K., & Cowell-Meyers, K. (2007). Sheer numbers: Critical representation thresholds and women's political representation. *Perspectives on Politics, 5*(3), 553–65.

Benhabib, S. (2004). *The rights of others: Aliens, residents and citizens.* Cambridge: Cambridge University Press.

Bernstein, M. (2005). Identity politics. *Annual Review of Sociology, 31 ,* 47–74.

Bickford, S. (1996). *The dissonance of democracy: Listening, conflict, and citizenship.* Ithaca, NY: Cornell University Press.

Bickford, S. (1997). Anti-anti-identity politics: Feminism, democracy, and the complexities of citizenship. *Hypathia, 12*(4), 111–31.

Brito Vieira, M. (2015). Founders and re-founders: Struggles of self-authorized representation. *Constellations, 22*(4), 500–513.

Collins, P. H. (1998). *Fighting words: Black women and the search for justice.* Minneapolis: University of Minnesota Press.

Dahl, R. A. (1956). *A preface to democratic theory.* Chicago: University of Chicago Press.

Dahl, R. A. (1989). *Democracy and its critics.* New Haven, CT: Yale University Press.

Deveaux, M. (1999). Agonism and pluralism. *Philosophy and Social Criticism, 25*(4), 1–22.

Dietz, M. G. (2003). Current controversies in feminist theory. *Annual Review of Political Science, 6*(2003), 399–431.

Disch, L. (2011). Toward a mobilization conception of democratic representation. *American Political Science Review , 105*(1), 100–114.

Disch, L. (2012). Democratic representation and the constituency paradox. *Perspectives on Politics, 10*(3), 599–616.

Disch, L. (2015). The "constructivist turn" in democratic representation: A normative dead-end? *Constellations, 22*(4), 487–99.

Dovi, S. (2002). Preferable descriptive representation: Will just any woman, black or Latino do? *American Political Science Review , 96*(4), 729–45.

Eisenberg, A. (2001). The medium is the message: How referendums lead us to understand equality. In M. Mendelsohn & A. Parkin (Eds.), *Referendum democracy: Citizen, elites and deliberation in referendum campaigns* (pp. 147–65). London: Palgrave Macmillan.

Eulau, H. (1967). Changing views of representation. In I. D. Sola Pool (Ed.), *Contemporary political science: Toward empirical theory.* New York: McGraw-Hill.

Forrest, D. M., & Hindman, M. D. (2015). *It's time to get over the pluralist heaven.* Unpublished manuscript.

Fraser, N. (1992). The uses and abuses of French discourse theories for feminist politics. *Theory, Culture & Society, 9* (1), 51–71.

Garsten, B. (2009). Representative government and popular sovereignty. In I. Shapiro, S. C. Stokes, E. J. Wood, & A. S. Kirschner (Eds.), *Political representation* (pp. 90–110) . Cambridge: Cambridge University Press.

Gaventa, J. (1980). *Power and powerlessness: Quiescence and rebellion in an Appalachian valley.* Urbana, Chicago, London: University of Illinois Press.

Geenens, R., et al. (2015). The 'co-originality' of constituent power and representation. *Constellations, 22* (4), 514–22.

Grant, J. (2014). 'Becoming one': Visions of political unity from the ancients to the postmoderns. *Constellations, 21* (4), 575–88.

Hayward, C. R. (2009). Making interest: On representation and democratic legitimacy. In I. Shapiro, S. C. Stokes, E. J. Wood, & A. S. Kirschner (Eds.), *Political representation* (pp. 111–38) . Cambridge: Cambridge University Press.

Heller, J. (1961/1999). *Catch-22: A novel.* New York: Simon & Schuster.

Judge, D. (1999). *Representation: Theory and practice in Britain.* London, New York: Routledge.

Krouse, R. W. (1982). Polyarchy & participation: The changing democratic theory of Robert Dahl. *Polity, 14*(3), 441–63.

Kymlicka, W. (1993). Group representation in Canadian politics. In L. Seidle (Ed.), *Equity and community: The charter, interest advocacy and representation* (pp. 61–89). Montreal: Institute for Research on Public Policy (IRPP).

Lukes, S. (1974). *Power: A radical view.* London: Palgrave Macmillan.

Lutz, H., Herrera Vivar, M. T., & Supik, L. (2011). Framing intersectionality: An introduction. In H. Lutz, M. T. Herrera Vivar, & L. Supik (Eds.), *Framing intersectionality: Debates on a multi-faceted concept in gender studies* (pp. 1–24). London: Ashgate.

Mansbridge, J. (1990, Spring). Feminism and democracy. *American Prospect, 1,* 126–39.

Mansbridge, J. (1994). Using power/fighting power. *Constellations, 1*(1), 53–73.

Mansbridge, J. (1999). Should blacks represent blacks and women represent women? A contingent 'yes'. *Journal of Politics , 61*(3), 628–57.

Mansbridge, J. (2011). Clarifying the concept of representation. *American Political Science Review, 105*(3), 621–30.

Mansbridge, J. (2003). Rethinking representation. *American Political Science Review, 97*(4), 515–528.

Mayo, H. B. (1960). *An introduction to democratic theory.* Oxford: Oxford University Press.

McNay, Lois. (2010). Feminism and post-identity politics: The problem of agency. *Constellations, 17* (4), 512–25.

McNay, Lois. (2017). Agency. In L. Disch & M. Hawkesworth (Eds.), *The Oxford handbook of feminist theory* (pp. 39–60) . Oxford: Oxford University Press.

Montanaro, L. (2012). The democratic legitimacy of self-appointed representatives. *Journal of Politics, 74* (4), 1094–107.

Näsström, S . (2006). Representative democracy as tautology. *European Journal of Political Theory, 5*(3), 321–42.

Näsström, S. (2011). Review article: Where is the representative turn going? *European Journal of Political Theory, 10* (4), 501–10.

Pennock, J. (1979). *Democratic political theory.* Princeton, NY: Princeton University Press.

Phillips, A. (1995). *The politics of presence: The political representation of gender, ethnicity, and race.* Oxford: Oxford University Press.

Phillips, A. (2004). Defending equality of outcome. *Journal of Political Philosophy, 12* (1), 1–19.

Plotke, David. (1997). Representation is democracy. *Constellations, 4*(1), 19–34.

Rogowski, R. (1981). Representation in political theory and in law. *Ethics, 91*(3), 395–430.

Rosanvallon, P. (2008). *Counter-democracy: Politics in an age of distrust* (A. Goldhammer, Trans.). Cambridge: Cambridge University Press.

Runciman, D. (2007). The paradox of political representation. *Journal of Political Philosophy*, *15*(1), 93–114.

Sandel, M. J. (1984). The procedural republic and the unencumbered self. *Political Theory*, *12*(1), 81–96.

Saunders, B. (2010). Democracy, political equality, and majority rule. *Ethics*, *121*(1), 148–77.

Saward, M. (2010). *The representative claim*. Oxford: Oxford University Press.

Saward, M. (2014). Shape-shifting representation. *American Political Science Review*, *108*(4), 723-736.

Schattschneider, E. E. (1960). *The semisovereign people: A realist's view of democracy in America*. New York: Holt, Rinehart & Winston.

Severs, E. (2010). Representation as claims-making: Quid responsiveness? *Representation*, *46*(4), 411–23.

Severs, E. (2016). Feminisme en constructivisme: Een 'catch 22'? *Sociologos*, *37*(1), 45–57.

Severs, E., Celis, K., & Erzeel, S. (2016). Power, privilege and disadvantage: Intersectionality theory and political representation. *Politics*, *36*(4), 346–54.

Severs, E., Celis, K., & Meier, P. (2015). The indirectness of political representation: A blessing or a concern? A study of the conceptions of members of the Flemish Regional Parliament. *Parliamentary Affairs*, *68*(3), 616–37.

Severs, E., & Dovi, S. (2018). Why we need a return to the ethics of political representation. *PS: Political Science & Politics*, forthcoming.

Shapiro, I. (2015). Against impartiality. *Journal of Politics*, *78* (2), 467–80.

Strolovitch, D. Z. (2006). Do interest groups represent the disadvantaged? Advocacy at the intersections of race, class and gender. *Journal of Politics*, *68*(4), 894–910.

Sunstein, C. R. (1991). Preferences and politics. *Philosophy and Public Affairs*, *20*(1), 3–34.

Urbinati, N. (2005). Continuity and Rupture: The power of judgment in democratic representation. *Constellations*, *12*(2), 194–222.

Urbinati, N. (2006). *Representative democracy, principles and genealogy*. Chicago: University of Chicago Press.

Urbinati, N. (2016). Postscript. *Critical Review of International Social and Political Philosophy*, *19* (3), 376–82.

Urbinati, N. (2000). Representation as advocacy: A study of democratic deliberation. *Political Theory*, *28*(6), 758–786.

Warren, M. E. (1992). Democratic theory and self-transformation *American Political Science Review*, *86* (1), 8–23.

Williams, M. (1998). *Voice, trust, and memory: Marginalized groups and the failings of liberal democracy*. New York: Princeton University Press.

Young, I. M. (1989). Polity and group difference: A critique of the ideal of universal citizenship. *Ethics*, *99*(2), 250–74.

Young, I. M. (1990). *Justice and the politics of difference*. Princeton, NJ: Princeton University Press.

Young, I. M. (1997). Deferring group representation. In I. Shapiro & W. Kymlicka (Eds.), *NOMOS XXXIX, Ethnicity and group rights* (pp. 349–76). New York: New York University Press.

Young, I. M. (2000). *Inclusion and democracy*. Oxford: Oxford University Press.

Young, I. M. (2001). Equality of whom? Social groups and judgments of injustice. *Journal of Political Philosophy*, *9* (1), 1–18.

Young, I. M. (2008). Structural injustice: The politics of difference. In G. Graig, T. Burchardt, & D. Gordon (Eds.), *Social justice and public policy: Seeking fairness in diverse societies* (pp. 77–104). Bristol: Policy Press.

Zerilli, L. (2017). Politics. In L. Disch & M. Hawkesworth (Eds.), *The Oxford handbook of feminist theory* (pp. 632–50). Oxford: Oxford University Press.

Chapter Seven

Representing Future Generations

Claire Dupont

Political representation in democratic political systems describes most commonly the notion of elected officials representing their constituents (see Chapter 2). Simple definitions of *representation* refer to the process of making citizens' voices and interests present in policymaking processes (Pitkin, 1967). Political representation is nevertheless a moving concept, with the representation of groups and other forms of representation gaining validity (Mansbridge, 1999; Saward, 2009). As such, and as is clear throughout this volume, political representation as a concept is being 'stretched' to accommodate new (types of) representatives and represented, and new ideas (Collier & Mahon, 1993; Sartori, 1970).

In this chapter, I discuss how the concept of political representation is being pushed to the 'edge', or rather pushed beyond its limits, when tasked to accommodate future generations in policymaking. When it comes to future generations, there is a growing body of literature describing the necessity of taking their interests into account in current policymaking—embedded in the concept of 'intergenerational justice' (Beckman, 2013; Hiskes, 2009; Weston, 2012). I ask whether representation can provide useful language and instruments to respond to calls for intergenerational justice. I bridge conceptual thinking in justice and representation literature to initial reflections on how to investigate such representation empirically, with the aim of assessing any potential of representation in this regard, focusing on climate policy as an example throughout.

Climate change is often called a 'wicked' policy problem: it is a complex issue, with multiple causes across many societal sectors and levels of governance, and, if not addressed, it will have negative effects for society, making action even more challenging in future (Peters, 2017). For climate governance, many of the consequences of climate change are (most likely) irreversible and will have long-lasting effects. The actions or inactions of present policymakers on climate change can therefore limit future generations' options for a comfortable and sustainable livelihood.

The push for consideration of future generations in current climate policymaking stems from the definition of sustainable development outlined by the World Commission on the Environment and Development in 1987: *sustainable development* is defined as ensuring that the needs of the present are met 'without compromising the ability of future generations to meet their own needs' (WCED, 1987). In other words, future generations have the right to enjoy a clean environment that will sustain their livelihoods. Using finite natural resources and damaging certain environmental systems today will have implications far beyond the current decision-making generation. It is therefore increasingly acknowledged in the literature, and in global governance structures generally, that the interests of future generations should be taken into account into today's decision-making processes (Beckman, 2008; Oxford Martin Commission, 2013). How this should be done is still up for debate, but much literature equates the idea of taking future generations' interests into account with the need for political representation in some form or another (Jensen, 2015; Weiss, 1990). I argue, rather, that this case clearly demonstrates the limits of representation. For effective and just policy decisions towards future generations, representation is an insufficient guarantee, but it may most effectively be combined with other governance forms.

I begin by discussing the rationale for 'representing' future generations in current policymaking from literature on justice. I then discuss how future generations can be imagined through representation in today's democratic systems, pointing out the practical challenges. Next, I analyze initial reflections on the empirical attempts to represent future generations through three categories of mechanisms of representation. Finally, I discuss the consequences of such representation for the quality of democratic governance (now and into the future), and conclude with an assessment of the appropriateness of representation in this context. In this case, political representation is pushed to the edges and is likely to serve as one source of instruments among several for the achievement of intergenerational justice and sustainable development.

JUSTICE THROUGH REPRESENTATION

Literature on theories of justice (Nozick, 1974; Rawls, 1971) and intergenerational justice (Beckman, 2013) forms the basis for any call for representation of future generations. This literature conceives of justice as requiring the (re)distribution of resources, recognition of rights, and/or participation in political processes. These conceptions differ in their discussion of rights and duties on various populations. They offer differing, and sometimes competing, accounts of who has rights, to what they have rights and towards whom a duty is owed. Such theories may also specify third-party beneficiaries of both rights and duties. Rights and duties are asserted, established and exercised through political institutions where policy decisions are made, and representation is considered a prime means to achieve these tasks. Moreover, we may, under any specific account of justice, have rights and/or duties with respect to representation itself, or more generally in the creation of common institutions and political mechanisms that are necessary to fulfil wider duties.

Democratic theory has understandings of justice at its core. The aim of democratic governance is to ensure that fair policy decisions are made for a certain population. As democratic governance has developed over time, considerations of the heightened participation of marginalized individuals and groups have been underlined to improve the justice (and legitimacy) of the democratic system. In practice, democratic governance traditionally involves elections of representatives from the general population to govern a society for a certain period (see Chapter 2).

While participation in political representation has expanded as democratic governance has evolved, democracies can nevertheless be considered as 'systematically biased in favour of the present' (Thompson, 2005, p. 246), with limited ability (or willingness) to consider the interests of future generations. This is summed up in the fact that electoral democracy works in short-term cycles of just a few years, although problems faced by future generations require solutions through more 'long-term' institutional, policy and governance arrangements. Therefore, our theories of justice, with contractually based understandings of distribution or participation, do not necessarily 'time-travel' well (Hiskes, 2009, p. 48). New concepts embedded in intergenerational justice are required, if justice towards future generations is considered legitimate. For future generations, past (or present) decisions may constrain their ability to decide for themselves. As Thompson points out (2005, p. 247), future generations 'will have to live with the consequences of the laws made by citizens of an earlier generation. They may try to change the laws when their time comes, but that may be difficult or futile. The effects of many laws are irreversible—the damage may have been done as precedents become established, laws entrenched and habits engrained'.

Some scholars argue that future generations can take care of themselves and will have the legal and democratic systems in place that allow them to change laws and policies to their own advantage (Beckman, 2013). Other scholars argue that aims for justice and distribution of access to resources in environmental governance should concentrate on ensuring that the most vulnerable populations within the current generation are taken care of before consideration of future generations comes into play (Ehresman & Stevis, 2010; Harris, 2010; Thompson, 2005). When it comes to climate change and environmental sustainability, however, it is clear that actions taken by the present generation will produce effects felt far into the future (Davidson, 2008). Therefore, our decisions are necessarily going to impact the lives of members of generations to come.

Justice in Environment and Climate Governance

Governing the environment is no easy task, even for the benefits of the present. Environmental governance has long been dogged with the problem of the 'global commons'—where common pool resources (such as the atmosphere or the oceans) are assumed to be used to such an extent that they may be eventually destroyed, depleted or irreparably damaged, because each user considers their own needs first in the short term. Hardin originally made this argument in his 1968 article 'The Tragedy of the Commons' (Hardin, 1968). Since then, numerous international environmental agreements have attempted to govern the global environment to mitigate the problem of unrestrained exploitation of common resources. Nevertheless, debates about equity in the distribution of access to natural resources or about the shared effort required to respond to environmental problems have grown in response to the perceived inadequacy of these global governance efforts (Beckman & Page, 2008; Eckersley, 2004; Ehresman & Stevis, 2010). Discussions on global environmental governance quickly move into the domains of global justice, with equitable distribution of both benefits and responsibilities as the core controversy.

Several theories of climate and intergenerational justice draw on the 'all affected' principle as a means to support the argument in favour of representation of future generations in current policymaking (Karlsson, 2006; Näsström, 2011; Owen, 2012). This principle argues that all those affected by a political decision have a right to participate in decision-making. Such a principle can include all policy domains. For future generations, there are myriad decisions taken today that will affect their ability to live as they choose (including city planning and pension reforms, for example). But environmental and climate justice towards future generations is perceived as particularly crucial, and the crisis of environmental degradation today is a clear motivating factor for calls for representation. As the effects of climate change are expected to be most greatly felt in the future, our decision to continue burning fossil fuels and emit greenhouse gases will have more impact in the future than today. This, coupled with the reality that such changes to the climate mean (irreversible) damage to the life-sustaining systems of the planet (water, soil, air), points clearly to future generations as being among the most affected by climate change. It can be argued that in other policy fields decisions may be made in the future that alleviate some of the challenges decisions made today may pose (Beckman, 2013). The very irreversible nature of many of the impacts caused by our present inaction on preventing climate change is a special case for intergenerational justice. Hence, the 'all affected' principle would argue, climate policy made without taking future generations' interests into account is unjust. But how can such representation be achieved?

REPRESENTATIVE DEMOCRACY
AND FUTURE GENERATIONS

Making future generations' voices 'present' in current governance systems is not without challenges. First, the communication of these groups' or individuals' interests to a representative is impossible—a representative cannot find out precisely the actual interests of future generations. Second, such representation raises serious questions about legitimacy and accountability: who assesses whether the representation is adequate? And it poses challenges for current democratic governance—why should current generations use valuable representation instruments to represent the future when several groups or individuals are marginalized in today's system (see Chapter 3)? Can such representation even be considered 'democratic'?

On the first point, we can only 'imagine' what could be the interests of future generations. Those who are not yet born cannot participate in political processes today and cannot communicate their wishes. But to represent a population's interests, we must first know what those interests are. Who are future generations? Can not-yet-existing people have interests? How can we know their interests? How can these interests be represented? How can their representation be democratic?

Defining who we are talking about when discussing 'future generations' can lead to further precision, or further confusion, for implementing any representation on their behalf. It is particularly difficult for human beings to conceive of people in the distant future. We struggle to imagine their lives, their civilizations, their desires. Even for those people just one or two generations into the future, we find it challenging to relate to any group beyond those of our own offspring or community. In some respects, this leads to the same difficulties for representation that broadened concepts for today try to resolve—the diversity of the human community in any given territorial state raises questions about just representation of groups, different ethnicities, genders, ages and so on (Mansbridge, 1999).

Several philosophical scholars have also pointed to a specific issue in thinking about future generations, known as the 'non-identity problem'. This refers to how our decisions today will impact who (which collection of individuals) will exist in the future. One can imagine that all potential future generations' have the interest to live. But decisions that we make today (such as increasing family planning awareness) may conflict with this interest. Therefore, taking account of future generations' interests may not always be in harmony with sustainability policies that we assume are for the benefit of the future. Torbjörn Tännsjö describes 'necessary people' as those in the future who will exist no matter what we decide, 'actual people' as those who will exist as a result of present decisions, and 'possible people' as those who could have existed had we made a different decision (Tännsjö, 2007). The temporal distance between present decision-making and future generations removes much of this philosophical debate from practical discussions on sustainability policies, with calls for the 'representation' of future generations ignoring the individual make-up of those generations (Jensen, 2015; Weiss, 1990). Rather, future generations are understood as a group, where the individual membership is unidentified and fluid. This understanding does not mean that the future is assumed to be a place of complete equality and inclusion, only that these group dynamics are impossible to identify and can safely be ignored for the representation of future generations. To represent this group's interests, a link is made between 'interests', 'needs' and 'rights'.

The response to our struggle to consider the interests of humanity as a whole or 'future generations' as a single entity long into the future is found in cosmopolitan ethics arguing for 'global citizenship' and human solidarity (Meckled-Garcia, 2008; Saward, 2003). These are ideals that, while noble, are challenging to implement practically in a world divided into territorially distinct units. However, for future generations, there is some value to keeping the notion undefined—it can mean many things to many people, but if representing future generations in climate and environment policy results in policies that help ensure that life-sustaining systems of the planet are protected, certain calls for intergenerational justice can be considered fulfilled.

Establishing what will be the interests of future generations can be achieved by a thought experiment that extrapolates from the interests of current generations. Scholars argue that in the case of both non-human interests (such as animals or nature) and future generations, it is possible to understand their interests as linked to the need to survive and prosper. Representatives of nature and animal rights, therefore, aim to promote policies that protect or ameliorate the conditions for the life of a species (Tănăsescu, 2014). For future generations, a similar thought experiment is possible. Understanding future generations' interests, at least in the context of sustainable development, as an extension of the present generations' interests for a healthy environment and prosperous living conditions, forms the basis for identifying interests to be represented in current policymaking. It can easily be assumed that future generations will want much the same basic necessities as today—a safe and healthy environment and the ability to sustain themselves and their families (Dobson, 1996). Future generations' interests are thus, at the most basic level, reduced to needs.

Under the definition of sustainable development, moreover, the needs of future generations for a healthy environment are a *right* conferred upon future generations (implying that it is a duty of present generations to help fulfil these rights) (Weiss, 1990). There is nonetheless a difficulty in quantifying what this would amount to: how much of a certain resource would be required for future generations to meet their needs? Current generations rely on general estimates of expected population growth (see, for example, the regular reports of the United Nations' Population Division) and understandings of the resources required to sustain a certain quality of life for the global population. Scholars draw on this data to identify the needs of future generations and the responses of current ones to natural resource use and environmental degradation (Lutz, Sanderson, & Scherbov, 2004; Oxford Martin Commission, 2013; Vörösmarty, Green, Salisbury, & Lammers, 2000; Wang, Ye, Cai, & Chen, 2014). When it comes to environmental justice, the needs of future generations are the same as the needs of today's generations and of all species—clean air, clean water, good quality soil for food production, and shelter. With much environmental degradation, and climate change in particular (IPCC, 2013), meeting the present generation's needs in an irresponsible manner may impede the fulfilment of future generations' needs. Therefore, the needs of the future become 'interests' that have to be represented in current policymaking. A decision to continue consumption of fossil fuels today for another decade or more may have little effect on the fulfilment of the basic needs of today's generation, but may prevent the ability of future generations to access the same quality of environmental goods to meet their needs. In this case, the key lies with the postponed effects of a certain policy decision that must be brought clearly to the fore in policymaking.

This idea that the needs of future generations are similar to the interests of future generations because of the long-term effects of the present generation's actions may ignore other potential interests of future generations—such as political freedom, security, and so on (Beckman, 2008). Highlighting the interests of future generations for a clean, safe and healthy environment that allows for a sustainable livelihood implies a hierarchy of interests for future generations, with democratic and political freedom thus considered secondary interests to those that can be broadly defined as necessary for survival. At the very least, the responsibility for ensuring the fulfilment of such imagined interests of future generations is passed on to the future generations themselves, allowing current democratic systems to assume few duties in this regard. Some argue that political, social and legal interests may be less locked in as a result of the decisions of the present, with future generations having some ability to change their inheritances (Beckman & Page, 2008). Nevertheless, basic or primary interests/needs should not be considered as excluding other interests, but as we are limited in our capacity to 'imagine' these interests, the pragmatic choice is for a narrow focus on interests as basic needs. Indeed, we could imagine that one political interest or need of future generations is that they are represented in current democratic governance.

Second, there are concerns about the democratic quality of political representation of future generations, both in terms of legitimacy and accountability towards those generations, but also in terms of interference in democratic processes for the current generation. Why should we worry about future generations who will make their own policies later? How can we ensure a high quality of representation for current marginalized groups or individuals while focusing on the representation of future generations? What sort of representation, anyway, is adequate for safeguarding the interests of future generations? Who represents future generations?

Calls for representation of future generations are based on concerns for intergenerational justice and the fact that future generations have no voice in policy decisions that may affect their interests. Usual responses of democratic systems to the lack of representation of those with no voice include allowing greater opportunities for participation and embedding more extensive representation into institutions (Dobson, 1996; Thompson, 2005). Institutions at many levels of governance have to some extent succeeded in ensuring that the interests of today's voiceless populations are represented, such as guaranteeing the representation of indigenous peoples outside usual jurisdictions in climate and biodiversity agreements (Ulloa, 2013; Wallbott, 2014), although representation may remain inadequate for certain marginalized groups (Haider-Markel, Joslyn, & Kniss, 2000; Mansbridge, 1999; see Chapters 3 and 6). Can mechanisms of political representation ensure that temporally voiceless populations are also heard?

Some theorists suggest ways of reconciling traditional representative democracy with the challenge of representing future generations through representatives in parliament (Dobson, 1996). But it is certainly challenging to ensure the representation of future generations (a temporal representation) through usual participatory mechanisms, especially since we can only estimate the interests of future generations based on our own interests and our own understandings of equity and justice. A broader understanding of representation may provide more potential in practice—including by considering claims of representation (Saward, 2009), quota-based representation, appointed representatives, representation as advocacy (Urbinati, 2000) or other mechanisms facilitating or guaranteeing representation (Meier, 2000). In each of these cases, assigning resources and political space to the interests of future generations may face a backlash from current generations who feel that their own interests are being diluted and marginalized. I return to a discussion of these mechanisms below.

MECHANISMS OF REPRESENTATION

There are several attempts in the literature to outline ways in which future generations could or should be represented in current policymaking. I group these attempts into three categories. The first category describes representatives for the future as members of parliament ('parliamentary representation') (Jensen, 2015); the second category describes representation taking place through advisory groups, committees or appointed officials ('appointed representation'); and the third category describes tools for highlighting interests of future generations without an assigned voice ('interest representation'). I discuss each of these three categories in turn.

Parliamentary Representation

Representation without temporal constraints traditionally involves a population electing a representative to parliament. This direct involvement in the choice of representative is impossible for future generations. However, Dobson (1996) suggests a model to overcome this problem and still ensure that representation in parliament takes place—representation by 'proxy'. This system aims to move the representation of future generations in a democratic direction by developing a 'proxy' future generation from the present one that would form the 'future' electorate. Candidates could then stand for election in the usual way, with the proxy electorate communicating their interests. In this way, future generations are represented through mechanisms that create a proxy constituency to whom the elected representative is accountable.

This option faces several challenges when it comes to composing the electorate or constituency. A first option is to use a random sample of the present population to form the proxy future generation, but there is no guarantee that such a proxy would put the interests of future generations before their own. Such a system may rather lead to the suppression of future interests and the sabotaging of future generations' interests in support of current generations' concerns. A second option is to develop the proxy electorate from the environmental or sustainability lobby that is used to considering the interests of future generations. This seems to be a solution that scholars consider the most useful, both in terms of ensuring that future generations' interests are not drowned out by present interests and for ensuring that a wide range of interests are included. From the perspective of democratic legitimacy, however, such a solution may prove too far from the ideals of the democratic system and too close to the notion of elite or expert governance for comfort (Beckman, 2013).

Ekeli (2005) proposes the 'extended franchise model' for political representation of future generations, or to give a voice to 'posterity'. This model draws on the 'all affected' principle to justify the need for such an action, asserting that 'collectively binding decisions can only be regarded as ethically justifiable if they result from a process of deliberation where all affected parties have had the opportunity to participate' (2005, p. 430). The model suggests that several seats in parliament ought to be reserved for representatives of future generations' interests. These representatives would be elected in the same way as others, but in a separate vote (so voters would have two votes), and they would have the same lawmaking duties and responsibilities as all members of parliament. While the proportion of future generations' representatives in this case is suggested (seemingly arbitrarily) at around 5%, they would be unlikely to wield significant veto power. The real power of their interventions in parliament would be in delaying policy discussions or prolonging negotiations and providing arguments for or against a particular measure. Ekeli thus assumes all voters have the ability and right to choose representatives of future generations, whereas Dobson proposes a proxy electorate to make this choice. In Ekeli's suggestion, the danger of future interests being pushed aside to accommodate current interests is reduced, with every member of the electorate casting a second vote. Whether this is a meaningful democratic process for the current generation and whether it leads to appropriate representation of the future remains a hypothetical debate. Neither the proxy delegate model nor the extended franchise model has been tested in practice.

These options for the representation of future generations face criticism from scholars who highlight the trade-offs that are likely to occur between present democratic ideals (such as political equality) and the representatives of future generations (who cannot be held accountable to constituents who do not yet exist) (Jensen, 2015). These mechanisms of political representation lack input legitimacy—representatives cannot guarantee that their actions will be legitimate towards a population they claim to represent. Furthermore, such representation places future interests in silos of a certain (small) number of representatives who may not have sufficient power to affect political decisions in favour of the future—thus also raising questions of 'output' legitimacy, or effectiveness. The second category of political representation tries to avoid these questions of democratic legitimacy (at least of 'input' legitimacy) by moving away from formal representation in parliament to representation through appointed advisory roles.

Appointed Representation

Several NGOs and organizations have been calling for the representation of future generations for many years (such as the World Future Council). However, on closer examination of their demands, these organizations envision representative mechanisms in the form of appointed committees, advisers, commissioners or ombudsmen, rather than (elected) representatives sitting in parliament. The role of these appointed representatives is to assess and review policy proposals from the perspective of future impacts and advise and report to legislative bodies on how to amend measures to safeguard the interests of the future (Orellana, Pearce, & Genin, 2012).

A few such institutions already exist in Europe. Finland established a 'Committee for the Future' in 1993 as a standing committee of the parliament. It comprises 17 MPs and prepares responses to the government's annual 'Report on the Future', to budget proposals and to proposals related to societal and technological development issues. It also prepares its own reports on future problems and opportunities.[1] Wales established a commissioner for sustainable futures in 2011, which was strengthened under the Well-being of Future Generations (Wales) Act 2015 to become the future generations commissioner. The commissioner advises public bodies, reports on progress towards 'well-being' objectives, makes recommendations and supports research on well-being and sustainable development.[2] Germany has a council for sustainable development and a Parliamentary Advisory Council on sustainable development, which aim to promote policies with a future-oriented outlook and advocate long-term responsibility in the political process.[3] Hungary established the Office of the Parliamentary Commissioner for Future Generations in 2008 (succeeded by the commissioner for fundamental rights in 2011). The commissioner aims to ensure that policies protect the rights of children, vulnerable populations, minorities and the interests of future generations.[4] From 2001 to 2011, the UK also had its own Sustainable Development Commission charged with providing independent advice to the government on sustainable development.[5]

None of these examples is appointed to take seats in parliament, but instead they act as watchdogs of policy development: to advise on potential impacts, to provide input for future policy directions and to provide research. Advocates for such an approach to the representation of future generations highlight the need for a voice that constantly pays attention to future interests across policy domains to enhance intergenerational justice and promote sustainable development (Jávor & Rácz, 2006; Orellana et al., 2012). Appointed representation thus avoids the criticisms of a lack of input legitimacy as it is a representative mechanism that does not strive to identify a specific set of future constituents to whom it is accountable. Rather it aims to advise present elected representatives about potential problems in their decision-making for future generations. Thus, the appointed representatives avoid the issue of input legitimacy and even dilute accountability of the elected officials they advise. There are still questions over the output legitimacy of mechanisms of appointed representation, however. Critics claim that creating separate institutions for the representation of future generations' interests may lead to these interests being sidelined in day-to-day majoritarian political processes, thus hampering effectiveness. Such scholars argue rather for interests of future generations to be integrated more precisely into the policy agendas of all elected officials—a move that seems to stretch the concept of representation beyond traditional understandings and uses and is linked to the third category (Jensen, 2015).

Interest Representation

This category moves beyond the notion of political representation as one where there are physical representatives responsible for ensuring the absent is made present, but remains valid within a broader understanding of what it is to make something (in this case future generations' interests) present, through whatever means possible. There are several suggestions for how future generations' interests can be represented (broadly defined) in political processes in democratic systems. First, a heightened awareness of policy implications on future generations (even into the distant future) can be institutionalized through policy procedures. These include constitutional measures promoting sustainable development and impact assessment procedures, for example (Ekeli, 2007). Such heightened awareness should not require any additional representatives for future generations, if all elected officials are anyway supposed to take care of their interests (Jensen, 2015). Second, representation can take place through sustainable development lobby groups and NGOs, acting as policy watchdogs, pressuring politicians from outside the legislative process, and 'claiming' to represent the interests of the future (Saward, 2006). This links to the notion of representation occurring as advocacy and places emphasis on output legitimacy (ensuring effective policies) rather than being concerned with input legitimacy (Rubenstein, 2013; Urbinati, 2000).

First, institutionalizing representation or consideration of future generations' interests is founded upon concerns for intergenerational justice, rather than concerns for appropriate mechanisms of representation. At the most legally basic, such institutionalizing measures mean constitutional requirements. Several (European) states have constitutional objectives promoting sustainable development. In Belgium's constitution, Article 7bis states that the 'Federal State, the Communities and the Regions pursue the objectives of sustainable development in its social, economic and environmental aspects, taking into account the solidarity between the generations'. The Czech Republic highlights its 'share of responsibility towards future generations for the fate of life on this Earth'. Estonia calls for policies for the general benefit of present and future generations in its Constitution. The French Charter for the Environment highlights in the preamble that 'choices designed to meet the needs of the present generation should not jeopardize the ability of future generations and other peoples to meet their own needs'. Article 20a of the German constitution states that, 'mindful also of its responsibility toward future generations, the state shall protect the natural foundations of life and animals'. Poland's constitution highlights that 'public authorities shall pursue policies ensuring the ecological security of current and future generations' in Article 74. The Treaty on the Functioning of the European Union, although it does not specifically mention future generations, highlights the objective of sustainable development in Article 11, which states that 'environmental protection requirements must be integrated into the definition and implementation of the Union's policies and activities, in particular with a view to promoting sustainable development'.

Second, there are a great number of NGOs and lobbyists pushing for their interests to be added to policy agendas, through more or less transparent methods and approaches (and not all in favour of future generations' interests) (Watson & Shackleton, 2003). Those organizations most concerned with protecting the interests of future generations are identified as the 'sustainability' lobby, which pushes policymakers to consider long-term impacts of policies (Dobson, 1996). Among the greatest criticisms levelled against NGOs or other organizations lobbying is their questionable legitimacy stemming from traditional understandings of legitimate representation through elected representatives (Jensen, 2015; Rubenstein, 2013). However, while NGOs are in the business of raising awareness, lobbying politicians and acting as watchdogs, they do not hold blocking or veto power over policy decisions. In some respects, calls for genuine or appointed representation of future generations is a further tool for the sustainability lobby to push its interests, highlighting an overlap among the three categories of representation described here.

In both the cases of constitutional requirements or procedures and external advocacy, representation of future generations is indirect. There is no single individual elected or appointed with the sole aim of representing the interests of future generations. Legal tools aim to oblige all policymakers to consider future generations in their policymaking, without specifications of what is sufficient or how to achieve this. Advocates outside the policy process (such as NGOs) use persuasion, lobbying and argumentation to push their agenda, which may or may not be in line with the interests of future generations. Nevertheless, an overarching aim of representative tools under the 'interest representation' category is to integrate a future-oriented approach into present policymaking and to safeguard long-term interests. This category moves beyond the traditional notion of an individual as a representative in parliament making present the interests of absent future generations, but it can still be contained within a broader notion of representation as any means or mechanism for making present what is absent.

CONCLUDING DISCUSSION

Literature on the political representation of future generations holds several normative assumptions at its core. First, it argues that democratic governance systems *should* take the rights of future generations into account in their decision-making, especially in areas such as environmental or climate governance where consequences of (in)action today are only likely to be felt in the future. Second, the literature is based on theories of justice and inter-generational justice that bestow rights and obligations on both future and present generations towards sustainability goals, forming the basis for calls for representation. Third, literature on political representation of future generations overcomes questions of 'who' are future generations and 'what' are their interests by treating the future as an undefined single group and their interests as extrapolated from the basic needs of survival inherent in current generations. Scholars build on the notion of the 'all affected' principle to require the political representation of future generations—or of their 'interests', at least.

The case of ensuring justice towards future generations in current policy-making pushes the notion of political representation to its limits. Literature proposes several solutions to the perceived problem of short-termism in democratic electoral systems to promote the interests of future generations—through parliamentary representation, appointed representation and interest representation. None of these proposals satisfy the criteria of just democratic governance for today. All the categories and mechanisms for representation of future generations described above face the problem of not providing opportunities for representatives to be held to account by the people they claim to represent. Future generations are not able to express their (dis)satisfaction with representatives in this time. All the mechanisms also face questions about their effectiveness vis-à-vis achieving the objectives of ensuring that policies agreed today are made with future generations' interests in mind. Limited empirical data hampers further assessment of the potential of these proposals.

'Parliamentary representation' through elected representatives in parliament suffers a lack of input legitimacy with no possibility for the representatives standing accountable to their true constituents (in the future), and suggestions for how to implement such representation in practice also lead to doubts about the output legitimacy of these measures. Further questions of legitimacy are raised due to the perceived unequal treatment of present and future generations. 'Appointed representation' avoids the issue of input legitimacy by falling outside the usual processes of selecting representatives through elections, but still raises issues of legitimacy, especially with regard to having any actual influence over policy and political decisions. Finally, 'interest representation' moves outside mainstream understandings of political representation and relies on constitutional requirements, decision-makers' awareness, external advocacy, lobbying and awareness raising to ensure that future generations' interests are integrated into political processes. Here, interest representation raises questions about the power or influence of un-elected officials or lobby groups in democratic systems, pointing to input legitimacy concerns—both in relation to current generations and future generations. Constitutional requirements face the least legitimacy concerns, but these are mechanisms with the least 'representative' element in that they are static objectives, and they still face problems of effectiveness (Bernauer & Gampfer, 2013; Jensen, 2015; Mansbridge, 1999). There is very little empirical analysis of how these mechanisms (could) work in practice, whether they provide meaningful and appropriate responses to calls for intergenerational justice through representation, and whether they increase and/or improve the representation of future generations. This is partly due to the limited empirical field, which makes an impartial assessment of the proposals difficult. Empirical work examining whether and how the mechanisms can be deployed in a coherent manner towards the overall enhancement of representation of future generations would also be welcome.

As such, it seems that none of the mechanisms in the different categories presents an ideal win-win scenario for both present and future generations. To resolve this issue, Jensen (2015) argues that it is sufficient for present generations to base their actions on moral judgement and sound principles of solidarity towards future generations. There is no need for specific representative mechanisms for future generations, he argues, if present generations take adequate consideration of future generations' interests into account. The moral argument is extended to one of obligations and duties by international legal scholars, where moral arguments are more than a sense of solidarity but place real obligations on present generations to make decisions that (at least) do not harm the potential quality of life of future generations (Hiskes, 2009; Weiss, 1984, 1990; Weston, 2012). Both of these positions bring us back to the notion of 'justice' as a basic function of good democratic governance and highlight the role of the judicial system in according rights to future generations and obligations on the present towards sustainability. For these scholars, political representation may provide some opportunities, but it is by no means the only way to ensure intergenerational justice.

In sum, we can say that making just decisions towards future generations requires a varied toolbox of approaches, which can include political representation, understood as making the absent present, by whatever (combination of) means are deemed appropriate. The language and instruments of political representation can provide the added value of identifying the beneficiaries of policies as future generations and can lead to policymakers acting upon what they imagine to be future generations' interests. But this understanding of intergenerational justice brings us far beyond a discussion of representation to a discussion of just governance. Sustainability requires some sort of holistic understanding of political processes across temporal divides, integrating long-term goals into short-term governance cycles, using multiple tools. Political representation can prove helpful, but when the objective is to achieve sustainability, several means can be (and probably should be) deployed in conjunction with each other. The case of future generations shows both the potential and the limits of political representation as a concept and a tool for just democratic governance in the long term.

NOTES

1. https://www.eduskunta.fi/EN/lakiensaataminen/valiokunnat/tulevaisuusvaliokunta/Pages/default.aspx , accessed February 23, 2016.
2. http://gov.wales/topics/people-and-communities/people/future-generations-act/?lang=en , accessed February 23, 2016.
3. http://www.bundestag.de/nachhaltigkeit and http://www.nachhaltigkeitsrat.de/en , accessed February 24, 2016.
4. http://www.ajbh.hu/en/web/ajbh-en/ , accessed February 24, 2016.
5. http://www.sd-commission.org.uk/pages/our-role.html , accessed February 24, 2016.

REFERENCES

Beckman, L. (2008). Do global climate change and the interest of future generations have implications for democracy? *Environmental Politics, 17*(4), 610–24.
Beckman, L. (2013). Democracy and future generations: Should the unborn have a voice? In J.-C. Merle (Ed.), *Spheres of Global Justice: Vol. 2. Fair Distribution—Global Economic, Social and Intergenerational Justice* (pp. 775–88). Berlin: Springer Press.
Beckman, L., & Page, E. A. (2008). Perspectives on justice, democracy and global climate change. *Environmental Politics, 17*(4), 527–35.
Bernauer, T., & Gampfer, R. (2013). Effects of civil society involvement on popular legitimacy of global environmental governance. *Global Environmental Change, 23*, 439–49.
Collier, D., & Mahon, J. E. (1993). Conceptual "stretching" revisited: Adapting categories in comparative analysis. *American Political Science Review, 87*(4), 845–55.
Davidson, M. D. (2008). Wrongful harm to future generations: The case of climate change. *Environmental Values, 17*(4), 471–88.
Dobson, A. (1996). Representative democracy and the environment. In W. Lafferty & J. Meadowcroft (Eds.), *Democracy and the environment* (pp. 124–39). Cheltenham: Edward Elgar.
Eckersley, R. (2004). *The green state: Rethinking democracy and sovereignty.* Boston, MA: MIT Press.
Ehresman, T., & Stevis, D. (2010). International environmental and ecological justice. In G. Kütting (Ed.), *Global environmental politics: Concepts, theories and case studies* (pp. 87–104). London: Routledge.
Ekeli, K. S. (2005). Giving a voice to posterity—Deliberative democracy and representation of future people. *Journal of Agricultural and Environmental Ethics, 18*(5), 429–50.
Ekeli, K. S. (2007). Green constitutionalism: The constitutional protection of future generations. *Ratio Juris, 20*(3), 378–401.
Haider-Markel, D. P., Joslyn, M. R., & Kniss, C. J. (2000). Minority group interests and political representation: Gay elected officials in the policy process. *Journal of Politics, 6*(2), 568–77. http://doi.org/10.1111/0022-3816.00026
Hardin, G. (1968). The tragedy of the commons. *Science, 162*, 1243–48.

Harris, P. G. (2010). *World ethics and climate change: From international to global justice.* Edinburgh Studies in World Ethics. Edinburgh: Edinburgh University Press.

Hiskes, R. P. (2009). *The human right to a green future: Environmental rights and intergenerational justice.* New York: Cambridge University Press.

IPCC. (2013). Summary for policymakers. In T. F. Stoker et al. (Eds.), *Climate change 2013: The physical science basis. Contribution of Working Group I to the Fifth Assessment Report of the Intergovernmental Panel on Climate Change.* Cambridge: Cambridge University Press.

Jávor, B., & Rácz, J. (Eds.). (2006). *Do we owe them a future? The opportunities of a representation for future generations in Europe.* Budapest: Védegylet—Protect the Future!

Jensen, K. K. (2015). Future generations in democracy: Representation or consideration? *Jurisprudence, 6*(3), 535–48.

Karlsson, J. (2006). Affected and subjected. The all-affected principle in transnational democratic theory. *Discussion Paper Wissenschaftszentrum Berlin Für Sozialforschung, SP IV 2006.* Retrieved from http://skylla.wz-berlin.de/pdf/2006/iv06-304.pdf

Lutz, W., Sanderson, W. C., & Scherbov, S. (Eds.). (2004). *The end of world population growth in the 21st century: New challenges for human capital formation and sustainable development.* New York: Earthscan.

Mansbridge, J. (1999). Should blacks represent blacks and women represent women? A contingent 'yes'. *Journal of Politics, 61*(3), 628–57.

Meckled-Garcia, S. (2008). On the very idea of cosmopolitan justice: Constructivism and international agency. *Journal of Political Philosophy, 16*(3), 245–71.

Meier, P. (2000). From theory to practice and back again: Gender quota and the politics of presence in Belgium. In M. Saward (Ed.), *Democratic innovation: Deliberation, representation and association* (pp. 106–16). London: Routledge.

Näsström, S. (2011). The challenge of the all-affected principle. *Political Studies, 59*(1), 116–34.

Nozick, R. (1974). *Anarchy, state and utopia.* New York: Basic Books.

Orellana, M., Pearce, C., & Genin, Y. (2012). The high commissioner for future generations: The future we want, (June). Retrieved from http://www.worldfuturecouncil.org/fileadmin/user_upload/Future_Justice/High_Commissioner_for_Future_Generations.pdf

Owen, D. (2012). Constituting the polity, constituting the demos: On the place of the all affected interests principle in democratic theory and in resolving the democratic boundary problem. *Ethics and Global Politics, 5*(3), 129–52.

Oxford Martin Commission. (2013). *Now for the long term: The report of the Oxford Martin Commission for future generations.* Oxford.

Peters, B. G. (2017). What is so wicked about wicked problems? A conceptual analysis and a research program. *Policy and Society, 36*(3), 385–96.

Pitkin, H. F. (1967). *The concept of representation.* Berkeley and Los Angeles: University of California Press.

Rawls, J. (1971). *A theory of justice.* Cambridge: MA: Harvard University Press.

Rubenstein, J. C. (2013). The misuse of power, not bad representation: Why it is beside the point that no one elected Oxfam. *Journal of Political Philosophy, 22*(2), 204–30.

Sartori, G. (1970). Concept misformation in comparative politics. *American Political Science Review, 64*(4), 1033–53.

Saward, M. (2003). Enacting democracy. *Political Studies, 51*, 161–79.

Saward, M. (2006). The representative claim. *Contemporary Political Theory, 5*, 297–318.

Saward, M. (2009). Authorisation and authenticity: Representation and the unelected. *Journal of Political Philosophy, 17*(1), 1–22.

Tănăsescu, M. (2014). Rethinking representation: The challenge of non-humans. *Australian Journal of Political Science, 49*(1), 40–53.

Tännsjö, T. (2007). Future people, the all affected principle, and the limits of the aggregation model of democracy. In T. Rønnow-Rasmussen, B. Petersson, J. Josefsson, & D. Egonsson (Eds.), *Hommage à Wlodek: Philosophical papers dedicated to Wlodek Rabinowicz.* Retrieved from http://www.fil.lu.se/hommageawlodek

Thompson, D. F. (2005). Democracy in time: Popular sovereignty and temporal representation. *Constellations, 12*(2), 245–61.

Ulloa, A. (2013). *The ecological native: Indigenous peoples' movements and eco-governmentality in Columbia*. London: Routledge.

Urbinati, N. (2000). Representation as advocacy: A study of democratic deliberation. *Political Theory, 28*(6), 758–86.

Vörösmarty, C. J., Green, P., Salisbury, J., & Lammers, R. B. (2000). Global water resources: Vulnerability from climate change and population growth. *Science, 289*(5477), 284–88.

Wallbott, L. (2014). Indigenous peoples in UN REDD+ negotiations: "Importing power" and lobbying for rights through discursive interplay management. *Ecology and Society, 19*(1). doi:10.5751/ES-06111-190121

Wang, C., Ye, M., Cai, W., & Chen, J. (2014). The value of a clear, long-term climate policy agenda: A case study of China's power sector using a multi-region optimization model. *Applied Energy, 125*, 276–88.

Watson, R., & Shackleton, M. (2003). Organized interests and lobbying in the EU. In E. Bomberg & A. Stubb (Eds.), *The European Union: How does it work?* (pp. 88–107). Oxford: Oxford University Press.

WCED. (1987). *Our common future*. World Commission on Environment and Development.

Weiss, E. B. (1984). The planetary trust : Conservation and intergenerational equity. *Ecology Law Quarterly, 11*(4), 495–582.

Weiss, E. B. (1990). In fairness to future generations. *Environment: Science and Policy for Sustainable Development, 32*(3), 6–31.

Weston, B. H. (2012). The theoretical foundations of intergenerational ecological justice: An overview. *Human Rights Quarterly, 34*(1), 251–66.

Chapter Eight

Understanding the Controversy of 'Black Pete' through the Lens of Symbolic Representation

Ilke Adam, Soumia Akachar, Karen Celis,
Serena D'Agostino and Eline Severs

Sometimes, salient political controversy arises about phenomena that for a very long time had no political relevance at all. The 'Black[1] Pete' commotion is a good illustration. For a long time, Black Pete was nothing more than a persona in a traditional festivity for children in the Netherlands and Belgium. However, all of a sudden it became associated with racism. How come long-standing traditions—such as Black Pete—and seemingly trivial issues, arguably belonging to the private sphere, suddenly get the status of a political issue of national importance?

As we will show in this chapter, the notion of Blackness in this particular instance has a bigger meaning, which explains the intensity of the controversy it engendered. In this debate, the figure of Black Pete relates to the question of whether its current portrayal still fits today's society that increasingly rejects racism. For some, the Blackness of Pete stood for the racist society. For others, in contrast, it was solely about innocent customs and private matters and should not be subject to political debate and intervention. The politicization of Blackness in the Black Pete controversy is not limited to this case only but also finds considerable overlap with contentious events related to a politics of resistance and struggle against anti-Black sentiments and racism experienced by the African diaspora in Anglo-Saxon contexts (see Cole, 1993; Maylor, 2009).

Our use of the concept of Blackness in this chapter deserves some elaboration. Blackness has been used in theories of race for both the external and internal characteristics attributed to the so-called black peoples (e.g. Hooks, 2001; Lipsitz, 2011; Pastoureu, 2008). Blackness, as referred to in relation to the figure of Black Pete in this chapter, refers not only to the colour of his skin but also encapsulates a set of internal and external stereotypes and associations about black groups, with some of its most frequently used stereotypes pertaining to their physical appearance, intellectual inferiority, malice, Black servitude to the white race, and so forth. In fact, the Blackness in the figure of Black Pete concerns both his black face, as well as the exaggerated painted red lips, the faux Afro wig and his gold hoop earrings—traditionally a slave token.[2]

This chapter attempts to find an explanation for the controversy: *What was actually going on in this debate? What was at stake?* The 'standing for' aspect of the debate and the fact that the symbolic dimension of the Blackness of Black Pete was so present point us in the direction of the concept of symbolic representation. The concept of symbolic representation serves as a heuristic tool to understand why this controversy took place (i.e. why it became politicized in the first place) and what the nature of the controversy actually was. The central point we make in that respect is that the political debate originates in the friction between the agent (i.e. the Blackness of Black Pete) and the principal (i.e. the ideal political community, seen as tolerant/non-racist). The controversy is a public questioning of whether a society's symbol supports, or at least does not harm, the way it sees and represents itself.

Beyond the heuristic contribution of the use of the concept of symbolic representation to understand the case, our analysis of the public controversy on Black Pete as an instance of symbolic representation generates a further development of the concept. Notwithstanding the fact that the notion of symbolic representation has been around since the 1960s when Hanna Pitkin (1967) coined it, the scholarship on symbolic representation is still very much in its infancy. Pitkin's well-known illustrations of symbolic representation concern the flag or the king, whose presence at certain occasions gives people the feeling of being represented.

In the sections that follow, we review the extant scholarship on the concept of symbolic representation as a timely topic for scholarly inquiry. The analysis allows us to deepen the concept of symbolic representation. By zooming in on the everyday politics of symbols, we push the scholarship of symbolic representation beyond its edges of the study of 'national symbols' (such as the flag) to also consider more 'everyday symbols' or practices of symbolization. Moreover, our analysis also helps to transform the concept into a model including processes involving the role of multiple audiences, context, power struggles and agency in the making, remaking and unmaking of symbols. The more subtle aspects of power exerted in the process of symbolic representation might well also affect other dimensions of political representation, such as descriptive and substantive representation.

SYMBOLIC REPRESENTATION

In *The Concept of Representation*, Hanna Pitkin (1967) defined political representation as 'the making present of something or someone absent' and conceived of symbolic representation as one means—in addition to formalistic, descriptive and substantive representation—for establishing a relationship between the representative (present) and those represented (absent). Her treatment of symbolic representation highlighted that representation does not necessarily need to involve human activity but may also be accomplished through inanimate objects, such as a flag or anthem *standing for* a nation (Pitkin, 1967, pp. 11, 93). A piece of cloth, a public statue or an anthem— just consider the "Star-Spangled Banner" or "God Save the Queen"— powerfully call a nation to mind. Similarly, political actors such as monarchs or presidents embody the unity of the nation and evoke images of its majesty, authority and place in international politics.

Like many of her counterparts (e.g. Edelman, 1964, 1971), Pitkin was wary of the evocative nature of symbolic representation and the risk that citizens' rational judgement of their representatives would be replaced by irrational beliefs or emotional identifications. In descriptive representation, the relation between parliament and the people is founded on the composition of the elected body and can be judged on the basis of rationally justifiable criteria, such as the extent to which it reflects descriptive characteristics that are considered politically relevant, such as geographical area of birth, occupation, ethnicity or gender[3] (cf. Pitkin, 1967, p. 100). In symbolic representation, there is no rational justification for accepting a particular symbol rather than another one. Because it is based entirely on conventional beliefs, emotions and affect, the connection between symbol and subject seems arbitrary. 'Symbol-making,' Pitkin (1967, p. 101) argued, 'is not a process of rational persuasion, but of manipulating affective responses and forming habits'.[4]

Given these associations with manipulation, it is not surprising that research on symbolic representation has traditionally centred on political manoeuvring. Edelman (1964, 1971) most famously studied the ways in which representatives employ political symbols to solicit constituents' trust. Later studies have also focused on descriptive representatives and the ways in which their presence in parliament evokes feelings of trust among historically disadvantaged groups or minority constituencies, such as women, migrants or ethnic minorities (e.g. Childs, 2008; Franceschet, Krook, & Piscopo, 2012; Lawless, 2004; Schwindt-Bayer & Mischler, 2005; Stokes-Brown & Dolan,

2010). Much of this research has drawn on the premise that the presence of descriptive representatives contributes to minority constituents' feelings of empowerment and inclusion. As such, scholars have predominantly treated symbolic representation as a by-product of descriptive representation, not as a dimension in its own right.[5]

This approach, however, ignores the ways in which other dimensions of political representation, such as substantive representation, may affect constituents' feelings of inclusion or identification with a polity (Akachar, Celis, & Severs, 2015; Bird, 2015). The tendency to conceive of symbolic representation as a mere by-product of other dimensions of representation has, moreover, the unfortunate effect of undervaluing the particular contributions this concept makes to broader processes of representation. While it is true that symbols' capacity to evoke meaningful relationships depends upon their relation to prevailing socio-historical, cultural and political repertoires, it is worth noting that symbols also have a capacity to reaffirm, or else reinterpret and transform, these repertoires. Because of their selective nature—highlighting some relevant characteristics of the nation to the detriment of others—political symbols become heavily involved in ongoing struggles to define a nation's core values.

This insight lies at the heart of Lombardo and Meier's (2014) recent work on symbolic representation. In *The Symbolic Representation of Gender: A Discursive Approach*, Lombardo and Meier (2014) argue that political symbols do not passively *stand for* political reality but actively contribute to constituting that reality (see also Disch, 2011; Saward, 2010). Political symbols only *appear* to be passive containers or mirrors of reality because they can draw upon conventional and routinized associations between symbol and subject. A flag's evocative power, for instance, originates from prevailing—invariably selective and potentially contingent—understandings pertaining to the characteristics that allow for conceiving of a set of individuals as 'a people'. As a reiteration or condensation of prevailing understandings of the people, a flag however also actively contributes to constituting that people in a particular way. Contrary to Pitkin (1967), who limited her treatment of symbolic representation to this notion of constitution, Lombardo and Meier's (2014) approach explicitly focuses on the human agency involved in symbol making and remaking, and explores the power differentials at play within such processes. The conventional and routinized associations that grant a political symbol its seemingly natural character are by no means neutral. The preponderance of male statues in the public sphere and the sheer handful of women that feature on national coins and bills reflect traditionally gendered conceptions of politics and continue to shape the public sphere and the nation in overtly masculinist terms. As a means to fully understand the ways in which symbols (re)produce privilege and disadvantage, Lombardo and Meier (2014) advocate a discursive approach to symbolic representation. The focus on discourse extends considerations beyond the symbol itself and allows for considering the ways in which people relate to particular symbols, and affirm or contest their relation to the subject represented.

In this contribution, we adopt Lombardo and Meier's (2014) discursive approach and conceive of symbolic representation as comprising the representative activities of a multitude of actors, elected as well as not elected (cf. Saward, 2010). While Lombardo and Meier (2014) focus on gender equality policies to study how political symbols mobilize processes of (re)constituting gender roles, we focus on specific debates in which the meaning of particular symbols, such as the children's festivity figure Black Pete, are actively contested. Similar to Lombardo and Meier's approach, our focus on contested symbols will provide more detailed insights into the ways in which power plays out in symbolic representation and how positions of privilege and disadvantage are (re)produced (cf. Severs, Celis, & Erzeel, 2016).

In order to adequately understand the role of symbolic representation in ongoing power struggles, it is important to first clarify the difference between symbolic representation and symbolizing. Like representation, symbolizing evokes a sense of proximity between the symbol and the people it stands for. This relation, however, is based on a vagueness or looseness that, in itself, does not define the subject. Consider the sign indicating that a particular parking spot is reserved for people with a physical disability (♿). This sign does not *stand in* for or represent citizens with a disability in the sense of being a genuine proxy of this social group. Although it makes an exact reference to disability, the parking spot is reserved for an indefinite group of people of which only some may need the assistance of a wheelchair (cf. Pitkin, 1967, pp. 97–98). In symbolic representation, in contrast, symbols become genuine proxies of the subject in the sense of propagating its core definitive characteristics, values, norms and beliefs. As proxies or stand-ins, they can be seen as genuine agents who not only embody but also transmit the nation's core values. Precisely herein lies the distinct prescriptive power of symbolic representation (Meier & Severs, 2017).

In order for a symbol to constitute a genuine principal-agent relationship with society, two conditions have to be met (see Figure 8.1). First, a minimal association between a symbol (i.e. the agent) and society (i.e. the principal) needs to be established, allowing the former to be conceived as a vehicle or carrier for the conception it symbolizes (cf. Pitkin, 1967, p. 97). This relation, however, depends on the establishment of a second association, namely between the symbol and society's prevailing repertoires of self (i.e. the referent). With the referent being a 'repertoire of self' in this model, we mean that the referent is a collection of more or less conflicting and overlapping interpretations of how society views and envisions itself, and how it seeks to be represented. This second relationship—between a symbol and society's core values, norms and beliefs—needs to tap into routinized processes of association in order to allow a people to identify with the symbol (cf. Meier & Severs, 2017). The referent, as the core values with which the society identifies, has clear political implications. It determines the objectives a society strives for, it influences political decision-making in a particular direction and has also a prescriptive and disciplinary character, as it determines which types of action and thinking are accepted and which are not.[6]

In *The Representative Claim* (2007), Michael Saward importantly conceives political representation as a creative and constitutive practice, in which a representative claimant attempts to convince the recipient of their relation through a portrayal of the claimant's self as representative of the recipient. For the portrayal to be successful, the recipient has to believe in the established connection (Severs, 2010). Symbolic representation, as we conceive it in this chapter, works similarly: a symbol's capacity to *stand in* for society, thus, depends on the stability and coherence of this triadic relationship—the claimant being the agent (i.e. symbol), succeeding in establishing a portrayal in which the recipient (i.e. society as the principal) can see and believe the connection invoked and the principal's ideas of itself (i.e. through the referent). When one of its constitutive elements becomes contested, or these three elements no longer neatly align, political symbols lose their representative qualities (see Figure 8.1). Such dis-alignment may occur when a

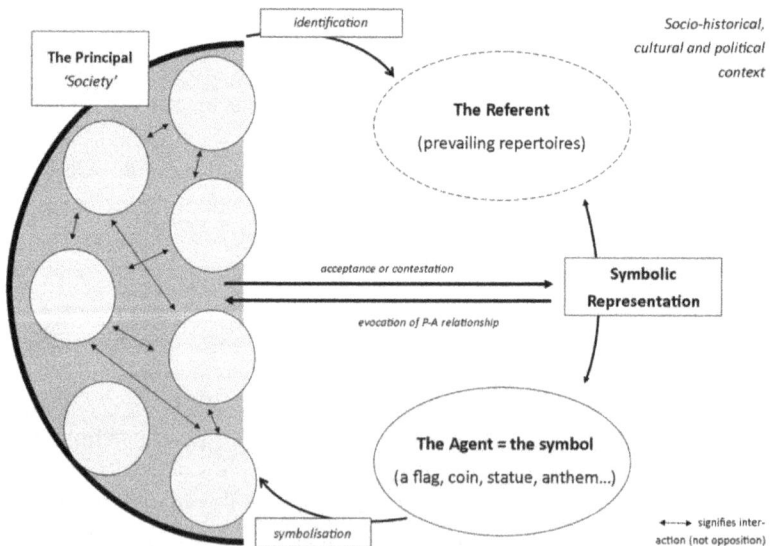

Figure 8.1. Symbolic Representation *Source:* **Authors' own compilation.**

society (or a particular subgroup) no longer identifies with the prevailing repertoire of a political symbol. In such cases, a society or a group can seek to have that repertoire amended because the political symbol is deemed harmful to society as a whole or, for instance, to the political standing of a particular group.

A key difference between ours and Saward's understanding of this relationship is the role we attribute to multiple audiences in establishing which ideas of their society as a whole (i.e. the referent) are accurately invoked through the symbol. Indeed, contestation of this kind may either signal a society's changing values and belief systems or the loss of consensus on the relevance of these values. Depending on the nature of contestation and the establishment of a new consensus, remediation of the principal-referent relationship may require an expansion of prevailing repertoires or, instead, a removal of contentious elements within these repertoires, allowing the latter to be conceived again as aligned with society as a whole. Dis-alignment may also occur when the association between a particular symbol and society is contested altogether (i.e. the association is conceived as nonsensical). This is most likely to occur when attempts are made to introduce new symbols which are insufficiently attuned to prevailing or dominant repertoires of self.

Because of the triadic nature of the principal-agent relationship, both forms of dis-alignment are likely to spill into each other and act as mutual restraints. This is not only the case for new symbols that are insufficiently embedded in a particular context. When society's prevailing repertoires of self become contested, it is also likely that symbols are no longer conceived as adequate vehicles or carriers of society's core values and become, in turn, contested themselves.

The outcome of contestation—be it a form of introducing, reinterpreting, recycling, or attempting to reject or abolish a symbol—is, in addition, strongly influenced by prevailing contexts that both shape the referent and structure relations between societal groups. As we will demonstrate in the empirical analysis, context and the particular power structures that prevail within it exert great influence on the outcomes of societal debates on the meaning of political symbols.

The principal-agent categories employed in our model facilitate our conception of representation as relational. Moreover, they also clarify the constitutive elements within the model. Theoretically, the principal-agent relationship has often been linked to discussions of democratic legitimacy and responsiveness, largely focusing on elections and processes of authorization and accountability (see Plotke, 1997). Indeed, conceiving the relationship between representative actors (agents) and constituencies (principals) allows for examining the conditions that undermine or enhance the two-directional linkage between agents and principals as well as conceiving the potential harmonious or conflicting courses of action that affect their relationship. The

role that contestation plays in our model, when the principal no longer be-
lieves in the agent's power to invoke their relationship, demonstrates the
relevance of these categories in the model as well as connecting it to representation theory as a whole.

We now turn to the case we briefly presented in the introduction. Analyzing Black Pete through the conceptual lens of 'symbolic representation' will
foster understanding of the controversies that took place around its understandings of 'Blackness'. While Black Pete is our main case and will be
analyzed in depth, the controversy around a similarly contested symbol will
be further explored in our concluding discussion. This discussion will serve
to explore whether our findings on one case of symbolic representation are
specific or, on the contrary, shed light on a broader set of cases.

THE TALE OF BLACK PETE

On November 12, 2011, Quinsy Gario, an artist and civil rights activist, and
three friends were arrested for wearing T-shirts with the slogan 'Black Pete
Is Racism' (Zwarte Piet Is Racisme). This happened during the annual parade
of Saint Nicholas in Dordrecht, the Netherlands. With the slogan, Quinsy
Gario protested against the blackfaced helpers of Saint Nicholas (Sinterklaas), the namesake of a traditional children's fest in the Netherlands and
Belgium. In comparison to the Anglo-Saxon figure of Santa Claus who typ-
ifies the spirit of good cheer at Christmas, the continental European figure of
Saint Nicholas more closely resembles the fourth-century Greek Christian
bishop of Myra (Byzantine Empire) who became famous during his life for
his generous gifts to the poor. On his name date, December 6, children
receive candy and presents.

Despite the shared emphasis on gift giving, the main characters of both
festivities differ greatly. The Anglo-Saxon figure of Santa Claus is generally
depicted as a portly, joyous, white-bearded man, who wears a red coat with
white collar and cuffs and is accompanied by elves and reindeer. The continental Saint Nicholas, in contrast, dresses in a white bishop's alb covered by
a red stole, wears a red bishop's mitre on his head and a red ruby ring on one
of his fingers. The bishop, in addition, holds a gold-coloured ceremonial staff
and rides a white horse. The bishop does not travel to Europe by magical
sledge, but by steamboat. The most remarkable difference, however, relates
to his helpers: he is assisted by companions that are referred to as his 'Black
Petes' (Zwarte Pieten). Actors portraying 'Black Pete' typically dress up like
17th-century pages in colourful attire and wear feathered caps. In addition,
they put on blackening make-up and wear curly wigs, red lipstick and golden
earrings. Historical research indicates that the figure of Black Pete was only
introduced in the mid-1850s (e.g. Boer-Dirks, 1993). Originally, the figure of

Saint Nicholas was often presented as some sort of a bogeyman who would treat well-behaved children and punish bad-behaved ones. Following the introduction of the figure of Black Pete, the execution of reward and, especially, punishment was subcontracted to Black Pete who wore a roe (i.e. a bundle of birch twigs) and a burlap bag. The bag contained presents but could, as popular Saint Nicholas songs caution against,[7] also be used to carry off bad-behaved children to Saint Nicholas's homeland. The repressive function of Black Pete only disappeared in the 1980s, as the result of evolving pedagogy (cf. Helsloot, 2008).

The earliest controversies over the figure of Black Pete go back to the 1960s. In the 1960s criticism of the tradition of blackfacing was mainly voiced by white intellectuals and gained little publicity (Helsloot, 2005, pp. 251–52). From the 1980s onwards, Dutch Surinamese youngsters in the Netherlands began to publicly voice their discontent with the figure of Black Pete. They created advocacy associations and distributed pamphlets to raise awareness of the racist character of Black Pete. One of the first mediatized protest activities was organized by the Solidarity Movement Suriname (Solidariteitsbeweging Suriname) in 1981 in the city of Utrecht. Activists called upon the organizers of the Saint Nicholas parade to cancel the figure of Black Pete and distributed pamphlets asking parents not to add a Black servant (chocolate figurine) to children's gift bags as slavery had been ended roughly 100 years previously[8] (Helsloot, 2005, pp. 257–58). In 1993, Petes with colour-painted faces were added to the annual Saint Nicholas parade in Amsterdam. The prevalence of Black Petes, however, stoked activists' protests during the following years (Helsloot, 2005, p. 259). In the absence of real policy change, a couple of mediatized incidents whereby Dutch celebrities of foreign origin were called Black Petes aided the activists' cause.[9]

It was not, however, until the mass mediatized arrest of Quinsy Gario in 2011 that the movement against Black Pete came into full force. Activists began to organize protests against shops that sold chocolate and candy figurines of Black Pete and who used the figure in their commercial leaflets and window displays. Gario's slogan 'Black Pete Is Racism' also gave way to the formation of various Facebook groups in which citizens voiced their grievances with regard to the racist character of Black Pete. In addition to the original Facebook page (@zwartepietisblackface) created by Quinsy Gario, at least six other Facebook pages were created that mobilized against the tradition of blackfacing. People's main criticism centred on the stereotypical depiction of a Black man in the servitude of a white man. People who endorse these pages often also refer to the 19th-century tradition of blackfacing in American theatre. Blackening make-up was used on white people to represent a black person, not seldom a stereotypical depiction of the 'happy-go-lucky darky on the plantation' or the 'dandified coon'. These practices were only abolished in the wake of the civil rights movement in the 1960s.[10]

If we now bring the model of symbolic representation in as a heuristic tool, we see the following: the controversy started with acts of symbolizing—giving symbolic meaning to—the Blackness of Pete. Quinsy Gario's claim was that Pete's Blackness referred to slavery, discrimination and submission of people of colour. Furthermore, holding on to Black Pete as part of an existing cultural tradition, even when confronted with the claim that at least for some Black Pete had an oppressive connotation, meant that society had not come to terms with its discriminatory and racist traditions. The Blackness of Pete was presented as proof that there was a schism between groups in society that tolerated and even cherished racist practices, and society's referent, namely it's self-conception as a tolerant and anti-racist society. Banning Black Pete would be a recognition of that past and a correction of a history judged as wrong. It would also reaffirm the values of tolerance, anti-discrimination and anti-racism as key features of the referent.

Many people, however, disagreed with this symbolization of Pete's Blackness and allegations that this historical tradition referred to deeply rooted and accepted racism. Countering accusations of racism, the proponents of Black Pete explained his blackened face as the result of his regular descents down houses' chimney to deliver gifts. Hence, Pete's Blackness was not at odds with the referent (a tolerant society). The proponents of Black Pete emptied the Blackness of all racist symbolic meaning and rejected the claim of the friction between society and its referent. Activists' pleas to change the appearance of Black Pete could then be accused of being illegitimate attacks against local traditions and customs, which were free of racism and discrimination. Reflecting this counter-mobilization, multiple Facebook pages stating that 'Black Pete should stay' (*Zwarte Piet moet blijven*) or 'Black Pete should stay black' (*Zwarte Piet moet zwart blijven*) were created, unifying a manifold of the people who defended the tradition of blackfacing.[11]

The attempts to get rid of the symbolic meaning of Pete's Blackness that puts him at odds with society's referent were, however, not sufficient for calming down the commotion. Reflecting policymakers' impasse over how to proceed, the city of Amsterdam ordered in 2012 a report on its inhabitants' attitudes to the Black Pete tradition. In their report, Greven and Bosveld (2012, pp. 10–12) stated that 53% of the respondents did not experience Black Pete as discriminatory and could not imagine that other people would experience the figure of Black Pete as such. This response was most frequent among so-called native Dutch (73%). Only about 25% of respondents of Ghanese and Antillean origin and 20% of respondents of Surinamese origin agreed with them. Overall, however, approximately 57% of the respondents stated that the tradition of blackfacing should continue in the future. The majority of these respondents were so-called 'autochthones' (74%).[12]

The survey is a good indicator of the degree to which the presentation of Black Pete as a contradiction with society's referent was accepted. More than anything else it showed that society was strongly polarized with, on the one hand, numerically dominant natives that reject the Blackness as being in contradiction with its referent (a tolerant society) and, on the other hand, a small minority of mainly Black citizens that opposed Pete's Blackness because it stood in contrast to society's referent. The symbolization hence mainly occurred before an audience (whites/native citizens) to whom the accusations of historical injustice and continuing structural inequalities are emotionally challenging: the claim that Black Pete refers to a racist past and tradition is at the same time an accusation that the native majority is racist, or at least tolerates racism and discrimination. The Black Pete proponents' preferred referent as the tolerant, non-discriminatory or post-racial society obviously clashes with the opponents' reference to a racist society. There exists nonetheless an important binding element, partially bridging both groups: the shared belief between the opponents and part[13] of the proponents that society should not tolerate discrimination and racism. In other words, neither the opponents nor a part of the proponents questioned the referent. They disagreed on whether or not there was a connection between Pete's Blackness and racism that would put Black Pete at odds with society's referent, of which tolerance and anti-racism are constitutive elements. In short, the opponents claim that a society that tolerates Black Pete is racist; part of the proponents, in contrast, claim that a society that rejects and fights racism can nonetheless have Black Petes.

In October 2013, the issue gained international media attention when Verene Shepherd, a social historian at the University of West India, Jamaica, and chair of the United Nations Working Group of Experts on People of African Descent, gave an interview to the Dutch broadcasting network NPO. In this interview, she explained the ongoing United Nations (UN) investigations on the tradition of Black Pete within the framework of the Office of the UN Human Rights Commission. Shepherd explained that the UN Working Group had sent a letter to the government of the Netherlands in January 2013. In this letter (OHCHR, 2013a), the UN Working Group indicated that it did not consider the Saint Nicholas and Black Pete tradition eligible for protection under the UNESCO Convention for the Safeguarding of Intangible Cultural Heritage. The Working Group, in addition, called upon the government to consult 'minority communities on issues that affect them' (OHCHR, 2013a, p. 2). This obviously gave leverage to the symbolization of Black Pete as racist and empowered the opponents' claim that a society that tolerates Black Pete also tolerates racism.

Following her intervention, Shepherd received death threats, and her connection to the United Nations was called into question. Activists, in addition, created the 'Pete-ition' (*Pietitie*, combining the Dutch words for Pete and petition), a petition (www.petitie.nl) that sought to gather support for the preservation of Black Pete. In two days' time, the accompanying Facebook page of the petition was liked or endorsed 2 million times, making the page the most trending Dutch Facebook page ever[14] (*De Telegraaf*, 2013; *Het Laatste Nieuws*, 2013). In reaction to these events, the United Nations Office of the High Commissioner for Human Rights (OHCHR) published a press release (November 21, 2013) in which it called on the government of the Netherlands to facilitate a national debate on Black Pete. In their press release, the OHCHR (2013b) expressed its concern for the safety of people of African descent living in the Netherlands and condemned the 'virulent intolerance expressed by those who could not understand that there might be problems with the way Zwarte Piet is presented or that the presentation might be perceived negatively'.

The high salience and explosive character of the controversy is remarkable. How can we understand why Black Pete, in the eyes of many and for a long time a trivial figure, engenders political debates involving high-level politicians and institutions and triggers violent reactions such as death threats? Conceiving the debate as one of symbolic representation helps us understand this high salience: society's very identity is at stake; it is accused of violating one of its central values, that is, non-discrimination and anti-racism. The controversy is caused by societies' uneasiness with the accusation that its behaviour is not in line with its own referent. It vehemently opposes that accusation because it is convinced that the referent is the right one: society hangs on to seeing itself as anti-discriminatory and anti-racist. Claims that society does not live up to its own ideals do not go unnoticed, and in that sense gain power. Put simply, a society that does not care about racism also does not care when it is called racist. The accusation of being racist is, in contrast, a challenging one for a society that self-defines as being tolerant and non-racist.[15] The level of controversy is therefore very telling of the degree to which the values at stake are key defining elements of society's ideals. Society's referent consists of some core principles that are clearly defined and consolidated, and others that are more at the periphery or are still in the process of (re)defining and (re-)consolidating. It is through controversies like the one about Black Pete that the very existence and weight of the principles of that ideal society are uncovered—at other times they often remain latent and unnoticed.

Notwithstanding the OHCHR advice, the controversy continued. In August 2014, Martin Bosma, member of the PVV and of the House of Representatives (Tweede Kamer) sent out a tweet: 'A country that gives in to whining allochthones will lose more than Black Pete. Boycott Hema'. This referred to attempts from the commercial chain Hema to change its advertisements and chocolate/candy figurines. White actors in society made appeals to organize against attacks on 'our culture'. There was a strong message: 'these are our final accommodations; we will not budge any further'.

In reaction to the international controversy over the figure of Black Pete, local governments began to make changes to their Saint Nicholas and Black Pete festivities. In the fall of 2014, the mayor of Amsterdam announced that many of the controversial features of Black Pete (the curly hair, the golden earrings, and the red lipstick) would be removed. As a transitional measure, Black Petes would participate in the parade beside more 'modern' Petes with soot smudges and Petes without make-up (*NOS NL*, 2014). In July 2014, the UN Working Group Experts on People of African Descent presented its final report on Black Pete during a press conference in The Hague, the Netherlands. It emphasized the importance of educating children on the problematic aspects of the Black Pete tradition and stated that it was pleased that at the local level changes had been made to the image of Black Pete and that the Ministry of Social Affairs and Development would facilitate further discussions with civil society organizations in order to find a joint agreement (OHCHR, 2014). By December 2015, the annual Saint Nicholas parade in both the Netherlands and Belgium replaced blackfaced Petes with so-called chimney Petes. The original thick all-covering black make-up was replaced by smudges of soot that link Pete's blackness to his descent along houses' chimneys. The chocolate and candy figurines, in contrast, continue to be modelled after the old Black Pete.

The Black Pete controversy hence shows that it is extremely hard to 'bury a symbol' which symbolizes the society. Power relations play an important role in the chances of the adaptation of a symbol. The more the contesters become an electorate by acquiring citizenship, and the more they are considered as consumers, the larger the chance of re-symbolization. Some 're-symbolization' tried to correct the symbol, thereby focusing on the meaning of blackness. The first option to re-symbolize was to claim that Pete's blackness is not about racist stereotypes dating from the colonial era; Pete is black from coming down the chimney. Historical documentation on the tradition was invoked to argue that Black Pete was never a slave. And even if he was, today we no longer see him as a slave. These actors also argue that children see the difference between Black Pete and Black people. Activists—through personal testimonies—reject this argument.

The second reaction to the contestation of the symbol was one of re-symbolization through 'reasonable accommodation'. It was similar to the first reaction in that it wanted to nuance Pete's blackness. Other-coloured Petes were added to counterbalance black Petes. Both the chimney Petes and the differently coloured Petes were considered to be 'reasonable accommodations' of the activists' critiques. The chimney and differently coloured Petes symbolize the reasonable society that recognizes the sensitivity of references to race and colonialism and accepts that it needs to be cautious in these matters and be ready to accept minor changes. Holding on to Black Pete and only trying to give another meaning to its blackness, however, was rejected by Black activists. It was interpreted as an unwillingness or inability to come to terms with a racist history.

The third response to the contestation of the symbol was one of resistance. The 'new' Petes were considered to be symbols of Black people 'stealing our traditions' and as 'asking for more than they would be willing to put up with themselves'. To them, maintaining the figure of Black Pete became a symbol of ownership over 'their own' history and society. Attempts are met with important resistance and processes of 'othering': the activists being called 'whining allochthones' reinforced their status of the cultural Other.

DISCUSSION: OTHER INSTANCES OF CONTESTED SYMBOLIC REPRESENTATION

Analyzing the Black Pete controversy from the perspective of symbolic representation is helpful for understanding its explosive as well as its long-lasting character. The previous section showed that the explosive character of the debate originated in the accusation of society's behaviour not being in line with a key feature of its referent: the tolerant, non-discriminatory, nonracist society. The controversy also showed that once the symbolic representation, even for a minority audience, was successful, the symbolization could not be undone. Quite the contrary, it set in motion alternative symbolizations and attempts at other symbolic representations (i.e. chimney and other-coloured Petes symbolizing legitimate accommodation according to some and illegitimate, giving up of their own traditions, according to others).

Beyond the Black Pete case, a cursory observation lets us presume that many other controversies on symbols can be interpreted as cases of symbolic representation. We could think about controversies regarding statutes or street names that go against society's views on the legitimacy of a nation's past; the salient debate regarding an obese minister of health which is at odds with the society's views on a healthy society (see the conflict on the Belgian minister of health, Maggy De Block[16]); or debate on the skin colour of St. Lucia, a traditional Swedish festivity for children. By discussing this last example, it is by no means our aim to include a second case to test the model presented in the chapter. Rather, the example serves to weigh in on the potential applicability of the model beyond the Black Pete controversy.

The figure of Black Pete is not the only tradition or children-oriented festivity that sparked heated debate in recent years. By the end of 2016, an advert for the Swedish department store chain Åhléns unleashed a heated online debate after it unveiled a new campaign featuring a dark-skinned child, whose gender wasn't obvious to all, dressed as a Lucia—who is otherwise represented by a stereotypically Caucasian-looking blonde-haired girl (The Local, 2016).[17] The festivity hails from St. Lucy, a young Catholic woman who was martyred in a city on the island of Sicily around 304 AD. Although Swedes are claimed to have adjusted to more eclectic representations of Lucia, the young dark-skinned boy featured in the advert received a fair amount of sexist and racist backlash from online trolls. Shortly after the campaign was launched, racist and sexist comments began to flood the group's Facebook page, questioning why Lucia was represented by a person of colour and whose gender prompted confusion. Although the negative comments were soon met with a strong response from people defending the Åhléns group's choice of Lucia, the ad was removed as a consequence of the large backlash.

It is still historically unclear how a Catholic-based figure worked her way into the predominantly secular Sweden, but what is more apparent, however, is that many Swedes have diverging interpretations of what Lucia should look like. The first recorded appearance of a Lucia in Sweden dates from 1764 (Tidholm & Lilja, 2013). However, the figure remained at the margin of Swedish society until the 1900s, when schools and local associations promoted the festivity all across the country. Today, despite the relative dislike towards competition and privilege in the country, hundreds of girls subscribe yearly to compete and become the new Lucia. Candidates are marketed and presented in newspapers weeks in advance of the televised competition. Most of the national Lucias were in fact Caucasian-looking girls, thereby reinforcing the idea of Lucia as the 'bearer of light' by connecting it to fair skin, blue eyes and especially lengthy blonde, straight hair. This representation of Lucia does not always remain unchallenged, however. There are yearly stories going viral concerning the ability of men to play the feminine character, which opposed the idea of Lucia as a national symbol of Swedish femininity (Henderson, 1988), as well as the beauty and identity-based aesthetics of its portrayal, which in turn put into question Lucia's representation as exclusively fair skinned and blonde.

The backlash that last year's advert unleashed can also be conceived as a case in which audiences became actively involved in the unmaking and re-making of symbols that stand for Swedish society as whole. The response to the store's choice of portraying a dark-skinned boy points to dominant ideas on what the symbol of Lucia should stand for and the presence of challenging or alternative ideas about how the portrayal of Lucia could be carried out. First of all, as a national symbol of Swedish womanhood, the gendered character of Lucia can only be adequately portrayed by a girl. Second, and perhaps more importantly, the contest and protest against dark-skinned representations of Lucia appears to dismiss the increasingly ethnically and racially diverse society Sweden is becoming and to reinforce the ideal of 'Swedishness' as inherently white. Although many portrayals of Lucia acknowledge the southern origin of the festivity and accept representations by girls with dark hair and eyes, the constant and dominant feature always included typically Caucasian traits, light skin and straight hair.

It could be argued that the company's pulling of the advert as a result of the sexist and racist comments that it prompted factored into the seemingly fast settling of the controversy. However, the department store did emphasize the versatile nature of the character, stating on their Facebook page that 'We are unbelievably proud of our Lucia picture which stands for every child's right to be and express themselves exactly how they want to—as a Lucia, an Epiphany singer, or a gingerbread person, regardless of sex, hair length, colour or background' (RT, 2016). Discussions on the portrayal of Lucia are typically recurring in the month of December but usually do not last very long. The controversy seemed to have sparked a very short-lived debate that might be expected to regain saliency when alternative representations and repertoires continue to be projected onto the symbol of Lucia as a typically Caucasian female.

At this point we can only provide preliminary hypotheses concerning the reasons behind the outcome of the Black Pete controversy vis-à-vis that of the case of Swedish Lucia. In the case of Lucia the controversy seems to take a middle-ground position: the case does generate yearly recurring debates when 'deviant' representations of Lucia are employed, but it ultimately does not seem to result in a nationwide discussion about whiteness, sexism or racism in Sweden. The lack of nationwide disputes over the symbol could also be explained by what Hübinette (2013) qualifies as "Swedish whiteness", which constructs Swedish identity as inherently white, antiracist, gender equal and detached from a colonial past. The dominant repertoire allows for dismissing racist and sexist responses as incidental and detached from Swedes' ideas of their national self.

We also see the following possible explanations for the differences in outcomes between Black Pete and St Lucia: a first reason might well be linked to the power status of the agents involved in the processes of symbolization. In the case of Black Pete the opponents belong to a historically disadvantaged minority. Speaking from this position, we suggest, might limit their potential to settle the symbolization to their advantage. Similarly, despite the presence of audiences keen to see multiple representations of Lucia, the store's decision to pull the advert in order to warrant the boy's safety from adverse reactions might have also unwillingly signalled some agreement to the claims pointing to Caucasian girls as the only adequate representatives of what the symbol of Lucia stands for.

In the case of Lucia, a strong divide between opponents and proponents of Lucia's representation by a dark-skinned boy was never solidified. We can see that the backlash that the advert initially prompted might signal a case of contested symbolization. However, the controversy around the racist and sexist backlash was rather short-lived, especially after December 2016. Compared to the Black Pete case, the roles were almost reversed: the features under attack were grounded in understandings of Blackness (and femininity), not because they represented a racist society, but rather because they failed to correspond to an ideal of Lucia as being feminine and Caucasian. The dark-skinned boy failed to invoke the referent that a vast majority of the Swedes associate with the portrayal of Lucia. The opponents of a non-Caucasian or masculine representation of Lucia, manifested in the racist and sexist backlash, were arguably a more articulated majority than the proponents of 'deviant' interpretations of who should be able to symbolize and portray Lucia. Referring to the reversed role of race in both cases, Sweden-based journalist Edina Masanga wrote an opinion piece in which she contended that 'there is something . . . hypocritical about Europeans fighting to continue a "cultural" event of celebrating Zwarte Piet while getting vehemently upset about a dark-skinned child representing St Lucia' (Masanga, 2016).

We suggest that in the Black Pete case, both groups are able to tap into a source of power—the opponents referring to a key principle; the proponents speaking from a majority position—which explains the polarization and the continued controversy. In the case of Lucia, the representations as typically female and typically Caucasian are still very much ingrained within Swedish society. The course of the case might change, however. It is possible to conceive a spillover of the anti-racist principle in the Black Pete case playing a role in future contestations over adequate and representative portrayals of Lucia as a symbol.

CONCLUSION

This chapter discussed a political controversy that arose around what many for a long time considered to be a trivial issue: a persona in a children's festivity. It set out to understand *why* it took place, and *why at that particular time*. The questions driving the chapter's analysis are thus: Why did Black Pete suddenly evoke strong political reactions of opponents and proponents? Why is the Black Pete controversy still salient? Because of its evident symbolic and political dimension, we opted for applying symbolic representation as a heuristic tool for better understanding the controversy around this issue. Without claiming that no other model or theoretically driven interpretation could have provided insight in the *why* and the *when*, we showed that symbolic representation does contribute to understanding the politics involved. Our chapter added to the work of Lombardo and Meier (2014) and beyond by demonstrating that the concept of symbolic representation can be applied beyond traditional national symbols such as flags and anthems to a far larger and extensive set of symbols representing the political community.

Because of our reading of the empirical case through the conceptual lens of symbolic representation, we understood that it provoked strong emotional reactions because Black Pete was considered at odds with the referent value of the non-racist society. Blackness was invoked to accuse society of not living according to its own principles of the ideal society. Why did the issue reach the status of national political debates at this particular moment in time? The short answer is because these principles were challenged by certain societal actors, and the principles were found important enough to be defended by other actors.

This chapter not only demonstrated that the use of the concept of symbolic representation can foster understanding of the controversy around Black Pete, but also that the analysis of the selected case allows us to transform the concept of symbolic representation into a model. Drawing on the constructivist approach to symbolic representation (Lombardo & Meier, 2014), our new model stresses the role of multiple audiences. Their agency and power positions play a role in challenging the capacity of a symbol to stand for the principal they envision (referent values such as anti-racism). The model thus allows moving beyond the bilateral relationship between the principal and the agent, and analyzes the controversies in light of a multidimensional relationship between principal, agent, referent and multiple audiences. It highlights the importance of ongoing power struggles and agency, which were neglected in former accounts of symbolic representation.

Our chapter showed that the minority-majority power position of the actors concerned in the Black Pete case matters. It also suggested that the degree of institutionalization of the values that are part of the referent, namely the codification of anti-racism into laws, matters to explain the contestation over symbolic representation. Hence, through a symbolic representation analysis, we can also understand how important certain values and principles are to a society and how they evolve. These findings suggest that the power position of the actors contesting and defending the symbols, the symbolization activity, as well as the degree of institutionalization of the values the symbol represents are key for the further theorization of symbolic representation.

The analysis of the controversies around Black Pete is the story of just one case. Hence this contribution to the conceptualization of symbolic representation is an invitation to further explore how agency, context and power matter in further studies of symbolic representation.

NOTES

1. We write *Black* with a capital *B* to honour the struggle for recognition and equal treatment by Black activists around the globe. While lowercase *black* is simply a colour, capital *Black* refers to the heritage of Black people, their diaspora and struggle for recognition in

racialized contexts. We write *white* in lowercase letters to problematize the arbitrary base of white persons' perceived superiority (Severs, 2015, p. 141).

2. We equally write *Blackness* to highlight the broad range of the set of internal and external associations and stereotypes that these concepts call into being.

3. Also see Chapter 3.

4. Pitkin's discussion of symbolic representation was limited to showcasing that there are forms of political representation that are symbolic. Unlike the field of semiotics, she did not offer a general discussion of symbols (i.e. cultural constructs) and their role in signifying processes. Because it is our goal to demonstrate the relevance of including symbolic representation when analyzing processes of political representation, we limit ourselves to a discussion of Pitkin's account of symbolic representation. Although a thorough discussion of semiotics would be useful for further unpacking how symbols work, it exceeds the scope and aims of this chapter.

5. For reasons of conciseness, this discussion makes omission of historical research on political symbols that has focused on the ways in which national anthems, myths, recitals, statues, rituals and public buildings give expression to prevailing political orders (e.g. Diehl & Escudier, 2014).

6. We acknowledge that processes of meaning production through symbols are not limited to the conceptual framework we discuss in this chapter (for more on this discussion, see Peirce's (1977) theory of signs or Hall (1997) on cultural representations). Similar to our analytical framework, semiotic studies traditionally deal with symbols as signs that stand for something else and which are made up of underlying meanings and signifiers. Although our approach to the analysis of symbolic representation reveals some overlap with these concepts, we limit our framework to political representation. A more general discussion on symbols as a signifying practice may distract attention away from our general argument, namely that the symbolic dimension of political representation defines a background to interest representation and helps us explain why political controversy and contestation arises.

7. A popular song still threatens that children who behave well will receive treats and those who behave badly will receive the roe (*wie zoet is krijgt lekkers, wie staat is de roe*). In the French language, Black Pete is known as 'Father Whipper' (*Père Fouettard*).

8. 'Stop geen zwarte knecht in uw Sinterklaaspakket. De slavernij is al honderd jaar geleden stopgezet' (Helsloot, 2005, p. 257).

9. In February 2003, the Dutch-Surinamese actor Gerda Havertong participated in a quiz programme on television. Before the broadcast, the live audience was entertained with music. When Havertong entered the studio, a popular Saint Nicholas song ('Zie ginds komt de stoomboot') was playing. When Havertong expressed her indignation—'How could I not think this song was meant for me?'—the audience showed little understanding for her reaction (Helsloot, 2005, p. 264).

10. Up until today, the practice of whitewashing—casting white actors to portray original characters of colour—takes place. See, for instance,http://www.theguardian.com/film/2015/nov/13/gods-of-egypt-posters-anger-whitewashed-cast-twitter-exodus

11. Facebook pages were consulted on February 18, 2016, using keywords such as 'Black Pete' (Zwarte Piet), 'Black Pete is . . .' ('Zwarte Piet is . . .'), and 'Black Pete should . . .' ('Zwarte Piet moet . . .'). We identified six Facebook pages mobilizing against the tradition of blackfacing and 136 Facebook pages mobilizing for the preservation of Black Pete.

12. Until 2016, the CBS (the Dutch Statistics Institute) institutionalized the terms *allochtoon* and *autochtoon* to differentiate between Dutch citizens who are native and non-native. Those who were born or have at least one parent born outside the country are traditionally referred to as allochthones. Both the CBS and the WRR (the Dutch scientific council for governmental policies) announced in 2016 to replace this terminology with, freely translated, 'individual with a Dutch background, non-Western migration background, second generation migration background, and so forth'. However, the everyday usage of the term *allochtoon* gained considerable traction when first introduced in the 1980s and has been typically connected to anyone with a visible non-Western background, particularly groups with a Surinamese, Moroccan or Turkish (migration) background. To give an example, a Belgian-born citizen in the Netherlands is officially an *allochtoon* but would pass as an *autochtoon* if not stating otherwise.

13. It cannot be denied that an important part of the proponents of Black Pete do not wish to live in a tolerant and anti-racist society but regret the old mono-cultural or hierarchical society wherein Black people were colonial subjects and did not have a voice. Seeing the legal interdiction of racism and anti-discrimination, they often hide behind the proponents of Black Pete claiming that Black Pete is not racism.

14. Approximately 150,000 people have withdrawn their support for the petition.

15. The post–World War II period indeed marked a gradual evolution of (Western) societies towards the official banning of racism. Two major developments in that regard are the adoption by the United Nations of the International Convention on the Elimination of All Forms of Racial Discrimination of 1965 and the victory of the American civil rights movement to end official racial segregation through the adoption of the Civil Rights Act of 1964 and the 14th and 15th Amendments to the US Constitution. In European countries, a gradual extension of immigrant rights in the post-war period (Soysal, 1994) as well as the inclusion of new anti-discrimination provisions under Article 13 of the Treaty of Amsterdam, followed by the adoption of the European Racial Equality directive in 2000 (Geddes & Guiraudon, 2004), also testify to these evolving views of the ideal society.

16. In October 2014, public controversy arose over the credibility of the newly appointed Belgian minister of health Maggie De Block. It all started with a tweet sent by a journalist of the Flemish public broadcasting network VRT. In his tweet, the journalist made reference to the weight of the newly appointed minister and compared the public's mellow reactions to the public controversy over the overweight American governor Chris Christie. He stated, 'Finding 1: in a country plagued by obesity a corpulent presidential candidate such as (Governor) Chris Christie is a problem. Finding 2: Belgium gets a Minister of Health that is obese. Criticism is dismissed as nonsense, but what about credibility?'

17. We recognize the reductive connotation and unstable definition of the term *Caucasian* but in this chapter, we employ it to refer to those who are typically denoted as white. The term is broad enough that it often downplays any biological or physical distinctions within this group (such as distinctions between Scandinavians on the one end and Spaniards on the other).

REFERENCES

Akachar, S., Celis, K., & Severs, E. (2015). *Citizens' feelings of (not) being represented: Towards a multidimensional and procedural approach of social group representation.* Paper presented at the ECPR General Conference, Montreal.

Bird, K. (2015). "We are not an ethnic vote!" Representational perspectives of minorities in the greater Toronto area. *Canadian Journal of Political Science, 48*(2): 247–79.

Boer-Dirks, E. (1993). Nieuw licht op Zwarte Piet. *Volkskundig Bulletin. Tijdschrift voor Nederlandse cultuurwetenschap, 19*(1), 1–35.

Childs, S. (2008). *Women and British party politics: Descriptive, substantive and symbolic representation.* London: Routledge.

Cole, M. (1993). Black and ethnic minority or Asian, Black and other minority ethnic: A further note on nomenclature. *Sociology, 27,* 671–73.

Diehl, P., & Escudier, A. (2014). La Représentation du politique: histoire, concepts, symboles. *Cahiers du CEVIPOF*, Sciences Po.http://www.cevipof.com/fr/les-publications/les-cahiers-du-cevipof/bdd/publication/1166

Disch, L. (2011). Toward a mobilization concept of democratic representation. *American Political Science Review, 105*(1): 100–114.

Edelman, M. (1964). *The symbolic uses of politics.* Chicago: University of Illinois Press.

Edelman, M. (1971). *Politics as symbolic action.* Chicago: Markham.

Franceschet, S., Krook, M. L., & Piscopo, J. M. (Eds.). (2012). *The Impact of Gender Quotas.* Oxford: Oxford University Press.

Geddes, A., & Guiraudon, V. (2004). Britain and France and EU anti-discrimination policy: The emergence of a EU paradigm. *West European Politics, 27*(2), 334–54.

Greven, J., & Bosveld, E. (2012). *Hoe denken Amsterdammers over Zwarte Piet?* Rapport in opdracht van Dienst Maatschappelijke Ontwikkeling, Gemeente Amsterdam. Amsterdam: Gemeente Amsterdam—Bureau Onderzoek en Statistiek.

Hall, S. (1997). *Representation: Cultural representation and signifying practices.* London: Sage.

Helsloot, J. I. A. (2005). De strijd om Zwarte Piet. In I. A. Hoving, H. T. Dibbits, & M. Schrover (Eds.), *Veranderingen van het alledaagse 1950–2000* (pp. 249–71). Den Haag: SDU. Retrieved from http://www.dbnl.org/tekst/hovi002cult01_01/hovi002cult01_01_0011.php

Helsloot, J. I. A. (2008). De ambivalente boodschap van de eerste 'Zwarte Piet' (1850). In De kleine Olympus. Over enkele figuren uit de alledaagse mythologie (pp. 93–117). Amsterdam: KNAW Press. Retrieved from http://www.meertens.knaw.nl/cms/images/nieuws2013/ambi.pdf

Henderson, J. (1988). Ancient myths and modern man. In C. G. Jung (Ed.), *Man and his symbols* (pp. 104–57). London: Anchor Press.

Hooks, B. (2001). Postmodern Blackness. In V. B. Leitch (Ed.), *The Norton anthology: Theory and criticism.* New York: Norton.

Hübinette, T. (2013). Swedish anti-racism and white melancholia: Racial words in a post-racial society. *Ethnicity and Age in a Changing World, 4*(1), 24-33.

Lawless, J. L. (2004). Politics of presence? Congresswomen and symbolic representation. *Political Research Quarterly, 57*(1), 81–99.

Tidholm, P. & Lilja, A. (2013). *Celebrating the Swedish way: Traditions and festivities.* Stockholm: The Swedish Institute.

Lipsitz, G. (2011). *How racism takes place.* Philadelphia: Temple University Press.

Lombardo, E., & Meier, P. (2014). *The symbolic representation of gender: A discursive approach.* Aldershot: Ashgate.

Maylor, U. (2009). What is the meaning of 'Black'? Researching 'Black' respondents. *Ethnic and Racial Studies, 32*(2), 369–87.

Meier, P., & Severs, E. (2017). *The flipside of role models: The symbolic representation of class.* Paper prepared for ECPR Joint Sessions of Workshops, Nottingham.

NOS NL. (2014, October 10). Van der Laan past Zwarte Piet aan. *NOS NL.* Retrieved February 18, 2016, from http://nos.nl/artikel/708573-van-der-laan-past-zwarte-piet-aan.html

OHCHR. (2013a, January 17). *Letter to the government of the Netherlands by the Office of the United Nations High Commissioner for Human Rights.* Reference AL Af. Descent 2012 Cultural rights (2009) Minorities (2005–4) G/SO 214 (78-15).https://spdb.ohchr.org/hrdb/23rd/public_-_AL_Netherlands_17.01.13_%281.2013%29.pdf

OHCHR. (2013b, November 21). *Black Pete and Sinterklaas: UN experts encourage respectful national debate on Dutch tradition.* Press release on the website of the Office of the United Nations Human High Commissioner for Human Rights. Retrieved February 17, 2016, from http://www.ohchr.org/EN/NewsEvents/Pages/DisplayNews.aspx?NewsID=14013&LangID=E

OHCHR. (2014). *Statement by the United Nation's Working Group of Experts on People of African Descent, on the conclusion of its official visit to the Netherlands, 26 June–4 July 2014.*

Pastoureau, M. (2008). *Black: The history of color.* Princeton, NJ, and Oxford: Princeton University Press.

Peirce, C. S. (1977). *Semiotics and significs.* Bloomington: Indiana University Press.

Pitkin, H. (1967). *The concept of representation.* Berkeley: University of California Press.

Plotke, D. (1997). Representation is democracy. *Constellations, 4*(1), 19–34.

Press release on the website of the Office of the United Nations Human High Commissioner for Human Rights (2014, July 4). Retrieved February 18, 2016, from http://www.ohchr.org/EN/NewsEvents/Pages/DisplayNews. aspx?NewsID=14840&LangID=E

Saward, M. (2010). *The representative claim.* Oxford: Oxford University Press.

Schwindt-Bayer, L. A. and Mischler, W. (2005). An integrated model of women's representation. *Journal of Politics, 67*(2): 407–28.

Severs, E. (2015). The limits of categorical refurbishment: Ethnicisation and racialisation in the Flemish debate on how to denote 'migrant' populations. *DiGeSt—Journal for Diversity and Gender Studies, 2*(3–4), 127–42.

Severs, E. (2010). Representation as claims-making: quid responsiveness? *Representation, 46*(4), 411–73.

Severs, E., Celis, K., & Erzeel, S. (2016). Intersectional theorizing on political representation: power, privilege and disadvantage. *Politics*, prepublished online. doi:10.1177/0263395716630987.

Soysal, Y. (1994). *Limits of citizenship: Migrants and postnational membership in Europe.* Chicago: University of Chicago Press.

Stokes-Brown, A. K., & Dolan, K. (2010). Race, gender, and symbolic representation: African American female candidates as mobilizing agents. *Journal of Elections, Public Opinion & Parties, 20*(4), 473–94.

PRESS CONTENT

De Telegraaf. (2013, October 23). 'Pietitie' met 1 miljoen likes grootste Facebook-pagina ooit. *De Telegraaf.* Retrieved February 18, 2016, from http://www.telegraaf.nl/binnenland/21995541/__Pietitie__1_miljoen_likes__.html

Gario, Q. (2012, November 12). *Mijn kunstproject is geslaagd omdat het zichzelf overbodig heeft gemaakt.* Retrieved February 17, 2016, from http://zwartepietisracisme.tumblr.com/post/ 35566690735/mijn-kunstproject-is-geslaagd-omdat-het-zichzelf

Het Laatste Nieuws. (2013, October 24). 'Pietitie' heeft de kaap van 2 miljoen likes overschreden. *Het Laatste Nieuws.* Retrieved February 18, 2016, from http://www.hln.be/hln/nl/960/Buitenland/article/detail/1728852/2013/10/24/Pietitie-heeft-de-kaap-van-2-miljoen-likes-overschreden.dhtml

Masanga, E. (2016, December 6). Swedish ad racism is shocking and hypocritical. TheLocal.se. Retrieved from https://www.thelocal.se/20161206/opinion-swedish-lucia-ad-racism-is-shocking-and-hypocritical

RT. (2016, December 6). Department store pulls festive ad following racist abuse of dark-skinned child. RT.com. Retrieved from https://www.rt.com/viral/369237-ahlens-lucia-racist-controversy/

Tidholm, P., & Lilja, A. (2014, December 1). Competing to be Lucia. Sweden.se. Retrieved from https://sweden.se/culture-traditions/lucia/

The Local. (2016, December 5). Swedish festive ad pulled following racist abuse of child. TheLocal.se. Retrieved June 13, 2017, from https://www.thelocal.se/20161205/swedish-festive-ad-pulled-following-racist-abuse-of-child

Chapter Nine

An Architecture for Hybrid Democracy in the EU

When Participation (En)counters Representation

Ferran Davesa and Jamal Shahin

Transformations in the way representative institutions deal with their voters are apparent, not least through the development of Internet-based tools that have changed the relationship between representative and represented. In the virtual arena, the conventional edges of political representation are challenged as a result of the proliferation of new forms of political engagement that transcend physical, cultural and idiosyncratic barriers. The venues in which political action takes place are not those of the old liberal democracies, but rather a result of hybridization and profound change. Innovative policy-making dynamics found fertile soil in the European Union (EU) and transformed the democratic functioning of multilevel governance. This forms the basis of our contribution to this volume. We wish to delve deeper into the relationship between *participation* and *representation* in this new context, understanding how the European Union's democratic landscape is being transformed, and the extent to which this is rebalancing its current political functioning and future stability.

EU institutions are trying to take advantage of the 'bundling' of participation and representation, with the two most archetypical institutions, the European Commission and the European Parliament, seeking to act as legitimate actors via their mixture of participatory and representative mechanisms. Both institutions are using new information and communication technologies (ICTs) for improving and enhancing their democratic functioning, yet they seek different goals when blending participation and representation. Hybridization within the EU follows two different paths: on the one hand, technocratic policymaking adopts a logic of 'representative participation', and on the other hand, representative policymaking digs into a logic of 'participatory representation'. For facilitating the interaction between these two classic principles of democracy, the Internet appears to play a crucial role.

In the formalized institutional structure of the European Commission, the claim to being representative is packaged as broadening participation. It is a collateral by-product of, first, enhanced stakeholder engagement processes developed by the innovative mechanisms of the 'good governance' reform presented in the White Paper on European Governance of 2001 (hereafter, the Governance White Paper) and, second, the European Commission's transition towards e-governance. This notion of policymaking generates a new ecology for political participation based on online engagement and consultation that takes the representativeness of the actors involved as a fundamental indicator of good governance. While the Internet enhances political accessibility by deactivating technical, economic and linguistic barriers, representation assures the inclusiveness and legitimacy of participatory governance.

Differently, the European Parliament (the only EU institution that has direct electoral legitimacy) is keen to use political participation as a decoupling mechanism to ensure the visibility and public support of the representatives and, ultimately, their public endorsement in the parliamentary elections through the votes of European citizens, which have proved to decrease since the first direct European elections of 1979. Participation, in that event, interacts with representation as a shortcut to get citizens' attention and to stimulate electoral mobilization, thus acting as a mechanism of 'opinion formation' more than a policymaking tool.

These institutions separately make use of online-based technologies to overcome the democratic deficits that emerge from a fragmented, complex and multilayered system of governance. The Commission's new model of *representative participation* and the Parliament's new logic of *participatory representation* attempt to strengthen their own legitimacy without altering the functional constraints deriving from the EU's decision-making structure. Yet, by entwining participation with representation via the Internet, the EU institutions adopt political repertoires that have been commonly used for collective action by social movements and advocacy groups.

The use of online-based technologies at both civil society and institutional levels has generated new opportunities for incipient forms of citizen involvement and interaction with the European Union. Hence, it could be argued that the rise of a digital European political space is generating more flexible, creative and transformative ways to reconcile European integration with citizens. By having an Internet presence, the question remains whether the Parliament and the Commission, together with social movements, political parties and other collective actors, might benefit from spillover effects that fortify EU democracy through 'hybridization'. That is, whether the emergence of a participatory momentum through the Internet at both societal and institutional levels can create synergies and connections between the public and the political, the participatory and the representative, the online and the offline. This chapter elucidates the main characteristics of such an incipient scenario, ending with a brief sketch of a policy issue around which several instances of these transformations have flourished: the Transatlantic Trade and Investment Partnership (TTIP) that the European Union started negotiating with the government of the United States in 2013.

'POLITICS AS USUAL' AND THE CRISIS OF DISAFFECTION

Public confidence in representative democracy has fallen dramatically over the last decades (see Norris, 2011). Rather than circumscribed to a specific institutional or geographical context, public alienation towards political leaders and institutions is challenging liberal democracies around the globe. At a time when, paradoxically, solid support is given to democratic principles and ideals (Wiklund, 2005), the disagreement between these principles and the actual functioning of democratic systems is growing. Scholars such as Dalton (2004, p. 199) claim that the "increasingly skeptical public has not posed a major challenge to the stability and viability of democracy", and Norris (2011, p. 142) states that "overt support for democracy as an ideal form of governance proves almost universal today". Hence, although democracy might not face its own recession, these same voices alert that the enduring alienation of citizens can ultimately harm the political process, affect the social legitimacy of decision-making, and alter the nature of electoral politics.

The large scope of citizen disenchantment has made the normative foundations of EU democracy tremble. One of its most important expressions has been the low turnout in European elections. Scholars like Blondel, Sinnott, and Svensson (1998); Carrubba and Timpone (2005); and Hix and Marsh (2007) confirm the link between citizen levels of support towards European integration and their electoral behaviour. While one typical outcome of the lack of trust is not casting a vote (the turnout in the European Parliament election of 2014 was 42.6%), another disruptive result is the rise of Eurosceptic sentiment across the continent. In line with this reasoning, recent events confirm the magnitude of this problem. These include the latest electoral results in countries as diverse as the Czech Republic, Germany, France, Greece, Austria, and the Netherlands, which gave renewed credit to Eurosceptic parties and confirmed a sound sentiment of disappointment amongst the population. Finally, the disenchantment with the EU brought Eurosceptic voices up to 25% of the seats in the European Parliament in 2014, and it pushed the UK's withdrawal from the EU that followed the 'Brexit' referendum of June 2016. The poor health of the EU's legitimacy is also exposed by public opinion surveys and indicators such as the Eurobarometer and the European Social Survey. During the last decades, these indicators have repeatedly shown sceptical attitudes towards EU institutions and the European integration project. It can be argued that a growing distance between citizens and 'politics as usual' (Margolis & Resnick, 2000) is damaging the link between the *representatives* and the *represented*. This tendency has often been explained through endogenous circumstances of EU politics, which include, for instance, the growing complexity and fragmentation of EU governance (Bartolini, 2005) and the fact that the "second-order effects" of European elections have increased instead of decreased (Føllesdal & Hix, 2006, p. 536). Having said that, important exogenous factors also need to be counted amongst the main triggers of this 'crisis in citizenship'.

These refer to a general engagement problem in Western societies that makes it difficult for conventional organizations (such as political parties) to incorporate new members and to engage with the public (Mair & Van Biezen, 2001; Putnam, 2000; also see Chapter 2). In advanced industrial democracies, particularly in the post–World War II era, political parties became the main vehicles of political representation (see Müller, 2000) by fulfilling a fundamental 'connecting function' between the public and policymaking (Key, 1961; Lawson, 1980; Sartori, 1976). The current decline of organizational membership has been interpreted as a form of 'diminished democracy' (Skocpol, 2003) in which only certain elites, rather than the general public, are interacting with the government. Inglehart and Welzel (2005) argue that the new patterns of citizens' political behaviour respond to a change in public values. According to this account, modernization revolves around post-materialist values linked to individualization, suburbanization, and an increasing focus on citizens' self-identity (Giddens, 1991; Putnam, 2000). This new political culture entails an erosion of deference towards traditional hierarchies of collective action, a dynamic that has been often linked to the abandonment of associational dynamics and the general loss of social capital (Putnam, 2000).

Although these explanations have encouraged pessimistic interpretations of the new political culture in advanced democracies, other perspectives challenge these views through an alternative set of explanations that focus on the increasing idealism, critical spirit or analytical capacity of citizens in post-industrial societies (Inglehart & Welzel, 2005). This so-called 'modernizing theory' makes a direct link between citizens' postmodern attitudes and the development of a more 'critical' conception of politics. The seminal work of Pippa Norris (1999) on the notion of the *critical citizen* relies upon the fact that "there is growing tension between ideals and reality" (Norris, 1999, p. 27). The new ideals of 21st-century critical citizens are expressed, as Beck,

Giddens, and Lash (1994, p. 20) anticipated, through the withdrawal from "old forms and institutions" and the "emigration to new niches of activity and identity". Thorson (2015) captures this attitudinal and behavioural change with the hallmark "it's up to you", a term that emphasizes citizens' new ethos of self-reliance and autonomy. Bennett and Segerberg (2012, p. 30) refer to this new political culture as "the current era of personalized politics" and use the term 'Do-It-Yourself' politics. All in all, these perspectives describe a situation in which postmodern society challenges elite-driven policies: since elites are seen as not being able to address key societal challenges, these are directly tackled by 'emancipated' citizens relying on 'new engagement repertoires'. According to Bennett (2012, pp. 21–37), that means varying combinations of the following conditions:

1. They rely upon *self-expression* logics. These follow the patterns of the 'Do-It-Yourself' politics and generate abundant personal action or identity frames.
2. They imply *direct, creative* and *short-term* actions that put individuals at the centre while including *new forms of coproduction and distribution* of content.
3. They develop large-scale *inclusive networks* that *form rapidly* and target *multiple actors*, ranging from parties, institutions, brands and transnational organizations.
4. They typically involve *Internet-based communication technologies* that allow individuals to activate their personal social networks.

It can be argued that European integration is exposed to both endogenous and exogenous pressures that compromise its legitimacy and long-term stability (in the guise of both challenges imposed by multilevel governance and a transformation of the political culture in the direction of the *critical citizens*). The EU has acknowledged on multiple occasions the need to transform its main governance structures so as to respond to such challenges. To date, the most recent attempt has been the European Commission's White Paper on the Future of Europe, a political initiative that was presented in March 2017 with the intention to activate inter-institutional debate on which would be the best scenario for the EU-27. This has been, however, the last of many attempts to define an enhanced model of governance for the EU that was able to reconcile both the endogenous and the exogenous pressures on its overall effectiveness and legitimacy.

BALANCING PARTICIPATION
AND REPRESENTATION IN THE EU

The constituents of a path towards a more democratic EU were subject to in-depth discussions during the Convention on the Future of Europe, a body established by the European Council in 2001. This was the formula chosen for developing a constitution for Europe in a way that the blockages of past treaty negotiations could be avoided (cf. Lombardo, 2007). The negotiations on the content of the treaty resulted in a very comprehensive phrasing of participation, which was conceived as a major legitimacy pillar of the new 'constitutional Union'. The Draft Treaty delivered by the convention in July 2003 incorporated a Title VI on the 'Democratic Life of the Union'. Its Article 46, 'The Principle of Participatory Democracy,' proposed three paragraphs to establish the legal basis of participation and a fourth one to define a specific participatory tool such as the European Citizens' Initiative (ECI), which was incorporated in the Lisbon Treaty in 2007 and made operational in 2012. Article 46 of the Draft Treaty reads as follows:

1. The Union Institutions shall, by appropriate means, give citizens and representative associations the opportunity to make known and publicly exchange their views in all areas of Union action.
2. The Union Institutions shall maintain an open, transparent and regular dialogue with representative associations and civil society.
3. The Commission shall carry out broad consultations with parties concerned in order to ensure that the Union's actions are coherent and transparent.
4. No less than 1 million citizens coming from a significant number of Member States may invite the Commission to submit any appropriate proposal on matters where citizens consider that a legal act of the Union is required for the purpose of implementing the Constitution. A European law shall determine the provisions for the specific procedures and conditions required for such a citizens' initiative.

In May 2005, France and the Netherlands rejected the Constitutional Treaty via referenda, which determined 'the beginning of the end' of the EU constitutionalization process. In spite of that, political participation as a legitimating source of the EU found a place in the Lisbon Treaty (TEU) in 2007 via Article 10.3. This has been considered a milestone in the development of the EU's participatory governance (Lindgren & Persson, 2011, p. 6). However, compared to Article 46 of the Draft Treaty establishing a Constitution for Europe, it is shorter and less ambitious. On the one hand, Article 10.3 was paradoxically not taken from Article 46 of the Draft Treaty establishing a Constitution (which was fully dismissed except for the part developing the

ECI) but from the third paragraph of Article 45, which was titled 'The Principle of Representative Democracy'. Showing no heading in the Lisbon Treaty other than Title II, 'Provisions on Democratic Principles', Article 10.3 reads, "Every citizen shall have the right to participate in the democratic life of the Union. Decisions shall be taken as openly and as closely as possible to the citizen". While this clause presents political participation as a way to reduce the gap between citizens and institutions, Article 10.1 underlines that "the functioning of the Union shall be founded on representative democracy". In its turn, Article 10.2 states that citizens are "directly represented" in the European Parliament and member states in both the Council of the EU and in the European Council. Lastly, Article 10.4 underlines that political parties contribute to express the will of citizens and to form European political awareness.

The legal definition of the concepts 'participation' and 'representation' in the treaty indicates how differently they are balanced in relation to how they were conceived in the convention. From one event to the other, the social and political background had changed profoundly, as did the institutional settings in which the negotiations took place. Instead of delivering a transformative benchmark of new governance for the Union, the Treaty followed a more conservative structure in which no major compromises were decided on the legal bases of such change. It could be argued, in consequence, that the so-called EU's 'participatory turn' (see Saurugger, 2008) lost momentum from one text to the other. However, the absence of a consensus for articulating in the EU's primary law an innovative conception of governance does not force the EU to be stuck with 'politics as usual' (see Margolis & Resnick, 2000) until the next eventual reform of the treaties. Instead, the lack of ambition of the Lisbon Treaty implied that each institution had to continue using its political and normative power for setting its own standards—using secondary legislation or instances of *soft law*. Unlike the Draft Constitutional Treaty, which established clearer normative bases on how to transform representative and participatory democracy in the EU, the Lisbon Treaty led to a competitive battle between institutions on new kinds of policymaking.

'REPRESENTATIVE PARTICIPATION' AS THE COMMISSION'S STRATEGIC CHOICE

During the first three decades of European integration, deals in the EU were cut by insulated elites who did not feel the pressure of a quiescent public opinion, nor of European constituencies (Hooghe & Marks, 2008, p. 5). In recent years, the political landscape in Europe has not been so accommodating. Since 1991, citizens have looked towards Brussels and to their national leaders with a much more demanding and sceptical opinion of the European

Union. This new scenario, which is highly consistent with the aforementioned cultural transition towards 'critical citizens', has been called 'constraining dissensus' by Hooghe and Marks (2008), in opposition to the previous 'permissive consensus' context, in which "citizens largely ignored the EU and its outcomes" (Schmidt, 2013, p. 13). By reforming both the meanings and the mechanisms of 'participation' and 'representation', the institutions of the EU wanted to offer new responses to such change regarding the social perceptions of the EU. One of the soundest reactions in that direction was the European Commission's White Paper on Governance.

After the crisis of confidence generated by the mass resignation of Jacques Santer's Commission in March 1999, Romano Prodi's pushed for a governance reform in order to reinvigorate the prestige of the institution and transmit a message of democratic consolidation to the public. The Governance White Paper was the outcome of that initiative, which was assembled by the vestiges of the 'Forward Studies Unit', an epistemic community of experts that was originally established under the presidency of Jacques Delors and took responsibility for designing the Commission's reform plan. A crucial aspect of that reform was to enhance and structure the direct participation of European citizens into policymaking.

Academic analyses have identified such reform as a 'participatory turn' (Saurugger, 2008) and linked it to the nature of the Commission's legitimacy, which emerges from its general efficiency and effectiveness in dealing with problems (Höreth, 1999, p. 251). The Commission is not a representative body but aims at defending the 'European interest' independently of member states or popular pressure, for which it has been characterized as a 'Platonic guardian' of the treaties. In that line, Kohler-Koch (2010, p. 108) states that "only the Commission has no constituency and the Treaties provide no mechanisms of linking the Commission to the citizens". Greenwood (2007, p. 343) argues that "organized civil society has become the natural constituency of the European Commission", to which Eder and Trenz (2003, p. 128) add that the goal of the Commission is to recollect the reactions of different European public constituencies in order to transform this knowledge into claims of public legitimacy. Thus, political participation appears to be the Commission's strategic choice against representation-based legitimacy.

The debate on the EU's 'participatory turn' is rooted in a rich political and academic debate on how to enhance the legitimacy of multilevel governance (also see Chapter 4). The 'participatory' approach to policymaking challenges the old democratic ideal based on aggregation of public preferences through devices such as voting and representation (Dryzek, 2000, p. v). The origins of the term are to be found in the activism narratives that emerged in the United States during the 1960s, specifically those of youth movements. Hence, 'participatory democracy' was originally linked to activist repertoires of the organized youth, which conceived it mostly in terms of empowerment. In that context, the terms *responsibility, autonomy, self-government* and *self-determination* were framed in opposition to the dynamics of "representation as delegation" (Floridia, 2013, p. 5).

According to Scharpf (1997, 1999), the way the Commission defines *participation* informs the main characteristics of its *input legitimacy*, or to put it in Schmidt's (2013, p. 2) words, the level of "responsiveness to citizen concerns as a result of participation *by* the people". The Governance White Paper not only builds a renewed strategy to enhance input legitimacy via the notion of participation (see Scharpf 1997, 1999) but also reclaims four other governance principles. By defining *effectiveness*, the Governance Paper structures the *output* legitimacy of the EU. And when the document addresses openness, accountability and coherence, it covers what goes in between the input and the output, which Schmidt (2013) refers to as *throughput* legitimacy. By connecting the reforms proposed in the document to these three normative values, the Commission aims at reinforcing EU democratic governance (European Commission, 2001, p. 10). While representation was not placed at the core of the new EU governance strategy, it was repeatedly mentioned throughout the document in relation, first and foremost, to the articulation of participation and the role of civil society organizations (CSOs). To exemplify, the text reads,

> Standards will reduce the risk of the policy-makers just listening to one side of the argument or of particular groups getting privileged access on the basis of sectoral interests or nationality, which is a clear weakness with the current method of ad hoc consultations. These standards should improve the representativity of civil society organisations and structure their debate with the Institutions. (COM, 2001, p.17)

The Commission's communication disentangles a pluralist understanding of participatory governance by accentuating that all the relevant stakeholders should have the opportunity to get involved in a consultative policymaking process as long as they represent a particular interest, regardless of their level of expertise, utility or financial and human resources (Quittkat & Kotzian, 2011, p. 403). We refer to this new governance approach through the term *representative participation*, a concept that is also stressed by the Commission to counter criticism of elitist policymaking, a complaint it had received in the years before launching this reform (Kohler-Koch & Quittkat, 2013).

One of the main values of representative participation via multistakeholderism relies on its deliberative nature. According to Elster (1998, p. 8), the notion of deliberative democracy includes collective decision-making with the participation of all who will be affected by the decision, by means of arguments offered by and to participants who are committed to the values of rationality and impartiality. The importance of dialogue and argumentation is also emphasized by Parkinson and Mansbridge (2012, p. 5), who define deliberation as a complex system of interactions that encompass a talk-based approach to political conflict and problem-solving. Although as stated by Floridia (2013, p. 3) "not all forms of deliberation are participative; and not all forms of participation are deliberative", the Commission's approach towards multistakeholderism emphasizes consensus rather than the mere aggregation of voices. This rationale has been used not only to integrate Green Papers in the EU policy cycle that summarize the different sectorial viewpoints around a topic; it has also informed new expressions of governance like the Open Method of Coordination (Sabel & Zeitlin, 2010), a framework that generated innovative structures of deliberation such as the Structured Dialogue with Youth (Davesa, 2018) and the European Integration Forum (García, 2012).

The Commission's white paper emphasizes the "important role" of new technologies (COM, 2001, pp. 11–12) to inform and structure the new initiatives of representative participation. On the one hand, the Commission assumed that the Internet is crucial to reaching expert publics beyond the Brussels bubble and to amplifying the scope of its calls for expertise. On the other hand, ICTs allow general coordination between the different Directorates General (DGs) and the development of a holistic participatory infrastructure (see Kohler-Koch & Quittkat, 2013). An initial step in this direction was the e-Commission reform programme, which paved the way for "modernising the administration and improving its communication and working methods" (European Commission, 2000, p. 8) through the renewal of the EU's information technology policies. Later, the Minimum Standards for Consultation (2002) ratified this strategy by highlighting the potential of online-based consultation tools such as Interactive Policy Making (IPM) or the Internet portal Your Voice in Europe (YViE).

Online consultations are the Commission's quintessential format for structuring representative participation and the most relevant mechanism for giving voice to the actors that constitute sectoral policy networks. Kohler-Koch and Quittkat (2013) establish three generations of the Commission's consultation regime (see also Kohler-Koch & Finke, 2007). The first one, which started in the 1960s, was characterized by an informal and hierarchical structure of cooperation with economic stakeholders that joined the debates irregularly and on a bilateral basis. The second phase goes back to the 1980s, with the consolidation of the 'partnership' principle based on multilateral social dialogue and collaboration. The third generation relies upon the Commission's governance reform to deploy the new online consultation paradigm, which has been characterized by Quittkat (2013, p. 110) as an efficient mechanism to formally guarantee "equal access to all those affected by a policy". Online consultations are open to contributions from all kinds of actors, from individual citizens to NGOs and interest groups. Participants can structure their visions on a certain policy initiative through the online forms prepared by the pertinent Commission DGs. Since the web portal was launched in 2000, online consultations have significantly grown; while in 2001 a total of 25 were launched, in 2009 the portal had published 117 (Quittkat, 2013, p. 103).

All in all, since the approval of the Governance White Paper in 2001 the Commission has dug into non-electoral legitimation structures for consolidating its power and for better informing its policies. The Commission's hybridization via the concept of representative participation relies on new ICTs to amplify the call for expert contributions and to better coordinate its online consultation regime. This builds upon a conception of legitimacy that, while reinforcing the Commission's role, decreases the participation costs and the 'representation' threshold for CSOs via the activation of online channels.

The question remains whether online-based representative participation is a valid mechanism not only for stimulating the participation of sectorial interests and expert elites but also for fostering deliberative problem-solving while opening the scope of participation to the ever-critical general public.

'PARTICIPATORY REPRESENTATION' AS AN ELECTORAL TOOL

With the intention to reinforce the democratic legitimacy of European integration, the functioning of the EU's representative democracy has also been amended. The main efforts have been directed towards reinforcing the European Parliament's role in policymaking and avoiding the 'second-order effects' of European elections, both initiatives seeking to gradually develop an EU-genuine representative policymaking structure (see Føllesdal & Hix, 2006). From this view, it is precisely the lack of strength of the EU's 'chain of representation'[1] that keeps citizens away from institutions and constitutes the biggest threat to the legitimacy of the European governance system. According to this view, Euro-parties should be able to engage in full electoral competition (Mair, 2006; Mény, 2003).

So as to complement (and balance) the reformist strategy applied to the participatory branch of the EU by the European Commission, abundant proposals were framed to strengthen the parliamentarian functioning of the EU. The adoption of the Lisbon Treaty confirms the significant steps that have been taken in that regard (see Reh, 2009, for a comprehensive review), thus validating Føllesdal and Hix's (2006, p. 536) argument that "successive reforms of the EU treaties since the mid-1980s have dramatically increased the powers of the European Parliament". One of the major modifications established in the treaty was the reform of the co-decision procedure into the

Ordinary Legislative Procedure (OLP). The update of the main EU policy-making structure took up the baton of the Maastricht reforms and strengthened the role of the Parliament by extending co-decision from 45 to 85 areas in which the Council votes by qualified majority. The Parliament was also given full parity with the Council in approving all expenditures related to the budget (Emmanouilidis & Stratulat, 2010), which had been one of the strongest claims of democratic deficit scholars (see Føllesdal & Hix, 2006). The Lisbon Treaty reforms further attempted to shore up the European election process and encourage voter turnout (it had fallen from 63% in 1979 to 43.1% in 2014) by modifying the process for choosing the Commission president.[2]

The normative modifications as regards the representative conception of the European Union have been accompanied by online-based transformations that intend to modernize the locus of representative democracy (i.e. the European Parliament) and its main agents (i.e. Euro-parties). So far, electoral campaigns have been the most innovative periods as regards political parties' adoption of online-based participatory repertoires. With the appearance of Web 2.0 applications, political parties count on more and better resources for increasing public engagement and incorporating citizens' voices into internal decision-making. Other than acquiring power and control over the organization through the ballot-box, citizens are offered tools for deciding on the content, the candidates or other areas of political parties' campaigns with the emergence of Web 2.0 campaigning. This new "architecture of participation" (O'Reilly, 2005) is based on the development of interactive apps, tools and platforms that, in spite of using complex software and sophisticated designs, allow political parties and public officials to employ them at a very low cost and reach massive audiences (Jackson & Lilleker, 2009; Vergeer, Hermans, & Sams, 2013). The adoption of online-based technologies for political purposes allows complex citizen-to-party and citizen-to-citizen interactions that were not possible before the Internet's rise (see Gibson, Nixon, & Ward, 2003; Jackson & Lilleker, 2009; Larsson & Moe, 2011). The new e-campaigning tools multiply citizens' *information* channels on parties' positions and ideology, their *communication* mechanisms with the organization and the candidates, the venues for *participation* in decision-making, and the *deliberation* mechanisms on the party's substantive priorities. Campaigns are to modern democracies the crucial periods when power is distributed, decision-makers selected, policies shaped, and leaders legitimated (Swanson & Mancini, 1996). Hence, these are also the events in which citizens' endorsement is most needed.

Most of the literature dealing with e-campaigning practices still refers to cases that were developed in the United States.[3] Studies such as Karlsen (2010) argue that the 'US campaign style' incentivizes the development of political ecologies based on Web 2.0 campaigning more than the 'West European campaign style'. Although European party-centred campaigns have re-acted to online politics later, this new participatory paradigm has been adopted by European countries (Gibson, Römmele, & Williamson, 2014; Kampitaki, Tambouris, & Tarabanis, 2008; Lilleker et al., 2011) and also by the European Union.

To date, most of the new mechanisms of 'participatory representation' in the European Union are generated during electoral campaigns and impact the way citizens are informed, as well as how they interact with the Euro-parties and their candidates. Post-electoral survey data indicate that for the European elections of 2009, 20% of citizens relied upon the Internet as their main source of information (see Anduiza, Cristancho, & Cantijoch, 2012). In the election of 2014, this paradigm grew stronger, and all parties and candidates developed innovative websites for disseminating information to citizens in multiple languages, owned multiple social media accounts from which to interact with citizens, and broadcast through web-streaming most public events of the campaign.

Significantly in that electoral campaign, the European Green Party (EGP) organized an unprecedented pan-European online primary to select its lead-ing candidates José Bové and Ska Keller in the race for the Commission's presidency. Although the party did not fully reach their original expecta-tions,[4] overall 23,000 green sympathizers from all EU member states voted during a two-and-a-half-month process, thus giving shape to the first-ever online-based Europe-wide constituency.

Davesa and Shahin's (2014) evaluation of how Euro-parties used digital tools for the 2014 European Parliament election campaign digs into the na-ture of hybrid democracy in the European Union and presents other signifi-cant examples. The analysis takes into account the websites of four electoral coalitions,[5] for which it describes their main participatory features and pro-vides different scores of e-campaigning. The work concludes that Euro-parties' main platforms presented high levels of *interactivity* and *engage-ment*, the typical repertoires of the Web 2.0 paradigm. Nonetheless, the anal-ysis shows less progress as regards the repertoires that target public collabo-ration and 'co-creation' (Davesa & Shahin, 2014, p. 14).

The attempts to adjust the gap between citizens and parties during the last European elections have been multiple, and these mostly relied upon the formulation of an embryonic European digital sphere in which both the 'po-litical' and the 'public' interact, thus defining a hybrid space of both mobil-ization and communication. We refer to the innovative EU (electoral) dy-namics as a new form of 'participatory representation'.

That said, electoral participation in 2014 was 43.1%, a worse record compared to the previous appointment. Scholarly literature on the 'three-dimensional' system of party families at the EU level (i.e. national parties, political groups in the European Parliament, and the extra-parliamentary

Euro-parties) claim that this institutional structure makes it very difficult to represent with a single voice the aggregation of political preferences shaped in the member states (Ladrech, 2010; Mair, 2006; Schmidt, 2013). This circumstance is reflected, for instance, in the little prominence that Euro-parties' manifestos have in national campaigns (Hertner, 2011). In spite of the fact that on the doorstep of the 2009 elections Euro-parties were given the right to campaign, electoral competition was not fully focused on European policy concerns but mainly on the internal struggles of member states (Hix & Marsh 2011). The constraints imposed by the current structure of the European Union are too prominent for fully transforming the EU representative system of governance. To introduce substantive modifications on the functioning of the EU would require a reform of the Lisbon Treaty through an international convention. Yet the limitations imposed by the current primary law of the Union are not the only factor threatening the proper functioning of political representation in the EU. The transformation of political values in the sense of 'critical citizens' implies an erosion of deference towards traditional mechanisms of political expression, and that inescapably includes elections. In this context, we wonder whether it is possible to establish a full-fledged model of hybrid democracy in the EU in which the new institutional expressions of 'representative participation' and of 'participatory representation' can grow in conjunction with the postmodern expressions of citizenship.

THE RISE OF HYBRID FORMS OF DEMOCRACY: THE EXAMPLE OF THE TTIP

The Internet's revolutionary impact on worldwide information structures has reached political communication and brought to conventional institutions (like the above-mentioned European Commission and European Parliament) the opportunity of enhancing the democratic quality of policymaking. Yet, as argued in the previous sections, we shall not refer to one single strategy of the European Union for countering the end of the 'permissive consensus'. Instead, two different institutionally dependent paths have been identified: first, an enhanced model of participatory governance in the shape of 'representative participation'; and second, a highly interactive type of party politics in the fashion of 'participatory representation'. The normative redefinition of both legitimacy principles (representation and participation) made them both salient in EU politics but scarcely interactive with each other, a fact that raises manifold questions on how this would change if Internet democracy was further developed in the European Union. The interaction and spillover effects among different new mechanisms of governance have the potential to transform citizen's relation with democracy into a more diverse, active and ultimately hybrid experience (cf. Cantijoch, Cutts, & Gibson, 2015). Present-day 'engaged', 'critical' or 'e-citizens' are relying on e-participation for, among other activities, petitioning to political institutions at all levels of administration (see Wright, 2015, for an extended work on e-petitions); joining policymakers online via deliberative polling (see Price, 2012); discussing the content of policies through public networks and blogging (see González-Bailón, Kaltenbrunner, & Banchs, 2010); and interacting with political and social groups through social media (Christensen, 2011).

Scholars such as Eriksen (2005) and Wright (2007) underline the potential of the Internet to facilitate transnational political discussion and mobilization. Similarly, Risse and Van de Steeg (2003, p. 21) argue that "there is increasing evidence for an emerging community of communication whereby European themes are discussed as issues that concern 'us by virtue of our common Europeanness'". The potential of an online-based European sphere of citizenship to influence the functioning of EU politics is clearly brought to the fore when analyzing some of the most vivid political debates in the current agenda of the European Union. That is the case of the Transatlantic Trade and Investment Partnership (TTIP) negotiations between the European Commission and the US government.

While the Commission's new paradigm of *representative participation* and the campaign-based *participatory representation* model of the Parliament had only incipiently blended into a single space where citizens could voice their concerns upon this trade policy arrangement, plentiful e-petitions and online mobilization campaigns have been arranged through non-institutional platforms such as Avaaz.org and Change.org. Table 9.1 presents a summary of the most successful initiatives, which add up to around 5 million European citizens. These online campaign websites have changed the way citizens engage with political processes. Avaaz.org is particular amongst the crop of new engagement initiatives in that it aims to build a platform that will allow people to participate in a range of different issues. On their website they claim that "Avaaz.org has a single, global team with a mandate to work on any issue of public concern", and in this way they differentiate themselves from most online campaigns, which are driven by issue-specific civil society groups. Similar to the United States' MoveOn.org (see Chadwick, 2007), Avaaz.org claims a certain degree of representation on behalf of its 42,960,804 members.[6]

The fact that the most successful petition to date has been organized by a coalition of advocacy groups and organizations across the EU (the association Stop TTIP) helps explain the multiple sides of hybridity that have been referred to throughout this chapter. This movement started as a European Citizens' Initiative (ECI) that was refused registration by the Commission when initially launched on September 12, 2014. Instead of accepting the institutional system's verdict, the organizers brought the initiative to a new

Platform	Promoter (user)	Title of the petition	Amount of signatures
Self-organised European Citizens' Initiative	Stop TTIP	European Initiative against TTIP and CETA	3.284.289
Campact.de	Stoppt TTIP	TTIP: Does not sell our future!	846.416
Change.org	Cynical Optimist	Do Not Sign Up to TTIP	11.290
Change.org	Europe of Freedom and Democracy	Stop TTIP	1.252
Change.org	War on Want	Help stop TTIPS	23.666
Change.org	INTERBEV	TTIP : Contre les viandes américaines	24.969
Change.org	Vote Leave	TTIP is a grubby EU deal	3.168
SumOfUs	Stop TTIP	Stop TTIP now!	171.552
SumOfUs	Stop the TPP and TTIP	Stop negotiating in secret and release the TPP/TTIP	120.339
Avaaz.org	Eloy H. R.	European Union: Stop TAFTA / TTIP Negotiations	3.625
Avaaz.org	Joe M.	Stop the EU-US free trade agreement	7.353
Avaaz.org	/	Schlimmer als TTIP!	345.044
Avaaz.org	Sven O.	Eu Parliament: Stop TTIP	1.077
Grand Total			4.844.040

Figure 9.1.   Instances of e-Petitions Against the TTIP Negotiations *Source:* Authors' own compilation. All data were checked in January 2017. Petitions with less than 1,000 supporters have not been included.

political space, which immediately connected with the minds and preferences of postmodern critical citizens. This fact makes even more evident that institutional constrains might not be an impediment for 'emancipated' citizens that try to influence the political agenda. In fact, it may work the other way around: in the digital age, citizens find alternatives that can capture public attention outside institutions. Political legitimacy is actually being transferred to places other than what we understand as traditional fora for 'politics'.

This new way of thinking about engagement is based intrinsically on a linkage between representation, legitimacy and participation. By making these linkages, however, the very nature of representation is 'redesigned'; its traditional edges are being pushed and broadened. Representation becomes something more malleable, flexible, and limited according to issue and context. People can choose to be represented (by actively or passively participating) by certain civil society groups, dealing with specific issues. The actual mechanisms by which they give permission to be represented by these groups are unclear, and most transfers of legitimacy are seemingly given (or more realistically, 'claimed') through signing an online petition or sharing an action frame through social media.

With regard to that last aspect, since 2013 there has been a great proliferation of Twitter accounts, to mention just one social media outlet that is highly salient within political analysis (see Barberá, 2015), that are monitoring and articulating the political debate around the TTIP and that aggregate thousands of 'followers'. These accounts vary in their political action perspective, ranging from countercultural activism (e.g. Twitter user @attac_fr) to expert reflection (e.g. Twitter user @trade_in_action), and not only do they provide abundant information on a topic that does not easily capture the attention of traditional media, but their diffusion power allows a great diversity of ideas, mottos and action frames to be rapidly transmitted to a wide audience. Similar examples could be found on most of the different social media, blogging, petitioning and online campaigning platforms. The actions conducted through these new political means, together with the more traditional on-street activism that still plays an important mobilization role (see Casas, Davesa, & Congosto, 2016, p. 87, about the 15M movement case), are key to explaining how it only took five days for the campaign Stop TTIP to get 500,000 signatures against the international agreement, and less than two months to get 1 million signatures.[7]

While the 'creative publics' (McFarland, 2010) of today's European society master 'repertoire switching' (see Chadwick, 2007) for mobilizing people's concerns and placing them into the political agenda, traditional political actors have also found ways to accompany those initiatives and switch their behaviours in accordance with the new modes of public mobilization. This 'organizational hybridity', as Chadwick (2007) calls it, allows EU institutional actors to approach citizens outside the constrictions of the formal policymaking structures and benefit from legitimacy gains. Regarding the TTIP case, different Euro-parties and groups such as the European Greens or the European Free Alliance have endorsed the e-petitioning campaigns by adopting online[8] and offline[9] action repertoires that are characteristic of 'networked social movements' (Castells, 2015). In its turn, the strong online presence of citizen movements has pushed the Commission to strengthen its visibility online, as well as to make its communication channels more flexible in accordance with this new reality. A good example of this is the creation of a specific TTIP Commission's Twitter account

(@EU_TTIP_team), which is devoted to opening a citizen dialogue on the matter.

Authors such as Pratchett (1999) and Chadwick (2006) emphasize how new ICTs can bridge both the public and the political spheres so as to generate incentives to engage those subjects who normally express apathy or lack of interest concerning traditional political institutions. By recognizing and even joining those (virtual) spaces in which the 'disaffected democrats'—to use Norris's (2011) term—find new incentives for political mobilization, the EU could better inform its policies or re-legitimize its institutions. Using the Internet, citizens might at the same time connect with any of the formulas of non-institutional activism and engage with online tools provided by political actors. By doing that, geographical, functional or communicative barriers might be bypassed, thus reconnecting the realms of participation and representation in a more effective way than the possibilities offered within the current EU governance system.

Yet the incipient dynamics of an EU democratic hybridity are not only (re)connecting the political and the public, but also the online with the offline. Deliberative democracy is often triggered via face-to-face dialogues, debates and discussions between a certain group of people or mini-publics. To integrate it with the emergent online dynamics of representative participation and participatory representation appears as one of the main challenges for the future of EU democracy. Although the mainstreaming of these democratic hybridities into common policymaking practices is still far away, the European governance has already generated prominent cases. A good example in that sense is provided by the European Youth Event (EYE). This initiative was taken up with the advent of the European elections in 2014 with the intention to stimulate debate on EU politics among the youth. The EYE2014 gathered in Strasbourg more than 5,500 young Europeans aged between 16 and 30 coming from all around the European Union and beyond.[10] During two days and a half, participants could join more than 200 panels and workshops that featured around 500 speakers, including members of the European Parliament (MEPs). Apart from allowing offline deliberation, the EYE generated an intense virtual participation structure. The debates were web-streamed, had tweet walls and ensured alternative means of audience participation to those who were not physically present.[11] In order to keep the impetus of the event going, and considering the interest of the ideas that were debated (among them, youth's vision of the TTIP and other international trade agreements[12]), the European Parliament decided that the conclusions should be presented before the Parliament standing committees in what was called the 'EYE Hearings'. Although the EYE was initially framed within the electoral context of 2014, the success of this new hybrid experience of deliberative policymaking compelled the European Parliament to establish that it would take place every two years, and thus a second and third edition were organized in 2016 and 2018 respectively, and a fourth one is expected for 2020.

CONCLUSIONS

As we see above, expert and scholar perceptions on the dynamics of representation in the EU tend to conflate participation and representation into one plot that centres on the legitimacy of the EU's institutions. Representation as a key political concept in the EU's polity is being challenged by the 'participatory turn' driven particularly by the European Commission and by the growth of social movements outside of the formalized institutional structures of the EU. Several EU-wide political groups in the European Parliament have attempted to follow the participatory momentum by renovating their electoral campaigns, therefore embracing a new Web 2.0 format of participation under the umbrella of their roles as representatives of EU citizens.

Yet in between elections' context, these same political parties are trying to catch citizens' attention and support by transcending the traditional policy-making venues and emulating social actors' more flexible and creative action repertoires. This has been the case of the opposition movement against the TTIP negotiations between the Commission and the US government.

The most recent EU governance reforms in the shape of 'representative participation' and 'participatory representation' generate limited interaction, thus not being able to provide adequate answers to the question of how the EU can seek greater legitimacy amongst post-industrial citizenry. Nevertheless, new mobilization synergies are taking place in an emergent European public sphere between different kinds of actors—political and non-political; environments—online and offline; and logics—participation and representation. Such alternative models of the functioning of democracy in the EU have been adopted in a rather tentative or informal fashion. While trying to incorporate the European public sphere's hybridity into the formal policymaking structure, they are still developed in an exploratory fashion. This makes these initiatives very much dependent on the policy context in which they take place. The question remains whether the EU will keep up the momentum and transform the boundaries of the concept of representation to make it more inclusive, more dynamic, and in consonance with the technological revolutions that challenge the political stability of the 21st-century EU.

NOTES

1. Chapter 4 in this volume also addresses how the long chains of representation that inform EU policymaking impact the overall legitimacy of the Union. However, while we address the debate on EU governance and legitimacy from an internal policy perspective, in

Chapter 4 Sebastian Oberthür focuses on the large distance between those representing the EU externally and those to be represented, the European people.

2. In the new Article 17, the treaty stipulates that the European Council shall nominate a candidate by qualified majority instead of by consensus, and more importantly, do it while "taking into account the elections to the European Parliament". As the wording of Article 17 is vague in addressing the power of the Parliament to put forth its own candidate, the EP was quick to seize upon the treaty change and the ability to involve the political parties in the mix. In a resolution passed on November 22, 2012, the European Parliament urged the European political parties to nominate candidates for president of the Commission. The idea behind the resolution was to raise the stakes of the vote, personalize the electoral campaigns, enhance their European dimension, attract more voters, and create a clearer democratic mandate for the European Commission (see Hobolt, 2014).

3. One of the first examples of a thorough Internet-oriented campaign was Howard Dean's race for the Democratic presidential nomination in 2003/04, which opened up the floor to citizens' online-based deliberation and participation in a rather unprecedented way (see Chadwick 2006, 2007). Also, Barack Obama's use of ICTs in the 2008 presidential election fueled online-based campaign processes and reached significant levels of interaction, collaboration and participation (see Greengard, 2009).

4. Results of the online primary were reported to Europe Decides by European Green Party campaign manager Johannes Hillje in an article of February 5, 2014, retrieved from https:// web.archive.org/web/20140702080740/http://europedecides.eu/2014/02/green-primary-pioneering-work-is-hard-but-worth-it .

5. European People's Party (EPP), Party of European Socialists (PES), Alliance of Liberals and Democrats for Europe Party (ALDE), and European Green Party (EGP).

6. Number checked at 3:21 p.m. on September 3, 2016.

7. On October 12, 2014, a tweet from the official account of the movement @eci_ttip read, "500.000 signatures in only 5 days!!! That's what the #Commission was afraid of . . . Please RT. #TTIP #CETA #ECI #O11Doa". A similar tweet celebrated reaching 1 million signatures on December 4, 2014.

8. See the Greens/EFA YouTube video on the TTIP campaign: https://www.youtube.com/watch?v=S7G3s2B-Hw8.

9. See the blog post "How low can you go? Greens rally outside the European Parliament against TTIP's 'race to the bottom'." Retrieved January 21, 2019, from http://ttip2016.eu/blog/Green%20rally%20summit.html

10. Among the participants, 92 came from candidate countries and 153 from non-EU countries. Source: see points (g) and (h) of the European Parliament's decision on discharge in respect of the implementation of the general budget of the EU for the financial year 2013, Section I—EP. Retrieved July 18, 2017, from http://www.europarl.europa.eu/sides/get-Doc.do?pubRef=-%2f%2fEP%2f%2fTEXT%2bTA%2bP8-TA-2015-0121%2b0%2bDOC%2bXML%2bV0%2f%2fEN&language=EN.

11. See page 9 of the EYE2014 Report "Ideas for a Better Europe", European Parliament Strasbourg, May 9–11, 2014. Report elaborated by the European Youth Press with commentaries by the European Youth Forum, June 2014. Available at the web portal of the EP: www.europarl.europa.eu/resources/library/media/20141010RES73702/20141010RES73702.pdf.

12. See Section IV of the EYE2014 Report (ibid.) on "Sustainability".

REFERENCES

Anduiza, E., Cristancho, C., & Cantijoch, M. (2012). La exposición a información política a través de internet. *Arbor , 188*(756), 673–88.

Barberá, P. (2015). Birds of the same feather tweet together: Bayesian ideal point estimation using Twitter data. *Political Analysis , 23*(1), 76–91.

Bartolini, S. (2005). *Restructuring Europe: Centre formation, system building, and political structuring between the nation state and the European Union.* Oxford: Oxford University Press.

Beck, U., Giddens, A., & Lash, S. (1994). *Reflexive modernization: Politics, tradition and aesthetics in the modern social order.* Stanford, CA: Stanford University Press.

Bennett, W. L., & Segerberg, A. (2012). The logic of connective action. *Information, Communication & Society, 15*(5), 739–68.

Blondel, J., Sinnott, R., & Svensson, P. (1998). *People and Parliament in the European Union: Participation, democracy, and legitimacy.* Oxford: Clarendon Press.

Cantijoch, M., Cutts, D., & Gibson, R. (2015). Moving slowly up the ladder of political engagement: A 'spill-over' model of Internet participation. *British Journal of Politics & International Relations, 18*(1), 26–48.

Carrubba, C., & Timpone, R. J. (2005). Explaining vote switching across first- and second-order elections. *Comparative Political Studies , 38*(3), 260–81.

Casas, A., Davesa, F., & Congosto, M. (2016). Media coverage of a 'connective' action: The Interaction between the 15-M movement and the mass media. *Revista Espanola de Investigaciones Sociologicas , 155*, 73–96.

Castells, M. (2015). *Networks of outrage and hope: Social movements in the Internet age* (2nd ed.). Cambridge: Polity Press.

Chadwick, A. (2006). *Internet politics: States, citizens, and new communication technologies.* New York: Oxford University Press.

Chadwick, A. (2007). Digital network repertoires and organizational hybridity. *Political Communication, 24*(3), 283–301.

Christensen, H. S. (2011). Political activities on the Internet: Slacktivism or political participation by other means? *First Monday, 16*(2).

Dalton, R. J. (2004). *Democratic challenges, democratic choices: The erosion of political support in advanced industrial democracies.* New York: Oxford University Press.

Davesa, F. (2018). *The EU's youth policy field: A new participatory governance?* (Doctoral dissertation, Vrije Universiteit Brussel).

Davesa, F., & Shahin, J. (2014). *Evaluating Europarties' use of digital tools for the 2014 EP election campaign.* Paper presented at the EDGE/SNES Conference on Elections and Democracy in Europe, Brussels.

Dryzek, J. S. (2000). *Deliberative democracy and beyond: Liberals, critics, contestations.* Oxford: Oxford University Press.

Eder, K., & Trenz, H.-J. (2003). The making of a European public space: The case of justice and home affairs. In B. Kohler-Koch (Ed.), *Linking EU and national governance* (pp. 111–35). Oxford: Oxford University Press.

Elster, J. (Ed.). (1998). *Deliberative democracy.* Cambridge: Cambridge University Press.

Emmanouilidis, J. A., & Stratulat, C. (2010). *Implementing Lisbon: Narrowing the EU's democratic deficit.* Brussels: EPC Policy Brief.

Eriksen, E. O. (2005). An emerging European public sphere. *European Journal of Social Theory, 8*(3), 341–63.

European Commission. (2000). *Reforming the Commission: A white paper—Part II action plan.* COM(2000) 200 final. Volume II. 01.3.2000. Brussels.

European Commission. (2001). *European governance: A white paper.* COM(2001) 428 final. 25.7.2001. Brussels.

European Commission. (2002). *Communication from the Commission: Towards a reinforced culture of consultation and dialogue—General principles and minimum standards for consultation of interested parties by the Commission.* COM(2002) 704 final. 11.12.2002. Brussels.

Floridia, A. (2013, September). *Participatory democracy versus deliberative democracy: Elements for a possible theoretical genealogy. Two histories, some intersections.* Paper presented at the ECPR General Conference, Bordeaux.

Føllesdal, A., & Hix, S. (2006). Why there is a democratic deficit in the EU: A response to Majone and Moravcsik. *JCMS: Journal of Common Market Studies, 44*(3), 533–62.

García, O. (2012). Transnational deliberative democracy in the context of the European Union: The institutionalisation of the European Integration Forum. *European Integration online Papers (EIoP), 16*, 1–22.

Gibson, R., Nixon, P. & Ward, S. (2003). *Political parties and the Internet: Net gain?* New York: Routledge.

Gibson, R., Römmele, A., & Williamson, A. (2014). Chasing the digital wave: International perspectives on the growth of online campaigning. *Journal of Information Technology & Politics, 11*(2), 123–29.

Giddens, A. (1991). *Modernity and self-identity: Self and society in the late modern age.* Stanford, CA: Stanford University Press.

Gonzalez-Bailon, S., Kaltenbrunner, A., & Banchs, R. E. (2010). The structure of political discussion networks: A model for the analysis of online deliberation. *Journal of Information Technology, 25*(2), 1–14.

Greengard, S. (2009). The first Internet president. *Communications of the ACM, 52*(2), 16–18.

Greenwood, J. (2007). Organized civil society and democratic legitimacy in the European Union. *British Journal of Political Science, 37*(2), 333–57.

Hertner, I. (2011). Are European election campaigns Europeanised? The case of the party of European socialists in 2009. *Government and Opposition, 46*(3), 321–44.

Hix, S., & Marsh, M. (2007). Punishment or protest? Understanding European Parliament elections. *Journal of Politics, 69*(2), 495–510.

Hix, S., & Marsh, M. (2011). Second-order effects plus pan-European political swings: An analysis of European Parliament elections across time. *Electoral Studies, 30*, 4–15.

Hobolt, S. B. (2014). A vote for the president? The role of Spitzenkandidaten in the 2014 European Parliament elections. *Journal of European Public Policy, 21*(10), 1528–40.

Hooghe, L., & Marks, G. (2008). A postfunctionalist theory of European integration: From permissive consensus to constraining dissensus. *British Journal of Political Science, 39*(1), 1–23.

Höreth, M. (1999). No way out for the beast? The unsolved legitimacy problem of European governance. *Journal of European Public Policy, 6*(2), 249–68.

Inglehart, R., & Welzel, C. (2005). *Modernization, cultural change and democracy.* New York: Cambridge University Press.

Jackson, N. A., & Lilleker, D. G. (2009). Building an architecture of participation? Political parties and Web 2.0 in Britain. *Journal of Information Technology and Politics, 6*(3–4), 232–50.

Kampitaki, D., Tambouris, E., & Tarabanis, K. (2008). eElectioneering: Current research trends. In M. A. Wimmer, H. J. Scholl, & E. Ferro (Eds.), *EGOV 2008.* LNCS, vol. 5184. Heidelberg: Springer.

Karlsen, R. (2010). Does new media technology drive election campaign change? *Information Polity, 15*(3), 215–25.

Key, V. O. (1961). Public opinion and American democracy. New York: Knopf.

Kohler-Koch, B. (2010). Civil society and EU democracy: 'Astroturf' representation? *Journal of European Public Policy, 17*(1), 100–116.

Kohler-Koch, B., & Finke, B. (2007). The institutional shaping of EU–society relations: A contribution to democracy via participation? *Journal of Civil Society, 3*(3), 205–21.

Kohler-Koch, B., & Quittkat, C. (2013). *De-mystification of participatory democracy: EU-governance and civil society.* New York: Oxford University Press.

Ladrech, R. (2010). *Europeanization and political parties.* Basingstoke: Palgrave Macmillan.

Larsson, A. O., & Moe, H. (2011). Who tweets? Tracking microblogging use in the 2010 Swedish election campaign. *ECIS 2011 Proceedings.* Paper 251.

Lawson, Kay (Ed.). (1980). *Political parties and linkage: A comparative perspective.* New Haven, CT: Yale University Press.

Lilleker, D. G., Koc-Michalska, K., Schweitzer, J., Jacunski, M., Jackson, N., & Vedel, T. (2011). Informing, engaging, mobilizing or interacting: Searching for a European model of web campaigning. *European Journal of Communication, 26*: 195–213

Lindgren, K.-O., & Persson, T. (2011). *Participatory governance in the EU: Enhancing or endangering democracy and efficiency?* New York: Palgrave Macmillan.

Lombardo, E. (2007). The participation of civil society. In D. Castiglione, J. Schönlau, C. Longman, E. Lombardo, N. Pérez-Solórzano, & M. Aziz (Eds.), *Constitutional politics in the European Union: The convention moment and its aftermath* (pp. 153–69). New York: Palgrave Macmillan.

Mair, P. (2006). Political parties and party systems. In P. Graziano & M. P. Vink (Eds.), *Europeanization: New Research Agendas* (pp. 154–66). Basingstoke: Palgrave Macmillan.

Mair, P., & Van Biezen, I. (2001). Party membership in twenty European democracies, 1980–2000. *Party Politics , 7*(1), 5–21.

Margolis, M., & Resnick, D. (2000). *Politics as usual: The cyberspace 'revolution'.* London: Sage.

McFarland, A. S. (2010). Why creative participation today? In M. Micheletti & A. S. McFarland (Eds.), *Creative participation: Responsibility-taking in the political world* (pp. 15–33). Boulder, CO: Paradigm Publishers.

Mény, Y. (2003). De la démocratie en Europe: Old concepts and new challenges. *Journal of Common Market Studies, 41,* 1–13.

Müller, W. C. (2000). Political parties in parliamentary democracies: Making delegation and accountability work. *European Journal of Political Research, 37*(3), 309–33.

Norris, P. (Ed.). (1999). *Critical citizens: Global support for democratic government.* Oxford: Oxford University Press.

Norris, P. (2011). *Democratic deficit: Critical citizens revisited.* New York: Cambridge University Press.

O'Reilly, T. (2005). What is Web 2.0: Design patterns and business models for the next generation of software. Retrieved from http://oreilly.com/web2/archive/what-is-web-20.html.

Parkinson, J., & Mansbridge, J. (Eds.). (2012). *Deliberative systems: Deliberative democracy at the large scale.* Cambridge: Cambridge University Press.

Pratchett, L. (1999). New fashions in public participation: Towards greater democracy? *Parliamentary Affairs, 52*(4): 616–33.

Price, V. (2012). Playing politics: The experience of e-participation. In S. Coleman & P. M. Shane (Eds.), *Connecting democracy: Online consultation and the flow of political communication* (pp. 125–48). Cambridge, MA: MIT Press.

Putnam, R. (2000). *Bowling alone: The collapse and revival of American community.* New York: Simon & Schuster.

Quittkat, C. (2013). New instruments serving democracy: Do online consultations benefit civil society? In B. Kohler-Koch & C. Quittkat (Eds.), *De-mystification of participatory democracy: EU governance and civil society* (pp. 85–113). Oxford: Oxford University Press.

Quittkat, C., & Kotzian, P. (2011). Lobbying via consultation—Territorial and functional interests in the Commission's consultation regime. *Journal of European Integration , 33*(4), 401–18.

Reh, C. (2009). The Lisbon Treaty: De-constitutionalizing the European Union? *JCMS: Journal of Common Market Studies, 47*(3), 625–50.

Risse, T., & Van de Steeg, M. (2003). *An emerging European public sphere? Empirical evidence and theoretical clarifications.* Paper presented to the Conference on the Europeanisation of Public Spheres, Political Mobilisation, Public Communication and the European Union, Science Center Berlin.

Sabel, C. F., & Zeitlin, J. (Eds.). (2010). *Experimentalist governance in the European Union: Towards a new architecture.* Oxford: Oxford University Press.

Sartori, G. (1976). *Parties and party systems: A framework for analysis.* London: Cambridge University Press.

Saurugger, S. (2008). Interest groups and democracy in the European Union. *West European Politics, 31*(6), 1274–91.

Scharpf, F. W. (1997). *Games real actors play: Actor-centered institutionalism in policy research.* Boulder, CO: Westview Press.

Scharpf, F. W. (1999). *Governing in Europe: Effective and democratic?* Oxford: Oxford University Press.

Schmidt, V. A. (2013). Democracy and legitimacy in the European Union revisited: Input, output and 'throughput'. *Political Studies , 61*, 2–22.

Skocpol, T. (2003). *Diminished democracy: From membership to management in American civic life*. Norman: University of Oklahoma Press.

Swanson, D. L., & Mancini, P. (Eds.). (1996). *Politics, media, and modern democracy: An international study of innovations in electoral campaigning and their consequences*. Westport, CT: Greenwood Press.

Thorson, K. (2015). Sampling from the civic buffet: Youth, new media, and do-it-yourself citizenship. In H. Gil de Zúñiga (Ed.), *New technologies and civic engagement: New agendas in communication* (pp. 3–23). New York: Routledge.

Vergeer, M., Hermans, L., & Sams, S. (2013). Online social networks and micro-blogging in political campaigning: The exploration of a new campaign tool and a new campaign style. *Party Politics, 19*(3), 477–501.

Wiklund, H. (2005). A Habermasian analysis of the deliberative democratic potential of ICT-enabled services in Swedish municipalities. *New Media & Society, 7*(2), 247–70.

Wright, S. (2007). A virtual European public sphere? The Futurum discussion forum. *Journal of European Public Policy, 14*(8), 1167–85.

Wright, S. (2015). E-petitions. In S. Coleman & D. Freelon (Eds.), *Handbook of digital politics* (pp. 136–51). Northampton, MA: Edward Elgar Publishing.

Chapter Ten

Conclusions

Mihnea Tănăsescu and Claire Dupont

This volume examined the conceptual and practical stretching of political representation. Whereas democratic rule has a millennial history, *representative* democracy can still be seen as a relatively young phenomenon, and one undergoing a current crisis, mainly of the representative part. In this sense, the concept of representation has seen unprecedented challenges and renewals, both theoretically and practically. By collecting contributions specifically designed to tease out the edges of political representation, we hoped to achieve a novel diagnosis of the problems of representation and to sketch out avenues for its future in theory and in practice. The subject matter therefore makes it impossible to provide a single, overarching conclusion. Instead, we draw out common lessons and particularly poignant insights that can take the scholarship and practice of political representation further.

What becomes clear from the chapters in this volume is that there are several lines of inquiry that are open for further development. As such, the chapters contribute to wider debates and discussions and outline interconnections among several issues. In these concluding remarks, we highlight five themes for future theorizing and research on political representation:

1. the exclusionary practices inherent in the concept of political representation;
2. the interconnections among representation, participation and deliberation;
3. social heterogeneity and political representation;
4. connections between theory and practice of political representation; and
5. links between the challenges of political representation and democratic governance.

First, several contributions to this volume remind us, implicitly, that an ahistorical treatment of political representation can only be a partial treatment. Situating representation within its political history allows one to more accurately identify structural, as opposed to merely contingent, elements of the concept. For example, representation is in some form or another fundamentally tied to the practice of elections. This is interesting to reiterate today, when scholarship has (rightly) developed the concept beyond its electoral forms. What the structural connection to elections tells us, even when no actual elections are present, is that representatives are always necessarily members of an elite that is chosen, at a minimum, for its capacity to stand out. Whereas in elections those elected are evidently those that convince that they are best placed to run for office and win, in non-electoral forms of representation a similar elite-formation process is in place.

This insight—that processes of selection, electoral or not, always give rise to anointed groups of representatives—can also be expressed by analyzing the ways in which representation is about exclusion. Inasmuch as representatives are necessarily a group apart, it stands to reason that the representative process must in every case exclude some. Furthermore, what representatives do is limited in their ability to accurately represent all that might fall under their constituency. This also means that there is a structural tension between the exclusionary tendencies of representation and democratic ideals of equal weight for those affected by political decisions. For example, Karen Celis shows in Chapter 3 how this tension has played out in the history of women's political inclusion, and how it is far from resolved in today's representative landscape.

In fact, it might be unresolvable. Several contributions suggest that exclusion is ingrained in the concept of representation and therefore can be considered an enduring edge, a hard border that, however much is chipped, retains enough thickness to be efficient. The democratic struggle for reinventing forms of representation can be read as a struggle against this hard edge of exclusion. Sebastian Oberthür shows in Chapter 4 how the long chains and various modes of supranational representation leave many unaccounted for, while Ferran Davesa and Jamal Shahin document in Chapter 9 the ways in which supranational institutions are trying to ameliorate the problem of partial representation (through participation and hybridization).

At stake in the struggle for representative inclusion are also the related concepts of legitimacy and accountability. In the supranational cases discussed in this volume, it is plain to see how the drive to reinvent the practice of representation is directly related to securing the legitimacy necessary for governing, particularly in the absence of direct mechanisms of accountability. Even when the classic accountability mechanism of recurrent elections is firmly in place, it no longer seems sufficient for securing legitimacy. Kris Deschouwer shows in Chapter 2, for example, that one of the more secure trends of the last decades is the electoral punishment of governing parties, irrespective of their performance.

We can therefore think of the stretching of the concept of representation as a struggle for more inclusion, both on the scholarly and practical levels. This recalls Plotke's now-famous formulation, "the opposite of representation is not participation: the opposite of representation is exclusion" (1997, pp. 26–27). The extent to which full inclusion is possible rightly remains a question for ongoing debate and is central to the exploration of the edges of representation. While Schweber (2016) argues in favour of maintaining limits in the content of representation, the contributions in this volume have highlighted that both practice and theory question the limits and edges of representation. The contribution of these chapters is in arguing that even when we no longer conceive of representation and participatory democracy as opposites, we are still left with a representative process that is intimately tied to exclusionary practices. It seems, then, that the reinvention of the concept of representation can most productively be seen as being concerned with securing more accountability and legitimacy in the representative process, via the increasing inclusion of those concerned. The crisis of representation need not be understood as a mortal threat, but it can also be read as a measure of vitality and reinvention in the face of empirical transformations.

Second, and in this vein, several contributions show the ways in which traditionally separated categories—representation, participation, deliberation—can also hybridize and form new conceptual terrain. Davesa and Shahin exemplify this hybridization in the case of supranational representation, where the new media of communication is inspiring a coming together of representation and participation, sidestepping the usual venues of representation in national politics. Similarly, albeit on a more theoretical level, Mihnea Tănăsescu reflects in Chapter 5 on how the representative process could incorporate the figure of the person (as primarily a moral category), more traditionally associated with participatory democracy (where each person represents themselves). These interventions of one theoretical tradition into another reveal important articulations of the concept of representation.

Third, contributors to this volume have tied the above insights to an historical trend for the increasing recognition of social heterogeneity. From the first to the last chapters, there is a common thread running through the volume claiming that the heterogeneity of the social body is partly behind the crisis of representation. We think the most productive way to read this is also in terms of exclusion/inclusion. It is not that heterogeneity is a recent invention, but rather that it has only recently come to play an important political role, therefore highlighting more than in any other historical time the exclusionary practices at the heart of representation. Even if everyone had an equal right and opportunity to vote, the heterogeneity of the social body would still be difficult to reproduce in representative bodies.

The importance of heterogeneity for challenging representative processes is one important lesson of this volume. Inasmuch as the social body was artificially restricted to select groups, representative processes had a relatively easy time of incorporating 'everyone' (as Deschouwer explains in Chapter 2). However, once everyone is literally counted in the representative process (at least in theory), then the issue of how extreme heterogeneity can be accurately represented becomes pressing. If there are no formal limits to who can count in the representative process, then it is to be expected that the process itself would need to undergo major revisions.

The precise meaning of *heterogeneity*, as well as its relation to the other common threads explored in this volume, is far from certain and still very much open to debate. The theoretical reach of the concept of heterogeneity is exemplified in Chapters 5 to 7 by Tănăsescu, Eline Severs, and Claire Dupont. These chapters all focus on the significance of heterogeneity for the representative process, from different angles. Dupont extends the concept of heterogeneity itself to incorporate future generations, thus revealing a challenging problem for an inclusionary ideal of representation that situates itself within the realities of present and future ecological crises. Severs argues that, despite tendencies towards exclusion, representation should remain about groups. Reading this chapter together with Dupont's raises the question of the significance of future generations in the definition of groups, something that needs further research. Tănăsescu argues that we should simply consider the basic unit of representation to be the person, though this would not be a guarantee that all are equally represented. Read together with Dupont and Severs, the argument for considering the person as the legitimate unit of representation challenges both the level of heterogeneity (extending it to individuals themselves) and its potential impact for inclusive representation. These arguments, in productive tension with each other, take the issue of heterogeneity seriously and define an important research agenda for future studies.

Fourth, the theoretical developments this volume presents, being as they are on the edges of the concept of representation, are not easily translated into practice. However, there are innovative ways of doing representation that might be getting closer to the theoretical imperatives explored here. The concluding, collaborative empirical chapters (8 and 9), display some of the array of innovation in representation practice. Though far from ideal, hybrid and symbolic forms of representation are at least trying to make up for some of the deficits identified in this volume. This uneasy alliance of theory and practice also opens up productive research avenues for scholars and practitioners.

Fifth, though we have only focused on the concept of representation, we are acutely aware of the interrelations between representation and democracy. The fate of representation is surely one of the most important determinants of the fate of democracy today. To this end, more needs to be understood on the link between the challenges of representation and democratic governance. Given the heterogeneity of both the social fabric and of individuals themselves, and given the interrelations between people in an increasingly small, and therefore common, world, how can we think of democratic practice in line with the imperatives for inclusionary representation? The arguments spearheaded by Plotke (1997) and Urbinati (2006), fundamentally tying representation and democracy together, along with the constructivist turn in representation theory (Disch, 2011, 2015; Saward, 2006; Urbinati & Warren, 2008), opened up the challenge of how representation can better conform to democratic norms. Are there ways to fundamentally transform representation in the interest of a more perfect democracy, and what do we risk losing in the process? These are crucial questions that no single contribution will be able to tackle. With this volume, we aim to provide many of the ingredients that are important for a fruitful continuation of the debate on the meaning and fate of political representation today.

REFERENCES

Disch, L. (2011). Toward a mobilization conception of democratic representation. *American Political Science Review*, *105*(1), 100–114.

Disch, L. (2015). The "constructivist turn" in democratic representation: A normative dead-end? *Constellations*, *22*(4), 487–99.

Plotke, D. (1997). Representation is democracy. *Constellations*, *4*(1), 19–34.

Saward, M. (2006). The representative claim. *Contemporary Political Theory*, *5*(3), 297–318.

Schweber, H. (2016). The limits of political representation. *American Political Science Review*, *110*(2), 382–96.

Urbinati, N. (2006). *Representative democracy: Principles and genealogy*. Chicago: University of Chicago Press.

Urbinati, N., & Warren, M. E. (2008). The concept of representation in contemporary democratic theory. *Annual Review of Political Science, 11*, 387–412.

Index

About the Contributors

Ilke Adam is research professor at the Institute for European Studies (IES) of the Vrije Universiteit Brussel (main affiliation) and a part-time lecturer at the Université Libre de Bruxelles. She coordinates the Migration, Diversity and Justice research cluster at IES. Her research interests include immigration and immigrant integration policies, multiculturalism, citizenship, discrimination, sub-state nationalism and comparative public policy.

Soumia Akachar received her PhD in political sciences from Vrije Universiteit Brussel (VUB). Her research focused on the political representation of Muslim youth in Flanders and their feelings of (not) being politically represented. This research was facilitated by the research programme Evaluating Democratic Governance in Europe. She is also a member of RHEA, the VUB Centre of Expertise Gender, Diversity and Intersectionality. Prior to that, Soumia obtained a master's in sociology and political sciences from the University of Amsterdam. Soumia is currently affiliated with the Sociology Department at the Free University of Amsterdam.

Karen Celis is research professor at the Department of Political Science, and co-director of Research of RHEA (Centre of Expertise Gender, Diversity and Intersectionality) of the Vrije Universiteit Brussel. She conducts theoretical and empirical research on political representation of groups, equality policies and state feminism. In her more recent work she investigates the political representation of groups from an explicit intersectional perspective. She is co-editor of *The Oxford Handbook on Gender and Politics* (2013), *Gender, Conservatism and Representation* (2015), the book series Gender and Comparative Politics, and founding editor of the *European Journal on Politics and Gender*.

Serena D'Agostino is a postdoctoral researcher at the Institute for European Studies (IES) and the Department of Political Science of the Vrije Universiteit Brussel (VUB). She coordinates the joint research programme Evaluating Democratic Governance in Europe (EDGE), together with Ferran Davesa, and is a member of the IES research cluster on Migration, Diversity and Justice. Serena is also a member of the VUB RHEA Centre of Expertise on Gender, Diversity & Intersectionality and an associate member of the European Academic Network on Romani Studies. She has worked in the International Development Co-operation sector in the Western Balkans and coordinated humanitarian aid interventions in Eastern Africa. Her research interests include Central Eastern Europe, Europeanization, intersectional mobilization, (political) intersectionality, migration and minorities, Roma activism, Roma women, and social movements.

Ferran Davesa is a postdoctoral researcher at the Institute for European Studies (IES) at the Vrije Universiteit Brussel (VUB). He coordinates the joint research programme Evaluating Democratic Governance in Europe (EDGE), together with Serena D'Agostino. He is part of the research project All Youth Want to Rule Their World (ALL-YOUTH), funded by the Strategic Research Council at the Academy of Finland (decision no. 312689). From 2008 to 2013, Davesa was a researcher of the Comparative Agendas Project (CAP) at the Institut Barcelona d'Estudis Internacionals (IBEI) and at the University of Barcelona (UB). His research interests include political participation, social movements, interest groups and youth policy, with special focus on the impact of new technologies and new media.

Kris Deschouwer is research professor in the Department of Political Science of the Vrije Universiteit Brussel. He has worked on political parties, elections, political representation, regionalism and federalism and consociational democracy. His latest book is *Mind the Gap: Political Participation and Representation in Belgium*. From 2018 to 2021 he has been the chair of the ECPR.

Claire Dupont is assistant professor of European and International Governance at the Department of Public Governance and Management at Ghent University and associate research fellow at the Institute for European Studies, Vrije Universiteit Brussel (VUB). Her research interests include EU climate and energy policies, governance of the transition to sustainability, and democratic systems' responses to long-term, complex societal problems.

Sebastian Oberthür is professor for environment and sustainable development at the Institute for European Studies (IES) at the Vrije Universiteit

Brussel (VUB). Trained as a political scientist with a strong background in international law, he is an internationally renowned expert on international and European environmental and climate governance.

Eline Severs is assistant professor in political science at the Vrije Universiteit Brussel (VUB). Her research interests fall within the field of democratic theory. She is especially interested in democratic representation, the relationships between civil society and democratic governance, representation fairness, and citizens' understandings of (representative) democracy. She has published various articles and book chapters on these topics. She recently edited, together with Suzanne Dovi (University of Arizona), a symposium on 'The Good Representative 2.0' in *PS: Political Science and Politics* (2018).

Jamal Shahin is a part-time research professor at the Institute for European Studies (Vrije Universiteit Brussel) and part-time senior lecturer at the University of Amsterdam. He holds a PhD in politics from the University of Hull (2004). In Amsterdam, he lectures on the BA and MA programmes in European studies. His courses concern the governance of the contemporary EU and the importance of linking theory and practice to inform better research and policy. His research interests focus on global Internet governance, political participation in the European Union, EU governance, and the impact of the Internet on policymaking. Jamal is keen to explore how new forms of social and political organization at the global and European levels influence the effectiveness and legitimacy of decision-making. Jamal is also very interested in the relationship between science and society and has carried out research on how to optimize dialogue between disciplines to ensure that relevant and useful research can help critique, design and improve policy.

Mihnea Tănăsescu is postdoctoral research fellow of the Research Foundation Flanders (FWO). His work focuses on the politics of nature conservation and rewilding, the political representation of non-human beings and entities, and the movement of securing rights for nature. His latest book is *Environment, Political Representation, and the Challenge of Rights*.

www.ingramcontent.com/pod-product-compliance
Lightning Source LLC
Chambersburg PA
CBHW020001290326
41935CB00007B/258